Liberating Exegesis

LIBERATING EXEGESIS

THE CHALLENGE
OF LIBERATION THEOLOGY
TO BIBLICAL STUDIES

Christopher Rowland

and

Mark Corner

Westminster/John Knox Press
Louisville, Kentucky

Unless otherwise stated, scripture quotations are from the Revised Standard Version of the Bible, copyrighted 1946, 1952, ©1971, 1973 by the Division of Christian Education of the National Council of the Churches of Christ in the U.S.A., and are used by permission.

This book was first published in Great Britain in 1989 by SPCK, as part of the series *Biblical Foundations in Theology*, edited by James D. G. Dunn and James P. Mackey.

First American Edition

Published by Westminster/John Knox Press
Louisville, Kentucky

PRINTED IN THE UNITED STATES OF AMERICA
9 8 7 6 5 4 3 2 1

Library of Congress Cataloging-in-Publication Data

Rowland, Christopher, 1947–
    Liberating exegesis : the challenge of liberation theology
to Biblical studies / Christopher Rowland and Mark Corner. —
1st American ed.
        p.   cm.
    Includes bibliographical references.
    ISBN 0-664-25084-X
    1. Bible — Hermeneutics. 2. Liberation theology. 3. Bible —
Criticism, interpretation, etc. — History — 20th century.
I. Corner, Mark. II. Title.
BS476.R695 1990   89-49129
220.6'01—dc20   CIP

To Tony Benn

Contents

Introduction

There is a sense in which this book has been in preparation for the last ten years. During that time we have both explored the implications of liberation theology for our own work and spent much time talking about it together. What we have written here arises out of that much longer dialogue, which is now given literary form in this book.

We have not attempted a systematic exploration of the use of the Bible in liberation theology. That is a task which is beyond the scope of the limited space available. In any case, we are aware of others who are now engaged in comprehensive studies in this area. For example, John Parr is completing a dissertation for the University of Sheffield on this subject, and his work has contributed to parts of the Biblical Perspective of the Poor (Chapter 2) and James Penney is looking at the way in which the Bible is being used in exegetical and pastoral work connected with the issue of the land in the Peruvian and Brazilian churches. There is now an enormous range of material being produced by exegetes in the Latin American countries, most of it untranslated. What is important is the way in which this work frequently relates closely to the pastoral practice of the churches, reflecting the close contact many exegetes themselves have with the struggles of the poor and marginalized.

Our book falls into five chapters. Chapter 1 sets out some contemporary readings of the parables of Jesus which have been influenced by a liberation perspective, albeit in rather different ways. In Chapter 2 we give some indication of the biblical and theoretical foundations of the theology of liberation and compare it with the dominant exegetical paradigm at work in the First

World. Chapters 3 and 4 attempt to explore the way in which the application of liberation exegesis affects our reading of the canonical stories of Jesus, our understanding of eschatology and the rehabilitation of the book of Revelation as an instrument of evangelical criticism and a testament of hope. Finally, in Chapter 5, we argue that liberation theology cannot be seen solely as a Third World phenomenon whose influence depends solely on circumstances of poverty and oppression and is therefore of limited relevance to Britain and the rest of the First World.

Our task in this book is threefold. First, we want to offer a sample of the kind of biblical interpretation that is now going on, particularly in Latin America. We have tried to include both the sophisticated 'materialist' exegesis which looks at the socio-political dimension of the text in its original context as well as the readings prevalent in the Basic Christian Communities which relate the biblical stories and images to contemporary struggles for justice

Second, we have sought to explore the impact of some of these exegetical approaches on the dominant method of reading the Bible in the North American and European churches and academies. We are convinced that it is necessary for all of us involved in biblical study to recognize the searching questions that are now being put to many of our assumptions about biblical study and use. One of the complaints of many Latin American exegetes is that we in the First World do not seem to take them seriously. One reason for this is that they do not have the opportunity to write in the kind of mode that would command a place in the learned journals of the First World academies. It is not that the exegetes cannot do this (after all, many have received their training at European and North American universities), but the facilities are not there for the kind of supportive detail which we have become so accustomed to expect. In addition, the pastoral demands of being in close contact with grassroots communities and accompanying them in their struggles hardly leaves the time necessary for that kind of activity. We both believe that this lack of dialogue is something which needs to be rectified, and we hope that what we have written may make some contribution to this.

Third, as the previous sentence indicates, we are also concerned to make sure that liberation theology does not remain just another 'theology' to be placed alongside other interesting subjects for discussion. Indeed, liberation theology cannot be properly understood if its close contact with action in favour of the poor is ignored. Once liberation theology becomes solely a matter for academic debate, and thereby a subject which merely becomes part of the syllabus, its power is reduced. So we want to write in such a way that those who read our book may understand something of what makes liberation theology such an important phenomenon in the contemporary world and why it is posing a challenge to the Churches in the First World about their pastoral priorities and understanding of the Christian tradition.

It will quickly become clear that we are not writing from a position of studied neutrality. If we have learnt one thing from our study of liberation theology, it is that such a position of Olympian detachment and insight is difficult, if not impossible, to find. We therefore make no apology for our sympathetic account of liberation theology, nor for the consequent sharp questioning which we want to make of aspects of the interpretative culture in which we were both brought up. Part of what we are both seeking to explore are ways in which we can engage in an appropriate liberation theology in Britain and relate to already existing experiments in various parts of the country where grassroots groups are reading the gospel of Jesus Christ in ways which are liberating both individually and socially.

Liberation theology is attracting considerable attention these days. Despite this there is a lack of understanding of its form and purpose. Even sympathetic commentators can suppose that it offers a theological justification for violent revolutionary change and Marxist politics. Those opposed to it regard it as a perversion of the gospel in which the language of Christian tradition is reduced to politics and the 'spiritual' dimension is evacuated in favour of a materialist view of the world. It is said to concentrate on externals rather than the internal life of faith where the action of God's grace is to be found, and on social relationships and structures rather than the individual's responsibility before God and neighbour. It is accused of abandoning the essence of Christian liberation, which is said to be liberation from sin (conceived of as an individual's accumulation of guilt and participation in a fallen world). It represents what has popularly come to be known as the 'politicization of religion', in which faith 'becomes essentially concerned with social morality rather than with the ethereal qualities of immortality'.[1] It is accused of reductionism as it seeks to evacuate an other-worldly divine element and reduce everything to politics.

Both views indicate a lack of knowledge of the writings of the major liberation theologians. Many of them have themselves been the victims of violence or death-threats and so are not starry-eyed in their support of armed struggle. Some indeed are unequivocal in their rejection of it. Simplistic links between violent movements for change and liberation theology are wide of the mark. Many liberation theologians stand closer to the rejection of the way of violence than many mainstream churches today. Likewise, a glance at the Peruvian theologian Gustavo Gutierrez' influential *A Theology of Liberation*[2] reveals how distorted a picture is offered of liberation theology by those who seek to suggest that it is only interested in translating the language of salvation into the language of political change (as if the whole world were to have nothing to do with the salvation of our God, to borrow the language of Isaiah). For one thing, Gutierrez along with others stresses the indivisibility of personal and structural/societal change. Repentance for them is not something that can leave those fallible structural projections of human sinfulness intact. Indeed, they would say that the combination of a concentration on the spiritual rather than the material and the privatized religion so preferred in conservative circles are themselves the classic examples of reductionism. God's sphere of influence is reduced to the inner life. The great Pauline themes of a cosmic triumph of Christ over a superhuman force of sin implanted throughout a fallen world – humans and structures and all – is ignored in favour of an inadequate dualistic approach to salvation. In it the world of politics and human suffering, and the impact of the liberating power of the gospel of the resurrection upon it, is by-passed. The ordinary world of material human history is left to the chill wind of a Manichean dichotomy which separates God from the concerns of history. That is hardly the picture to which the biblical tradition calls us to be faithful. As in other areas of our theological activity, liberation theology is demanding that our understanding of tradition and what is traditional needs to be re-examined, and assumptions about the relation between faith and politics, the sacred and the secular and the sphere of divine activity be explored anew. Our hope is that in this book we can share something of what we have learnt from the theology of liberation and how it has affected our approach to the theological task.

We are aware that as contextual theology becomes ever more popular old certainties about boundaries of acceptable exegesis begin to crumble. The abandoning of old certainties leads to a situation of bewilderment, even anarchy, as the old signposts disappear and anything goes. In this book we review several readings which will seem to many to come fairly close to that. Neither of us would want to jettison the historical-critical method which is an important resource for questioning readings which may tend to be self-indulgent and careless of the form and content of the text. What is necessary is a renewed quest for guidelines in our biblical reading, assuming that a fixed Archimedean point is no longer possible. We feel that we are still some way from being able to do more than offer the broadest outline of such guidelines in this book.

A prime task of the exegete is to watch the way in which the biblical material is being and has been *used*. There is more than meets the eye in the way in which we are wont to read and use the Scriptures. We should accept the inevitable eisegesis (i.e. reading into texts, whether consciously or not, our own social and political preferences) which is an unavoidable part of the complex process of finding meaning in texts – what we call exegesis. By recognizing this process at work we will enable one another to be aware of the various kinds of eisegesis which we practise in all their subtlety and sophistication. We will thereby seek to lay bare the various human interests which may be at work in the maintaining of particular theological or political positions of individuals and groups. That is going to necessitate that we take seriously the patient analysis of the particularity of each situation and of whose interests are being served by various interpretations. It is easy to see how biblical material can be extracted from its context and function as the support for particular causes. It can offer the reader a way of escape from the wider context of the scriptural witness. Just as easily a facile resort to the demands of Scripture can ignore the other world of injustice and oppression which intersects with our creation of biblical worlds and systems. Standing four-square on particular doctrines or scriptural principles may lead us into a world of fantastic speculation which is out of touch with the reality of our divided world.

Readers who seek a critical awareness should seek to maintain a critical distance from the institutions of the old order. Accordingly, the temptation to wrest verses out of their context in a particular book must be resisted and the wider fabric of the narrative heeded. Nor should those of us who are on the 'left' of contemporary theology ignore those parts of the canon which do not fit so easily with our particular views of the world. Most middle-class Christians like ourselves actually practise the compromises which characterize the outlook of books like the Pastoral Epistles, with their social conformity and theory of male supremacy. We may not be comfortable with these solutions, but we cannot fail to recognize that such compromises are the normal stuff of our existence. At the very least the unpalatable parts of the canon can place a mirror before our rhetoric and remind us of the distance which exists between our preaching and our practice. A realistic self-criticism must accompany the critique of contemporary ideology. This must be a corporate activity which recognizes the fallibility of our judgements while affirming the necessity of keeping to the task of proclaiming justice and peace, however costly that may be.

Something like this seems to be what the New Testament witness is demanding of those of us who are seeking to bear witness to and work for the reign of God. It is going to have a decentred quality consistent with an identification with the one who died 'outside the city', reflecting the distorted world in which we live and the incompleteness of God's project of establishing a reign of justice and peace. When the gospel offers satisfaction and wholeness, questions need to be asked when that claim to wholeness ignores those at the fringes of our world whose fractured existence is a reminder of the pain of the suffering Son of Man and the struggles still endured and to be shared before the Kingdom comes.

NOTES
1 E.R. Norman, *Christianity and the World Order: The BBC Reith Lectures 1978* (Oxford: Oxford University Press, 1979), p.2.
2 G.Gutierrez, *A Theology of Liberation* (London: SCM Press, 1974, 2nd edition 1988).

1

Sampling Liberation Exegesis

It is not uncommon for works on the theology of liberation to begin (and sometimes continue) with the kind of abstruse theoretical analysis which the very principles of liberation theology ought to make us cautious about employing. There is, after all, a certain irony about the sort of highly technical discussion of 'theology as praxis' which is itself very much an exercise in 'theology as theory'! In our own discussion we intend to begin with a chapter that simply offers examples of liberation exegesis, concentrating upon readings of the parables. We try to keep technical arguments to a minimum in this section, and then in Chapter 2 move on to a more theoretical discussion, some of which will have arisen out of the practical exegesis offered in this chapter.

Clearly a very important area for examination by liberation exegesis will be the parables of Jesus, since the parable represents the form in which much of Jesus' teaching was encapsulated. Our understanding of the nature of that teaching derives in considerable part from our assessment of the 'message' conveyed by those parables. It is not difficult to think of well-known examples which are recalled time and time again in the teaching of the Church. Often they have been given titles which have become phrases in their own right, embedded in our language and culture, so that people are referred to, for instance, as 'good Samaritans' or 'prodigal sons' in circumstances which are obviously very different from those of the biblical narrative itself.

Thus parables not only convey much of Jesus' teaching, but they convey it in a way that subsequent generations can appropriate and apply to their own time. At the same time, parables are open to misinterpretation. In one example, from Mark 4, Jesus provides his own interpretation of the parable of the sower (vv. 13–20), following a comment to his disciples:

> To you the secret of the kingdom of God has been given; but to those who are outside everything comes by way of parables, so that (as Scripture says) they may look and look, but see nothing; they may hear and hear, but understand nothing; otherwise they might turn to God and be forgiven. (vv. 11–12, NEB)

This text has proved difficult to scholars, since some have wondered whether it suggests that parables are a means of concealing rather than revealing the truth. More likely the point is simply that those outside the fold of the disciples have to rely entirely on parables, without the additional teaching which the twelve received. But clearly there is also a warning here. Parables can as easily end up preventing insight as facilitating it. As with the slogan, their very effectiveness as a teaching device can make them dangerous.

It is unsurprising, therefore, that the theology of liberation has looked closely at the parables of Jesus, together with some of the shorter sayings that have themselves to some extent become slogans applied at random – for instance: 'Render to Caesar the things that are Caesar's, and to God the things that are God's' (Mark 12.17). In this section we shall look at some familiar biblical stories, and our treatment will attempt to bring out ways in which the parables are understood by certain theologies of liberation today. In particular we shall argue that the parables are intended to be understood in terms of a particular social context, both that of their writing and that of their reading. This must question the tendency to discover 'universal messages' in parables, moral home-truths that have been let down from on high and which can be applied and re-applied without difficulty from one generation to the next.

In the first section of this chapter we examine briefly a number of different parables and sayings from the collection *Parables of Today*. In the second section we concentrate more closely upon a liberation understanding of two particular parables, the stories of the labourers in the vineyard and of Dives and Lazarus.

PARABLES OF TODAY

1. THE LOST SHEEP

1
John Bosco was going to be ordained.

2
The bishop liked him very much. He had known him since he was a boy.

3
John studied and worked in the community.

4
The community was so happy that John Bosco was going to be ordained that they decided to have a big party.

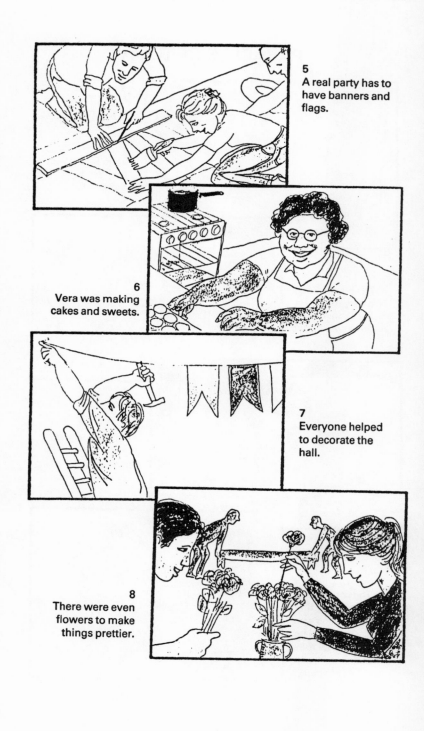

5
A real party has to have banners and flags.

6
Vera was making cakes and sweets.

7
Everyone helped to decorate the hall.

8
There were even flowers to make things prettier.

9
Maria trained the children to sing.

VIVA O BISPO E O

10
Everyone was there, talking and waiting for the bishop.

11
It was time for the ceremony to start and the bishop hadn't arrived. Someone went to phone him . . .

12
and got this message: a factory worker had been arrested.

13
The bishop had gone to the police station.

14
The ordination would have to be postponed.

15
Late at night, the man was set free . . .

16
and the bishop took him home.

2. THE LAST JUDGEMENT

1
The migrant workers spend the day cutting sugar cane.

2
The plantation owner transports them from field to field . . .

3
in an old truck, with bad brakes and old tyres.

4
And one day the worst happened!

5
The nurse and the catechist ran to help.

6
There had been so many accidents that the two of them called the community together.

7
The migrant workers started to discuss how they could get more security.

8
At supper time, an employee went and told everything to the plantation owner.

9
He went straight to the parish priest and started to accuse the nurse and the catechist.

10
'They stick their noses into everything. They're subversive: they visit the jails . . .

11
go to care for the sick . . .

12
they help the village idiot, giving him clothes . . .

13
now they've even
worked out how to
build houses
together. But I
don't want them
interfering with my
plantation.'

14
The priest
remembered a
parable from the
Gospel that
answered the
plantation owner's
complaints.

15
But the plantation
owner became
furious and
threatened: 'Do
you know who you
are talking to?
Things won't go on
like this!'

16
But the people,
united, went
marching through
the street in
support of the two
women.

BÓIA FRIA TAMBÉM É GENTE

TIVE FOME...
ERA BÃ...RU
TIVE SEDE...

E VOCÊS, O QUE
FIZERAM?

1 PARABLES OF TODAY

This is a series of slide sequences based on the parables of Jesus which relates stories told within the Basic Christian Communities in São Paulo, Brazil, together with commentary and suggestions for use.[1] The groups start with the slide sequence which gets them in touch with the familiar scenes of ordinary life, because many Christians feel that the biblical text is far too sacred for them to be interacting with it in any critical way. After the short slide sequence (a method which has been widely used in the educational programmes of the archdiocese of São Paulo on subjects like land and political involvement, as well as more 'religious' issues) a group is asked to discuss the story. They should recall similar experiences, identify with various characters in the story and share what their feelings might have been. At another meeting the biblical text is read and discussed and a comparison made with the story from life. It is only at the end of the process that a commentary prepared by the experts is read and discussed and any insights drawn from the reflection which relate to the present call to discipleship in the community.

The commentary consists of a summary of recent scholarship on the parables. Users of the study pack are told that Jesus used these stories so that everyone could understand what he wanted to say, particularly the poor to whom they were in the main directed. Jesus' parables were an invitation to change things according to God's justice and goodness. The conviction that God's bias is to the poor is evident in the statement that the parables explain why this Kingdom is of the poor and why the powerful didn't like Jesus' parables. The powerful, we are told, were satisfied with their own ideas and their way of acting. They were responsible for their country's politics. They organized religious life and made sure that the domination of people they exercised in society extended to the values proclaimed in church of submission to the rich and powerful.

(i) THE LOST SHEEP In the commentary relating to the parable of the lost sheep (Matt. 18.10–14), it is stressed that the power of the community is in its preoccupation with the needy and in its search for those who are lost and most need the community's support. The community of God's people does not exist for itself. It was called by God to serve those who are lost, because they have no land, no job or no home, because they are hungry, sick or suffering persecution. So the parable shows that the model of the Church is *not* to preserve the ninety-nine sheep who at the moment are gathered together. The model of the Church is to search unendingly for the needy. Mercy is at the centre of daily life. Jesus tells us that the church that acts this way is imitating his ministry. Matthew, whose account is used, thought that the Church of his time had forgotten this, because his community was too directed to its own needs.

Reactions to the way of reading this parable in *Parables of Today* may be various. First of all, those of us brought up on an approach to the parables which seeks first the meaning of a parable in its original context[2] may feel some unease that the socio-economic realities of modern Brazil can so dominate the reading. In the story from life the pastor's concern is in no way confined to the religious realm. The flock is not identified with those assembled for worship and specifically religious activities. Indeed, the Brazilian reading seems to relegate the religious occasion to the practical mission of support to the detained activist. Mission and pastoral work thus take on an overtly political garb which poses questions to the way in which we separate religion from politics, the sacred from the secular. The activity of God's Church, not least its leading ministers, is going to be alongside those who fall foul of the political system for their political involvement. The Brazilian parable does not tell us whether or not the union activist in the accompanying story from life was a practising Christian or not. However, his activity is not outside the concern of God's people. What is more, the sphere of that activity involves dealing with situations of arbitrary arrest and real fear for the safety of those arrested. In the First World it is tempting to react by saying: 'that *couldn't* happen here.' While the focus of attention in the story is on a bishop as the provider of help for the union official, and joy or disappointment for the Christian community, the message for the community is to challenge its assumptions about pastoral involvement both for itself and its ordained ministers.

(ii) THE LAST JUDGEMENT   In the commentary on this parable (Matt. 25.31–46) it is pointed out that this is one of the clearest texts about the meaning of the gospel. Christianity is a practice, an urgent action for the transformation of the world. The sheep are separated from the goats. Christian love cannot be neutral; it has to take sides. The question is: But whose side should one be on? Jesus' parable states explicitly: That of the little ones, those who are hungry, thirsty, migrants, sick, and prisoners. These are the poor of the gospel. In other narratives Jesus speaks of prostitutes, public sinners, the tired and weary, the children. These are the people with whom Jesus identifies. Jesus separates himself from the 'goats'; those who don't recognize *him* in the *poor* are responsible for their suffering. In Jesus' time and today, sheep and goats are mixed. The goats (oppressors) try hard to convince us that the truth is with them. Jesus preached this parable to help us to remember that the struggle against injustice is the criterion of our faith. The message of the parable is so clear that no one should be surprised when the Church, like Jesus, says to the goats: 'To hell with you.' Those who don't know the parables – like the plantation-owner in the accompanying story from life – are scandalized by the Church's option for the poor.

Two things stand out in the Brazilian version. First of all, there is a wider perspective than that offered by the Matthean original. There is a reason given for the suffering of those little ones in whom the Son of Man is to be met: oppression. Second, the identity of those in need is not confined to members of the Church. It encompasses all those who are victims of injustice and violence. As in the case of the treatment of the parable of the lost sheep, the role of the priest is held up to examination. In the Brazilian version of the last judgement it is the issue of political involvement which is raised for discussion. The separation of religion and politics is implicitly criticized as enabling the pressing demands of a God of justice to be ignored, so that the interests of the economically powerful can be safeguarded. The role of the priest as the guardian of spiritual as opposed to temporal values is implicitly criticized. Also, the fact that the approach to Scripture is firmly rooted in Catholic teaching is borne out by the involvement of two of its ordained ministers in the modern parables: liberation theology is consistent with Catholic social teaching.

It is a disturbing matter for Christian theology that the picture of Jesus offered in the Gospel of Matthew in particular seems to sit so light to the need for formal confession and doctrinal absolutism. The emphasis of the Gospel is on the need for a righteousness that will exceed that of the scribes and Pharisees (Matt. 5.20), not on the purity of belief. Indeed, the major criticism of the Pharisees in Matthew 23.2–3 is that they preach but do not practise. The adequacy of the practice of Christians is thus seen as the criterion for true discipleship, and it is that which the apostles must communicate to the nations as the substance of following Jesus ('. . . teaching them to observe all that I have commanded you', Matt. 28.20). Elsewhere in Matthew's Gospel a way of life is encouraged in which care for 'normal' provision is not paramount (e.g. Matt. 6.25–33). Poverty and homelessness are ideals for discipleship. Indeed, when the disciples are sent out on their mission in Matthew 10 they are encouraged to practise such ideals of the Kingdom. Jesus declares that any kind of service done to them will be rewarded as though done to him, and indeed to God: 'He who receives you receives me, and he who receives me receives him who sent me' (Matt. 10.40). This is reflected in the story of one whose whole career is identified with the marginal and whose style of life is a demonstration of the injunctions he offers. It would be hard in the light of this to be too confident about tying down precisely where the risen Son of Man is to be found.

It is a measure of the pervasiveness of the ideas that social ethics is a consequence of the gospel rather than of its essence and that what is Christian is to be found in areas of belief and grace rather than ethics and law. Liberation theology is putting a question mark to such a subordination of ethics to other items of the good news. It finds ready support in the priorities of Jesus in the synoptic Gospels. What the São Paulo approach to the Matthean parables reminds us of very forcibly is the way we in the First World approach such stories with clear-cut assumptions about what is religious and what is not, and about where Christ is to be found and where he is not. It subverts our concern for tidiness and order, and even our understanding of what is specifically Christian.[3]

Throughout these readings of the parables there runs the conviction that Bible study is above all understanding what God is saying *today*. In this process there are three key elements. First of all there is reality: the things that happen to people today . . . the social situation in which the Bible is read. Then there is the Bible itself: the written text and the situation of God's people in the past; and finally there is the community. As Carlos Mesters has put it:

> The Bible must be read with the 'head', with the 'heart' and with the 'feet'. The feet are very important. The Bible was written as the product of a journey. It is only by following with our own feet the same journey that we can get to know all the meaning of the Bible for us.[4]

Within the 'reality' of the Brazilian poor that journey is one of hope and promised liberation. That reality may be different in the comfortable First World, where the journey may mean hanging on to our comforts and spiritualizing the journey, but that different reading at the very least puts a question mark against the legitimacy of our assumption that we have grasped the meaning of the biblical story of God's people

The two stories which we have been examining began their life in the experiences of the Basic Christian Communities in Brazil. The vitality and ingenuity of these contexts is a major contributory factor to the emergence of liberation exegesis. We can gain some insight into some of the main characteristics of Bible study in a Basic Christian Community via this extract from the diary of James Pitt:

> I went to a first communion class on the periphery of São Paulo where I experienced a practical lesson in liberation theology. The theme that fortnight was that Jesus was born poor and humble and shares our life, and the question was 'why?' The women present were all poor. None had much formal education. Most were migrants from rural areas. All knew real hardship. They could easily identify with a poor family on the move whose baby had been born in a stable. Indeed a one-minute reading of St. Luke's account of the nativity provoked a one-hour discussion of the injustices, humiliations and hardships that the mothers themselves experienced . . . They swapped accounts of having to wait in shops while better dressed people were served first and how as domestic servants they were treated without respect by their mistresses. After an hour the catechist put the question: why did Jesus choose to be born poor and humble? Maybe, said one woman (a mother of ten of whom three had died and only two were working),

Maybe it was to show these rich people that we are important too. A ripple of excitement went through the room. Was God really giving such a clear statement about their humanity? About their rights as people? The discussion progressed, but with an electric charge in the air. Half an hour later a young woman said, I think we still haven't got the right answer to the first question. A complete hush. I think, she went on, that God chose his son to be born like us so that we can realise that we are important. It is not just to show the bosses. It's to show us too. And suddenly I saw what it means to say that the Gospel has the power to set people free, that the good news to the poor is a message of liberation . . . these women [were] fired by a sudden consciousness of their own worth, of their identification with Jesus Christ . . . they went on to discuss what they should be doing about the high food prices, about how a particular chain of shops had cornered the market and was overcharging, and how they themselves would link up with catechists' groups and basic church communities across the sector to organise a boycott.[5]

There are superficial similarities between this and the approach of that form of Protestant Bible study which goes straight to the text with no concern to ask questions about its original historical context or meaning. In Evangelical circles a naive reading of the text serves to encourage faith and bolster confidence in the individual's relationship with his/her Lord. The Bible then becomes a treasury from which the spiritual nuggets can be quarried to assist in the 'pilgrim's progress'. But while it may be true that the lay character of the Basic Christian Communities and their resort to the Bible as a collection of paradigms of contemporary discipleship is akin to what we find in this Evangelical reading of Scripture, the major differences are at once apparent. While there is also a clear repudiation of the more 'distanced' approach of the historical-critical method (with its concern to ascertain what the text originally *meant*), the difference from the naive Evangelical reading is the communitarian setting and the avoidance of a narrowly individualistic 'religious' reading. The setting for the reading is not primarily the inner life of an individual Christian but a world of poverty, disease and death in which good news comes to offer hope and a path to life. The story is that of the people of God as a whole, in which the historical perspective dominates and the oppression is not confined to the world of the spirit but is to be found in the structures of society which keep the poor poor and maintain the hegemony of the rich.

What we see in the liberation approach to the parable material is the interpenetration of the specific social reality of the Brazilian poor, as they meet to share their experiences of oppression, with the story of the people of God as set out in the Bible. The mission of the Church as the people of God is to be on the side of the marginalized. That kind of model undergirds the understanding of the biblical story. There is an affinity between the lot of millions of peasants who have left home and family and set out for a 'promised land' and the biblical narrative of the quest of God's people for their promised land. The stories of Israel's ancestors are potent reminders to the poor of not just the uncertainty and fragility of life but also the identification of God with those in that state. So, for example, Abram's story is told because he refused to live according to the conventional urban models of his day. He obeyed the insistent call of God and left the security of home and country (Gen. 12.1–4).[6] He preferred the life of a shepherd on the steppes. God's purpose is fulfilled and revealed through the story of one who had no part in the power structures of the city. Abram is presented in Genesis as the antithesis of the social structure created by the kings and the state. The story of Abram is a blessing for the clans who are made up of the families of the farmers who work and produce (Gen. 12). He exists on the margins of the settled life of the kings and the princes, yet his position is one which demands respect from them (Gen. 14) and ought not to be abused (Gen. 12.17). So justice is seen as the understanding of history and of the structures of society from the perspective of the Abramic minorities. It is in this tension that discernment and hope are born (cf. Ezek. 33.24; Isa. 51.1–8).

It is with the wandering shepherds that God's intervention on behalf of humanity first comes about. The story of Cain and Abel (Gen. 4) is read as an example of the kind of struggle which goes on in society between the landed and the landless, the farmers and the shepherds (a prime feature of contemporary Brazilian economic and political life). The cause of Abel's death is the division of labour, which creates social classes and the ensuing struggle for the land. Just as in contemporary Brazil, where there is (and has been) an unremitting struggle between the people who subsist by rearing animals and tending smallholdings and those who wish to exploit the resources of the country to the full, so in ancient Israel there was a struggle between farmers and shepherds endemic to the socio-economic system of the Canaanite city-state. In this situation Yahweh is on the side of the shepherds without land. God was pleased with the sacrifices of Abel, the shepherd.

The second part of the story of Cain and Abel tells how the oppressor became the oppressed and how he was accepted by God (Gen. 4.8–16). There is now a reversal of values. Cain will be under constant threat of vengeance from the oppressed, who will not forget Abel's murder. But just as Yahweh sought to avenge the death of Abel, so he is against the death of Cain. The punishment of Cain is to become like Abel. He is obliged to live without land, and this is his salvation! He becomes like the landless and the marginalized. Cain is no longer an oppressor but has been transformed into the class that he persecuted before.

J. P. Miranda notes the significant links with the previous story of the Fall in Genesis 3.[7] It is a consequence of the Fall that there is division between the brothers and a tension that originates from the division of labour (Gen. 4.1–7). The links between the two stories are evident, both in their juxtaposition and in the verbal echoes: for example, the questions of God to Adam and Cain after both have transgressed (Gen. 3.9; 4.9) and the curse on Cain (Gen. 4.11) being linked with the earth, which has been cursed in Genesis 3.17. The consequences of the Fall find their first expression in fratricide, the injustice of humanity. Cain and Abel's story is the first story of humanity outside Paradise. Death entered history in the fratricidal behaviour of Cain. Equally God intervenes to respond to the cry of Abel's blood which cries from the cursed ground, just as later in the story of Israel he was to respond and intervene on behalf of the oppressed people whose cry had come (Exod. 6.5). God acts as judge on behalf of the oppressed.

There lies behind the first part of this interpretation the conviction that the story functions as a reflection on the tension in Israelite society between the nomadic ideal and Canaanite culture which is prevalent throughout the Old Testament. But the story of Cain and Abel in Genesis presents us with a problem. At first sight the division of labour does not seem to be the subject of the narrative.[8] Indeed, there is something inexplicable in the origins of this inequality in God's treatment of the two brothers. The lack of an explicit rationale for the acceptance of Abel's offering and the rejection of Cain's need not leave us totally pessimistic about offering a reason, however. We must ask ourselves: On what grounds do we reject the Latin American interpretation?

The Gospel in Solentiname

A well-known collection of biblical interpretation by the poor of Latin America is found in the series of reflections on the Gospels collected by Ernesto Cardenal.[9] In place of the sermon each Sunday there would be a dialogue between Ernesto and the *campesinos* who attended the Sunday Mass on the island of Solentiname in Lake Nicaragua. As the following extract (which is the comment of a young Nicaraguan, Laureano) indicates, it reflects the situation in Nicaragua before the Sandinista revolution in 1979, where the links between the oppressive conditions in twentieth-century Central America resonate with the colonial oppression of first-century Judea.

> It isn't that the money belonged to the emperor; the money belonged to the people, but Jesus tells them to notice the coin, so they can see what imperialism is: a coin with the face of a man there. He wanted them to see that from the time when the emperor puts his name and face on a coin he's making himself boss of everything in the country, of everybody, of the money that belongs to everybody. And Jesus is showing them that Caesar's a complete dictator because he's putting his portrait on the coin and taking for himself what belongs to the people. He's telling them that he's grabbing the money, because he's pictured there as owner and lord of everything; then he wants to make himself owner even of the people, because he was on the money with which the people were buying. Let's say that it's like this now in Nicaragua, with Somoza, because Somoza is on the money, and we're all used to seeing him as the owner of Nicaragua; that's the way it was at the time. I believe he wants to tell them that all things belong to God, but that the emperor wants to make himself owner of everything when he makes himself owner of people's money.[10]

This contribution owes much to the revolutionary commitment of Laureano, but even so it is remarkable for its perception about the character of the dialogue. Another thing that marks this collection is the part which Ernesto Cardenal plays. Throughout it he injects the insights of conventional historical-critical exegesis, and these either offer a corrective to more outrageous interpretations or form the basis of interpretation and application in the Nicaraguan context. This is hardly ever slavishly carried out, and, as is the case with Laureano's reading of the passage about tribute money, the insight offered has little root in Cardenal's comment and so is not dependent on the preferences of the theologically sophisticated priest.

It is quite remarkable that the interpretation offered by Laureano has some similarity with the approach to this passage (albeit in its Marcan version) adopted in the following example of European materialist exegesis:

> The fig-tree and the vineyard (in Mk. 11 and Mk. 12), in fact, are symbolic images of Israel whose centre is the Temple. The fig-tree is sterile (11.12ff); the vineyard has been taken over by tenants who no longer recognize their owner (Yahweh) or his envoys (12.1ff); and the Temple has been turned from its role as a house of prayer into a means of commercial benefit . . . [Jesus' presence in Jerusalem] showed the perversion which the society of classes had brought about in the area of Palestine, and in so doing it subverted it . . . It is no less clear in the taxes for Caesar (12.13ff). The envoys . . . are not interested in Jesus' reply. They have set up the question as a trap and whatever his answer Jesus must be taken in by it. In fact, if he replies, 'No we must not pay,' they will accuse him before the Romans, which is what Luke actually reports (Lk. 23.2). If Jesus answers, 'we must pay', the crowd that admires him as the Zealot messiah will abandon him to the hatred of the chief priests (11.27). Now the text shows . . . the movement and subversion introduced by Jesus. Confronted with the coin symbolizing the Roman occupation and the power of the ruling classes collaborating with the Romans . . . Jesus gives an answer that shows his adversaries are simply forgetting what 'belongs to God'. And what belongs to God if not Israel – a fig-tree made sterile by its exploiters, a vineyard stolen by tenants from its owner, the Temple, which is a symbol of the society of classes? Thus the instruction 'Pay Caesar what is due

to Caesar and pay God what is due to God' means reconquering
from Caesar, that is, the Jewish sub-Asiatic system integrated
into Roman imperialism, what belongs to God.[11]

In both interpretations of the tribute money, one of the most
politically pertinent stories in the Gospels – the one arising from
the immediacy of the world of the *campesinos* in pre-revolutionary
Nicaragua, the other from the sophisticated materialist exegesis of
Michel Clevenot – we find similar themes being enunciated. Yet,
perhaps surprisingly to some critics of liberation theology, in
neither case is there a hint of the explanation favoured by those
who would argue that Jesus was a Zealot: that paying Caesar what
is his due means the expulsion of the Romans by force from the
Holy Land to enable the due deserts to be offered to God.[12]
Instead there is a recognition that the division between God and
Caesar is not what God wants and does not represent the way the
world should be – it is an imposition by the powerful which
should not be accepted by those who really want to do their duty
to God.

2   A STUDY OF TWO PARABLES

(i) THE   LABOURERS   IN   THE   VINEYARD   (MATT.
20.1–16)   The interpretation discussed here is based on Luise
Schottroff's contribution to the book *God of the Lowly: Socio-
Historical Interpretations of the Bible*.[13] It is a useful example to
begin with, since it provides an interesting contrast with other
interpretations of the parable in the history of the Church. The
liberation theologian's interpretation is built up out of a critique
of social conditions, both those of first-century Palestine and
those of the contemporary reader. Whether or not an understanding so clearly different from traditional views of the parable seems
convincing, it is an excellent example of the liberation theologian's approach to the text.

The parable compares the kingdom of heaven to a householder
who hires labourers for his vineyard. He hires some at first light,
some later in the day, and some only one hour before the end of
work. Yet the householder pays each labourer the same wage.
When those hired at the beginning of the day complain, the

owner asks whether they begrudge his generosity to those who worked for only an hour. The parable concludes with the words: 'So the last will be first, and the first last' (Matt. 20.16).

From a liberation perspective, it is essential not to overlook the socio-economic context of a gospel passage. This parable describes a land-owner who recruits workers on a day-to-day basis from the market-place. Although they are described as 'standing idle' (Matt. 20.3), their position was not an easy one. They were guaranteed employment only for the day, having no expectation of a longer-term contract, and because of a high level of unemployment there was always an excess of workers available over need, even at harvest-time. It was a 'buyer's market', brought about partly by the concentration of land in fewer and fewer hands and partly by the consequent displacement of workers who had to survive in insecurity, finding jobs when and where they could. They would appear in the countryside at harvest-time in the hope of finding temporary employment, but with no expectation of more.

The labourers would live from hand to mouth. They would be paid, as in the parable, on the day of working, and would have no assurance of being employed by the same land-owner on the following day. Many land-owners preferred to hire different day-labourers each day in order to keep them in a weak position, unable to organize. Sometimes they went unpaid, which to those on the breadline had dire consequences. For this reason, Jewish tradition emphasized that the wages of a hired servant should not be kept back from him until the following day (Lev. 19.13).

Arguably the position of labourers such as these was one of the most exploited in society. Unlike slaves, who were kept for long periods of time and therefore had to remain productive if they were to be of use to their owners, the day-labourers could be worked to the bone and then discarded to make room for the plentiful supply of replacements. In a situation where surplus labour was assured, and where not even self-interest operated to protect the worker (as it did to some extent in the case of slaves), there was little that the day-labourers could do.

The recognition of the labourers as an exploited and suffering group in society provides a key to interpreting the text because it highlights their need to organize. Only collaboration could provide the means by which they might improve their situation. But the temporary nature of their employment made organization difficult. They wandered from place to place in a desperate search for work, picking up jobs wherever they were available, in competition with one another. Those who were in effect hired and fired in a day were those least able to come together and unite against injustice.

In this context, Schottroff argues that the parable highlights the labourers' situation of vulnerability by pointing up their disunity in contrast to the unity that alone would enable them to break out of their situation. They are a group divided and thereby weakened. They are a household divided against itself that cannot stand (Matt. 12.25).

Therefore the sense of injustice which should be turned against those who exploit them is instead turned against each other. Solidarity is lost. They end up complaining about each other rather than about the way in which they are exploited as a group.

Unity and solidarity are important principles in the Christian community. Hence the Gospels provide a number of warnings against some Christians claiming privileges over against others. Indeed we can see this from the wider context of the parable of the labourers in the vineyard itself. Matthew's Gospel continues with the story of the mother of the sons of Zebedee, who wishes to obtain privileges for them in God's Kingdom. In response to her, Jesus distinguishes between the rulers of the world, who 'lord it over their subjects', and the community of disciples, among whom 'whoever wants to be first must be the willing slave of all' (Matt. 20.25-6, NEB). There must be no jealousy and one-upmanship within the group, no attempts to claim privileges over against other members, for this is to reproduce the divided and hierarchical structures of Gentile society.

The unity of which the parable speaks is a unity to resist oppression. The vision expressed in the final verse of the parable – 'Thus will the last be first, and the first last' (Matt. 20.16, NEB) – is incapable of realization, Schottroff argues, where those who are oppressed quarrel with each other. The socio-economic context of the parable points up the weakness of the labourers' situation in society and the way in which Jesus outlines a condition for overcoming it. Only by uniting among themselves can the last make themselves first.

So far the liberation interpretation of the parable has concentrated on the socio-economic context of its writing, but it is important to remember that the theology of liberation also concentrates on the ways in which a text can be received by another age to that of its original composition. Liberation theology questions, as our section 'The Form of Liberation Exegesis' in Chapter 2 makes clear, the familiar idea that exegesis is simply the attempt to understand the text 'as it was originally meant'. It must not be supposed that the point of studying the socio-economic context of the parable is only to reinforce the historical-critical method with a fuller account of the circumstances in which the text was originally written. The point of socio-economic analysis is not merely that of reaching further into the mind of the author. By bringing out the fact that labourers were an exploited and divided body of workers, made use of on a hire-and-fire basis, we are not simply adding a further refinement to the process of elucidating what the writer of the Gospel meant to say to us. In the best tradition of evangelism, the concern of the liberation theologian is to ask what the text meant to the writer of the Gospel only in order to ask what it means to us as readers. The text is only a vehicle – one that is designed expressly for the purpose of moving the reader to faith (John 20.30–1).

For this reason, H.-G. Gadamer's principle of a 'fusion of horizons'[14] is important to the liberation theologian, who will want to consider not only the socio-economic context of the writer but also that of the readers/interpreters, those who make the labourers in the vineyard (like the good Samaritan and the prodigal son) into markers belonging to different languages and cultures.

A well-known appropriation of the parable, particularly from the time of the Protestant Reformation, understands the story in terms of God's free self-giving in faith. The grace of God is not a reward for human works but a condition of such works. That those who begin working at the eleventh hour are paid the same rate as those who have toiled for the whole day is seen as an indication that acceptance by God is not earned through human works but is freely given to all.

This interpretation also speaks of human solidarity – the solidarity of the equally undeserving, a solidarity in sin. The divisions among men and women which are created by their different levels of achievement and worth are cancelled out and replaced by their common failure to measure up to perfection. Speaking in terms of 'faith' and 'works', the theology of the Reformation undermines the hierarchical character of the medieval theocratic state, in which political and spiritual power are inseparable (although in terms of practical politics most of the Protestant Reformers drew back from this implication, as witnessed in Luther's reaction to the Peasants' Revolt). The labourers in the vineyard become those whose struggle is at once for equality in the sight of God and of their temporal rulers, who 'lord it over them' not only with secular but also religious authority.

This interpretation of the parable, which thinks in terms of God's grace that makes the last first and the first last, could fairly be seen as the traditional understanding of the text. However, for the theology of liberation solidarity in sin cannot be measured simply in terms of the individual's relationship to God. It has to be understood in terms of the 'sinful structures' within which Christians work to overcome the divisions produced by injustice. Moreover, the liberation theologian will want to examine ways in which the parable of the labourers in the vineyard, the nature of whose employment makes it difficult for them to organize together, can be applied to the situation of those in the modern context who are tempted in different ways towards a fatal disunity. In contemporary Britain the liberation theologian might see the parable in terms of the tendency of today's victims to oppress each other, rather than to unite in resisting a form of social organization from which they all suffer. Those in low-paid employment turn against the unemployed, black people or women are blamed for taking jobs from white males, the South is blamed for robbing the North, one union of workers blames another – in each case those who in reality share a solidarity as victims of injustice fail to discover the unity which alone can enable them to 'make the last first'. Recent trends in the British and North American economies away from heavily unionized manufacturing towards the often non-unionized service industries, where rates of pay are relatively low, provide another contemporary *Sitz im Leben* for reading the parable.

By looking at the social context of the parable's reading today, the liberation theologian sees ways in which it illustrates how injustice can prevail only while there is a lack of perception concerning its origins. In the modern world there exist sophisticated techniques of persuasion to encourage division among victims of social and economic discrimination. Newspapers encourage poorly paid workers to complain of dole-scroungers, the ethnic majority to see job prospects blighted by immigration, or men to feel that women are creating dole queues for them by leaving the home and going out to work. By such means the modern household is divided against itself, and becomes a house built on sand. Rather than making the first last, the last argue among themselves as to who should be at the back of the queue.

The work of interpretation, the liberation theologian claims, must always draw into the equation not only the socio-economic context of the writer but also that of the reader. This can be a controversial process when the reader is set in contemporary Britain. Socio-economic analysis is widely accepted as a necessary ingredient of exegesis, but often only at a distance. The distance may be temporal, as in the case of the sociology of the New and Old Testaments, which concentrates on the *Sitz im Leben* of the writers but not on that of the readers of Scripture. Or the distance may be spatial, as in the early tendency of liberation theology to concentrate on Third World contexts which are assumed to be very different from those of the First World. Socio-economic analysis is extended the hand of toleration so long as it is concentrated on cultures or times other than our own.

What the liberation theologian sees in much contemporary British exegesis is a preparedness to study any socio-economic environment save that of contemporary Britain. Ancient Israel, first-century Palestine, the Mediterranean world of the Roman Empire – all have been opened up by experts who are now recognized by scholars as household names.[15] Their work is then taken over by and subsumed within the historical-critical method. Although their task is sometimes called the sociology of the New and Old Testaments, they tend to be treated as historians filling out in greater detail the sort of background to the biblical text that used to be meted out by histories of Israel and ancient Rome. The work of Meeks, Gager, Theissen and others is accepted so long as they are content to be updated versions of John Bright's *A History of Israel*, establishing more fully the original context of the most famous Galilean without allowing his shadow to fall on to their own times.[16]

As historians, these scholars can safely be presented in the role of understanding the past for its own sake, rather than possessing a sociological interest in using the past to analyse the present. In similar manner, much of the early writing in liberation theology could safely be presented as belonging to a different culture to our own. Its concern for the contemporary socio-economic environment was limited to the particular conditions of Latin America, South Africa or Asia. But such a limitation was never likely to be more than arbitrary. Black theology, for instance, was bound to reach out to the black communities in the First World, particularly the United States. Movements that had strong links with liberation theology, such as feminist theology, were indeed to emerge primarily in the First World, while the nature of the global economy and international economic and social forces was bound to suggest that there might be similarities between the situation in First and Third World countries. This is examined more closely in Chapter 5.

In this decade there has been an increasing concern to develop a liberation theology for First World countries, including Britain. The effect of this must be to make the political and economic conditions of contemporary Britain an inevitable ingredient of exegesis. Alongside Tiberius' Rome in the ancient world, or Somoza's Nicaragua and Botha's South Africa in the modern, will be Thatcher's Britain. This is not to suggest that Mrs Thatcher is able to govern Britain in the way that Tiberius could rule Rome. It is merely to point to the fact that an analysis of contemporary Britain, its political and economic structures, including those of the Church, forms part of the exegetical task.

The analysis of the parable of the workers in the vineyard offered by the theology of liberation includes not only comments about the socio-political structure of first-century Palestine but also comments about that of twentieth-century Britain. Liberation theology seeks to apply the biblical tradition to the situation of today. In the modern economy, as in the ancient, many work from day to day without security of employment. In a society which is increasingly recognizing that low-paid, part-time work is as much of a problem as unemployment, the parable of the labourers in the vineyard provides a tradition that can readily be appropriated by those who most need to organize today and yet are often least able to do so.

(ii) DIVES AND LAZARUS (LUKE 16.19–31)

Wealth and its attitudes

In this well-known parable, a rich man (traditionally referred to as Dives) feasts 'in great magnificence' (NEB) while a poor man lies at his gate covered in sores. Both die. The rich man goes to torment, while the poor man, Lazarus, is carried by angels to be with Abraham. Dives seeks to persuade Abraham to send Lazarus in order to cool his tongue with water, but Abraham reminds him that in life he had all the good things while Lazarus had all the bad. Between the two of them there is now a 'great chasm fixed' (NEB). Dives, the rich man, then asks for his family to be forewarned of the fate in store for them if they do not repent. Abraham tells him that they have Moses and the prophets to warn them. Dives argues back that someone from the dead will be listened to, but Abraham replies that if they do not listen to Moses and the prophets, neither will they listen to someone returning from the dead.

The parable has led to the accusation that Christianity commends 'pie in the sky when you die'. Lazarus receives 'consolation' after death; Dives receives punishment. Is this the sort of interpretation that we should arrive at in our own day?

We can understand the parable as falling into three parts. The first presents the contrast between Dives and Lazarus before their deaths. The text draws attention to the fact that Dives feasted in great style. There is not only a suggestion of great wealth ('dressed in purple and the finest linen', NEB), but also one of generosity. The peasants of Solentiname see in Dives a man who gives lavish parties for his friends.[17] Certainly he shows concern for the other members of his family, even when suffering torment. He is not a man who doesn't show any consideration for others; but the others for whom he is concerned are only those who are rich like himself.

Lazarus is described as lying at Dives' gate, but there is no suggestion of contact between them. Rather than being despised by the rich, the poor exist in silence under their noses. Such a situation is familiar to the Latin and Central American poor, their shanty towns a circle around the wealthy suburbs and a stone's throw from some of the beaches where the rich tourists flock to soak up the sun along lines of hotels. There is no need to put the poor in a ghetto; the rich are masters of the discretion that turns away from evil and remains with 'their own kind'. Just as there is a 'great chasm fixed' between them after death, so there is a great chasm between them in life, but one that is created by their different social and economic circumstances. The chasm in life is made all the more shocking by the suggestion of Dives' generosity. He is not a man unaware of the needs of others, but his situation in life provides the boundary to that awareness. Poverty is at his door, but it does not disturb him at his parties.

In the second part of the parable, their conditions are reversed after death. But it is noticeable that the attitude of Dives towards Lazarus is still one of the master towards the servant, of rich towards poor. 'Send Lazarus to dip the tip of his finger in water, to cool my tongue' (Luke 16.24, NEB). He still cannot perceive the common humanity which he shares with the poor. They are still beneath him, whether beneath his vision so that he doesn't perceive their physical needs, or beneath his respect so that they must be treated as servants to satisfy his own.

In the third part of the parable, Dives asks for a warning to be given to his family. He is told that they have 'Moses and the prophets' (Luke 16.29). We find here a revealing comment upon exegesis itself. They had Moses and the prophets, just as Christians today have Moses and the prophets, together with their own New Testament. But there is no guarantee that the rich will discover in their Bibles a warning to themselves. Even the story of a man come back from the dead – the resurrection of Jesus, here alluded to in the reference to Lazarus returning to life – will not convince them. Indeed, they may read the Bible from a perspective that reverses the message which is read there by the peasants of Solentiname. They may read a parable which consoles the poor, rather than a parable which threatens the rich. If so, even the account of the resurrection will contain no message in which they will be able to see a challenge to their lifestyle and lack of commitment to the poor.

As we have outlined above, the theology of liberation concerns the appropriation of this parable not only by the poor of the Third World but also by those of the First. The juxtaposition of rich and poor is increasingly apparent in contemporary Britain. Many British cities, like those in the Third World, contain adjacent areas of inner-city dereliction and poverty on the one hand, and suburban wealth on the other. British society is increasingly unequal, the rich receiving cuts in taxes that make them richer, the poor receiving cuts in benefit that make them poorer. And there is in British society, as elsewhere, an insidious ideology that seeks to remove the poor from sight, and to suggest that everyone is in fact participating in the oil-based bonanza of the late twentieth century.

The parable of Dives and Lazarus, we have affirmed throughout the discussion, is interpreted in different ways in different contexts. In the first century it could have suggested the exclusion of the Gentiles from the messianic feast in the Kingdom of heaven. Dives is befriended by dogs who lick his sores, and we read that he 'would have been glad to satisfy his hunger with the scraps from the rich man's table' (Luke 16.20–1, NEB). In similar terms the Phoenician woman spoke to Jesus when he made the comment that 'it is not fair to take the children's bread and throw it to the dogs' (Mark 7.27, NEB). She replied, 'Sir, even the dogs under the table eat the children's scraps' (Mark 7.28, NEB). Jesus was moved by her words to recognize the common humanity of Gentiles with Jews, and to accept that he could not heal only the children of Israel. Similarly, Dives is condemned for failing to recognize his common humanity with the poor, and for sharing his wealth only with those as rich as himself.

In the oppressed communities from which the theology of liberation is generated today the parable of Dives and Lazarus is read in terms of the exclusion of the poor. Poverty not only means a lack of material wealth; it means a lack of personal significance, the social invisibility of the man with sores who lies unnoticed at the gate while the rich guests go by.

In *The Gospel in Solentiname* one of the peasants, Oscar, connects Jesus' blessing of the poor with his blessing of children:

> Do you know what I understand by a child here? It's the poor people! They are children with respect to the rich. I mean that we, then, since we're poor, we're always beneath the rich . . . We ourselves, even though we're adults, are like children: the poor. But, the child is not always going to be tiny.[18]

Oscar's appropriation of Jesus' teaching about children in terms of the situation of the poor in society shows how far the use of this parable by the theology of liberation is from the idea of 'pie in the sky when you die'. Though the child is weak and dependent now, they will grow to adulthood and have power and independence on earth. Similarly, those who are made weak and dependent by poverty and oppression will overcome their difficulties. They are the 'children' who will grow to maturity. They are the meek for whom only the earth will do as an inheritance (Matt. 5.5).

For some of those mentioned in the parable, of course, there is nothing like 'pie in the sky' after death. About this question *The Gospel in Solentiname* has an interesting comment: 'There are now advanced sectors among Christians who don't believe much in hell. It seems to me a very revolutionary dogma: that there is a place of damnation and that the rich are in it.'[19] The revolutionary character of the parable lies not simply in its condemnation of the rich, however, but in its condemnation of them for no other reason than their wealth: 'Christians usually believe that the good rich man is saved and only the bad rich man is condemned. But that's not what is said here. The rich man isn't called evil, he's just called rich.'[20] The parable is concerned with circumstances, not attitudes. It does not focus on Dives' character, and indeed as we have said there are hints that he may have been generous to his circle of friends. It does not concern itself with his behaviour towards others, or his treatment of his servants and family. It identifies only his wealth, the riches which make his feasts, unlike the messianic banquet, occasions when those along the highways and byways are left to lick their sores. The revolutionary character of this parable is perceived to lie in the fact that everything of significance about Dives is subordinate to the fact that he is rich. Whatever his manners, the suggestion is that material circumstances make the man.

In many passages of the New Testament the rich are condemned simply for their wealth, as in the Lucan 'Woes' (Luke 6.24), or in the famous saying about it being easier for a camel to pass through the eye of a needle than for a rich man to enter the Kingdom of God (Mark 10.25). It is true that emphasis is also put upon attitudes to wealth. Immediately before the parable of Dives and Lazarus the Pharisees are described as a group 'who were lovers of money' (Luke 16.14), and the warning is given that 'You cannot serve God and mammon' (Luke 16.13). But the point of interspersing passages which condemn attitudes to wealth and passages which condemn the sheer having of it is to emphasize that the two are unfortunately very closely linked. In other words, those who are rich tend to love and to serve money (even if their piety compels them, like the rich young man who comes to Jesus seeking the secret of eternal life, to try to serve two masters at once and love God too). Many of the attitudes towards life which are condemned in the wealthy are created by their wealth itself. That is why the Bible warns so strongly against being rich. Like a drug, wealth will take you over and rule your personality. It will also distort your vision of reality. There is a clear warning here against any view which tries to isolate individual attitudes from material circumstances.

In contemporary Britain the parable of Dives and Lazarus is not only a challenge to the process by which the rich become richer and the poor poorer. It is also a challenge to the view which supposes that charitable sentiments in the rich will supply gaps in provision to the poor. The realistic view, particularly for a society in which advertising encourages an acquisitive attitude, is that most of those who receive tax cuts will consume more themselves. They will not wish voluntarily to share their wealth with the poor. They are far more likely to behave like Dives than like Zaccaeus, who gave half his possessions to charity (Luke 19.8). Their very wealth will create the desire to retain what they possess and indeed to acquire more of it. It will also encourage them to develop the attitudes which render invisible the poor at their gate.

There is no doubt that those who say that the love of money, rather than money itself, is the root of all evil, can claim support from biblical tradition.[21] At the same time, however, it has to be asked why that same tradition is also prepared to condemn riches in themselves, irrespective of the attitude taken towards them. The implication of the straightforward condemnation is that the love of money is something created by money itself. In a society which encourages acquisitiveness, moreover, there is no such thing as enough. The seriousness with which the biblical text takes the possession of wealth, and the manner in which it is condemned so strongly, indicates a perception of its danger. Pious comments about having the right attitude to riches ignore the way in which, time and time again, the situation of becoming rich itself alters attitudes. It very easily leads those who become wealthy to lose sight of the experience of being poor.

So far as the contemporary rulers of Britain are concerned, growing social and economic inequality will lead to a spirit of generosity and giving, of which they would say there is plentiful evidence in the experience of individual charities.[22] But in the view of others there can be no liberation for the poor by this route. Riches will curl around their possessors and cocoon them in further desire for wealth. They will take away from them any vision of the needs of others in society, and encourage them to believe that everyone is benefiting from increased wealth. Rather than a spirit of generosity, there will be a spirit of self-interest and decline. Dives need not have been a man with an evil character. Wealth may have taken hold of him rather than vice versa. The oppressor is always a victim alongside the oppressed in a situation of injustice. From the perspective of the British poor, there is little room in the present economic situation for individual goodness to overcome social forces. That is why the poor can appreciate a text in which little is made of individual attitudes and the weight of the condemnation is placed upon the material circumstances of the wealthy. The poor perceive through this text that they are struggling not against evil individuals but against an unjust social and economic system from which, even if the best in human nature is demanded, the worst in human nature is encouraged.

The treatment of this parable is sub-titled 'Wealth and its Attitudes' rather than 'Attitudes to Wealth'. For attitudes and circumstances are closely bound together. All too easily the situation of being wealthy creates the attitudes that seek to preserve and enhance that wealth. This is not an inevitability – the camel may always find its way through the eye of the needle! (cf. Mark 10.27, 'all things are possible with God') – but it is hardly uncommon for those with a great deal of money to find reasons why they should have it. In Chapter 5 we look more closely at the idea of helping the poor through charitable giving from the wealthy rather than the provisions of social legislation. But whatever the merits of 'charity' as a method of redistributing wealth, it is unlikely to happen anyway. The scepticism of the biblical tradition concerning wealth makes it clear that human beings do not easily achieve a dispassionate judgement of need irrespective of their own personal circumstances. They are more likely to allow their generosity to be expressed in terms of the limited benevolence of a Dives than the total self-renunciation of a Zacchaeus.

3 CONCLUSION

Parables are intended to be universal in their application, and indeed, as this chapter has pointed out, they have been taken and applied throughout history to the different circumstances of their readers. But they can possess such universality only if they are open to reinterpretation in the present context. To give an obvious example: no one who reads the parable of the good Samaritan in contemporary Britain can apply it to his or her own life if they think of it as a story addressed to Samaritans today. In order to understand that this is a parable addressed to them, and demanding a response from them, they have to be able to ask: Who is the good Samaritan in contemporary British society? Who is the priest and who is the Levite? Certainly the answers to these questions will be controversial and provoke debate, but that is precisely what parables are intended to do. Jesus provoked his own hearers with the parables he told; in applying them to their situation today, Christians will expect to provoke their own hearers too.

The parables of the labourers in the vineyard and of Dives and Lazarus are neither mere portraits of life in bygone age nor moral home-truths which can be expressed as slogans for all time ('Don't be envious'; Help the needy'). They are stories deliberately earthed in the material circumstances of their time which can be appropriated through the material circumstances of another time.

A parable is not a truth 'made easy' for simple hearers by way of illustration, an attempt by Jesus to teach the philosophically backward by means of examples that can simplify the message. The truth expressed in parables can be expressed in no other way. It exists only in the life of those around Jesus, in their personal, social and economic relations with one another. By describing that life, Jesus presents the 'truth' that cannot be grasped abstractly apart from it. Similarly, the modern interpreter has to appropriate the parable as it is embedded in life today. Its capacity to illuminate, to provoke opposition, to teach, must be discovered in the conditions of modern Britain. It cannot any longer be found only in the conditions of the ancient world.

For this reason, the methodology of teaching by parables is better understood by the theology of liberation. The principle that truth can be arrived at not by abstract discussion but by attention to life (arguably another important link between liberationist and existentialist thought) is accepted. The idea that Jesus had recourse to parables in the way that a schoolteacher with a backward class has recourse to a diagram is firmly rejected. Rather, the parabolic mode of discourse is the mode appropriate to 'truth as praxis'. The liberation theologian knows that only in the life of those around him or her today will the meaning of Jesus' parables be found – and will therefore not be afraid to describe that life as he or she interprets the text.

NOTES

1 *Parables of Today*; the text, pictures and commentary are published by Edicões Paulinas, São Paulo.

2 See the comments of C. M. Tuckett, *Reading the New Testament* (London: SPCK, 1987), p. 175, and F. W. Beare, *The Gospel According to Matthew: A Commentary* (Oxford: Basil Blackwell, 1981), pp. 375–6.

3 See also Beare, *Gospel According to Matthew*, p. 496, and W. Meeks, *The Moral World of the First Christians* (London: SPCK, 1987), p. 143.

4 C. Mesters, *God's Project*; English translation by the Theology Exchange Programme, Athlone, South Africa, and the St Dominic's Translation Group, São Paulo, pp. 26ff.

5 J. Pitt, *Good News for All* (Catholic Fund for Overseas Development, 1978).

6 These ideas regarding the Genesis narratives are from unpublished papers by Ana Flora Anderson and Gilberto Gorgulho, who teach in the Roman Catholic Seminary in São Paulo and are theological advisers to the Cardinal Archbishop of São Paulo, Paulo Evaristo Arns. Gen. 4 is mentioned at the start of *The Road to Damascus: Kairos and Conversion*, a document signed by Third World Christians (London: Christian Aid 1989).

7 J. P. Miranda, *Marx and the Bible: A Critique of the Philosophy of Oppression* (London: SCM Press, 1977), pp. 88ff.

8 See, for example, C. Westermann, *Genesis 1–11: A Commentary* (London: SPCK, 1984), pp. 293–4.

9 E. Cardenal, *The Gospel in Solentiname*, 4 vols (Maryknoll, NY: Orbis Books, 1977–84).

10 ibid., vol. 3, p. 284.

11 M. Clevenot, *Materialist Approaches to the Bible* (Maryknoll, NY: Orbis Books, 1985), pp. 78f.

12 See, for example, S. G. F. Brandon, *Jesus and the Zealots* (Manchester: University Press, 1967), and cf. F. F. Bruce, 'Render to Caesar' in E. Bammel and C. F. D. Moule (eds), *Jesus and the Politics of his Day* (Cambridge: University Press, 1984), pp. 249–64.

13 L. Schottroff, 'Human Solidarity and the Goodness of God' in W. Schottroff and W. Stegemann (eds), *God of the Lowly: Socio-Historical Interpretations of the Bible* (Maryknoll, NY: Orbis Books,1984), pp. 129–147.

14 H.-G. Gadamer, *Truth and Method* (London: Sheed & Ward, 1975). See also A. C. Thiselton, *The Two Horizons: New Testament Hermeneutics and Philosophical Description with Special Reference to Heidegger, Bultmann, Gadamer and Wittgenstein* (Exeter: Paternoster Press, 1980).

15 See, for example, J. G. Gager, *Kingdom and Community: The Social World of Early Christianity* (Englewood Cliffs, NJ: Prentice-Hall, 1975); H. C. Kee, *Community of the New Age: Studies in Mark's Gospel* (London: SCM Press, 1977); *Christian Origins in Sociological Perspective* (London: SCM Press, 1980); *Miracle in the Early Christian World: A Study in Sociohistorical Method* (New Haven, NY/ London: Yale University Press, 1983); W. Meeks, *The First Urban Christians: The Social World of the Apostle Paul* (New Haven, NY/London: Yale University Press, 1983); G. Theissen, *The First Followers of Jesus: A Sociological Analysis of the Earliest Christianity* (London: SCM Press, 1978); *The Social Setting of Pauline Christianity: Essays on Corinth* (Edinburgh: T. & T. Clark, 1983).

16 But note G. Theissen's *The Shadow of the Galilean* (London: SCM Press, 1987), a highly original attempt in narrative form to let Jesus' shadow fall on to our own age.

17 See P. and S. Scharper (eds), *The Gospel in Art by the Peasants of Solentiname* (Maryknoll, NY: Orbis Books, 1984), p. 36, and Cardenal (ed.), *Gospel in Solentiname*, vol. 3, pp. 251–6.

18 P. and S. Scharper (eds), *Gospel in Art*, p. 18. Note the way in which, in the passage cited by the Scharpers about Dives and Lazarus (p. 36), Cardenal attempts to steer the discussion along lines of the 'correspondence of relationships' rather than 'correspondence of terms' (on which see pp. 85–101 below). When one of the peasants remarks that letting in the poor will make the houses of the rich dirty (p. 36), Cardenal recalls the point that 'the parable was not to console the poor but rather to threaten the rich', a point which allows the tradition to be applied to the situation of his day.

19 Cardenal, *Gospel in Solentiname*, vol. 3, p. 256.

20 ibid., p. 251.

21 Margaret Thatcher's speech along these lines to the General Assembly of the Church of Scotland in May 1988 is discussed in Chapter 5, below (see pp. 238–41).

22 See the discussion in Chapter 5 below (see pp. 241–8), where it is argued that this is a principle already shown to be unsuccessful as a method of relieving the plight of the international poor, but which is increasingly being suggested as a solution to the problem of the national poor.

2

The Foundation and Form of Liberation Exegesis

---

1 THE BIBLICAL PERSPECTIVE OF THE POOR: THE CHALLENGE OF GRASSROOTS EXEGESIS

Most faculties of theology and religious studies have not moved too far from the well-trodden paths of the historical-critical method, with its painstaking quest for the text's original meaning and context. The hegemony of this interpretative approach is firmly rooted in theological education and the Churches. Indeed, successive generations of ministers have been taught to read the Bible using the historical-critical method.[1] In the process of acquiring the tools of historical scholarship we have all been enabled to catch a fascinating glimpse of the ancient world as it has been reconstructed for us by two hundred years of a biblical scholarship of increasing sophistication. But all too often our devotion to the quest for the original meaning of a Pauline text or a dominical saying has left us floundering when we are asked to relate our journey into ancient history to the world in which we live and work. While the journey into the past has offered us insights aplenty, our historical preoccupations have left us with the feeling that the biblical world we have constructed is alien to us. So the biblical text, instead of being a means of life, can become a stumbling-block in the way of our contemporary discipleship. When we use the Bible in wrestling with the contemporary problems of Christian discipleship we find that our exegetical efforts frequently have not been matched with the skills necessary for the provision of illumination from the Bible on the exploration of those questions which our generation is asking.

There is a deep divide among contemporary interpreters of Scripture. On the one hand there are those who think that the original meaning of the text is not only retrievable but also clearly recognizable, and that it should be the criterion by which all interpretations should be judged. On the other hand there are those who argue either that the quest for the original meaning of the text is a waste of time or that, even if it is possible to ascertain what the original author intended, this should not be determinative of the way in which we read the text. It believes that whatever the *conscious* intention of the original author, different levels of meaning can become apparent to later interpreters, granted that the text is free from the shackles of the author's control and has a life of its own in the world of the reader.

Understandably, the first group is worried that the freedom implied in the second approach might lead to exegetical anarchy.[2] It wants some kind of control over interpretation, and where better to find it than in the original meaning of the text? No doubt most biblical exegetes would chafe at the imposition of any kind of hermeneutical control on their endeavours, yet there is today a 'magisterium of the historical-critical method' in the Church. The magisterium of the Holy Office has been replaced by the critical consensus of the biblical exegetes, preoccupied as most of them are with the original meaning of the text and its controlling role in the quest for meaning of the Scriptures.[3] As part of that quest, the search goes on for 'history', whether it be that of Jesus, the mind of the evangelist or Paul, or the situation of the early Christian communities. But history is such an allusive quarry. Not only is it never directly accessible to us, but our involvement in the search casts such a shadow over the whole process that the significance of our investment in time and effort itself demands an explanation. Frederic Jameson reminds us:

> History is *not* a text, not a narrative, master or otherwise, but that, as an absent cause, it is inaccessible to us except in textual form, and that our approach to it and to the real itself necessarily passes through its prior textualization, its narrativization in the political unconscious.[4]

Of course, that political unconscious has been at work in the multifarious attempts to get at the real meaning of the text during the last two hundred years (though all too frequently it has remained unrecognized). That said, the *quest* for the original context (or for better contexts of the biblical texts, since many of them show signs of being part of an ongoing community of interpretation) is necessary as a component of any historical approach to the reading of texts. It is part of the history of the interpretation of a text. But the starting-place is the way in which and the place in which the texts are being used in the contemporary world, whether by millions of ordinary Christians or the sophisticated researchers of the First World academic institutions.

But it is not just *ancient* history that is important. Recently, the application of sociological theory to the study of early Christianity has enabled us to look at familiar issues in a new light.[5] The new insights which the sociological approach affords, however, present a challenge to a preoccupation with the original meaning of the text. Sociology of the New Testament must involve a penetrating analysis of the social formation of the contemporary reader too.

Of course, the truly historical method will also attend to the specific historical situation of the various interpretations on offer. But it must be conceded that we have been singularly negligent over the application of historical criticism to our world, and to ourselves as interpreters. We may want to suppose that the exegetical enterprise is an autonomous one, to be kept distinct from the various ways in which the text is being *used*. Nevertheless, we have to accept the fact that the historical-exegetical project owes everything to the interpreter and the interpretative culture of which he or she is a part. The reconstruction of that past world in which the texts originated can therefore enable the contemporary reader to view present prejudices in a fresh light.[6] The world of the New Testament is, after all, *our* creation from the fragments, both textual and otherwise, that have come down to us. The sort of people we are and the kind of interests that we have must necessarily determine, or at least affect, the biblical world we create.

There is an unease among many biblical readers about the way in which the Bible has been studied. Those who use the Bible as part of Christian ministry wonder at the enormous investment in biblical interpretation which seems to enable so little fruitful use of the foundation documents of the Christian religion. Something similar is said about the crisis facing biblical interpretation by Carlos Mesters as he writes from the perspective of one whose work has involved him in interpreting the Bible with the poor of Brazil.[7]

Mesters points out the indebtedness of liberation theology to Enlightenment methods and contrasts its original vitality with the weariness which characterizes its contemporary use. He regrets the way in which the 'scientific' study of Scripture has had the effect of distancing the Bible from the lives of ordinary people, so that its study has become an arcane enterprise reserved for a properly equipped academic élite. In its early career the historical-critical method had the power and courage to contribute greatly to the revival of interest in the Bible. Its historical concern played a major part in the critique of the ideology of ecclesiastical dogma. But that negative function, now so well established, has not been matched by the positive encouragement of methods of reading which would enable the people of God to respond to the needs which the life of faith in a changing world is placing upon them.

Mesters points out that the same weariness was also to be found in Brazilian biblical study, with the growth of learned works on exegesis which had little appeal or relevance for the millions seeking to survive in situations of injustice and poverty. In that situation, however, a new way of reading the text has arisen, not among the exegetical élite of the seminaries and universities but at the grassroots. Its emphasis is on the threefold method: *see* (starting where one is with one's experience, which for the majority in Latin America means an experience of poverty), *judge* (understanding the reasons for that kind of existence and relating them to the story of the deliverance from oppression in the Bible) and *act*. Ordinary people have taken the Bible into their own hands and begun to read the word of God not only in the circumstances of their existence but also in comparison with the stories of the people of God in other times and other places. Millions of men and women abandoned by government and Church have discovered an ally in the story of the people of God in the Scriptures.

This new biblical theology in the Basic Christian Communities is an oral theology in which story, experience and biblical reflection are intertwined with the community's life of sorrow and joy. That experience of celebration, worship, varied stories and recollections, in drama and festival, is, according to Mesters, exactly what lies behind the written words of Scripture itself. That is the written deposit which bears witness to the story of a people, oppressed, bewildered and longing for deliverance. While exegete, priest and religious may have their part to play in the life of the community, the reading is basically uninfluenced by excessive clericalism and individualistic piety. It is a reading which is emphatically communitarian, in which reflection on the story of a people can indeed lead to an appreciation of the *sensus ecclesiae* and a movement towards liberative action. So revelation is very much a present phenomenon: 'God speaks in the midst of the circumstances of today.' In contrast, the vision of many priests is of a revelation that is entirely past, in the deposit of faith – something to be preserved, defended and transmitted to the people by its guardians.

So for Mesters the Bible is not just about past history only. It is also a mirror to be held up to reflect the story of today and lend it a new perspective. Mesters argues that what is happening in this new way of reading the Bible is in fact a rediscovery of the patristic method of interpretation which stresses the priority of the spirit of the word rather than its letter. God speaks through life; but that word is one that is illuminated by the Bible: 'the principal objective of reading the Bible is not to interpret the Bible but to interpret life with the help of the Bible'.[8] The major preoccupation is not the quest for the meaning of the text in itself but the direction which the Bible is suggesting to the people of God within the specific circumstances in which they find themselves. The popular reading of the Bible in Brazil is directed to contemporary practice and the transformation of a situation of injustice. That situation permits the poor to discover meaning which can so easily elude the technically better equipped exegete. Where one is determines to a large extent how a book is read. This is a reading which does not pretend to be neutral, and it questions whether any other reading can claim that either. It is committed to the struggle of the poor for justice, and the resonances that are to be found with the biblical story suggest that it may not be unfaithful to the commitments and partiality which the Scriptures themselves demand.

Of course, Mesters recognizes the difficulties of this approach.[9]

He expresses his unease about the way in which the biblical story can become so identified with the experiences of the poor that any other meaning, past or present, can be excluded. So the story of the deliverance of God's people from oppression in Egypt can become for the poor *our* story, its message being directed solely to the outcast and impoverished. Mesters' emphasis on the importance of a historical dimension to scriptural study in a quest for the original meaning is a remedy against this kind of tendency. It can remind readers that the text has been the property of many who have read it in many different situations. The original readers would not have had identical concerns with the contemporary poor, whatever else they may have had in common.[10]

Mesters asks us to judge the effectiveness of the reading by its fruits: is it 'a sign of the arrival of the reign of God . . . when the blind see, lepers are clean, the dead rise and the poor have the good news preached to them'? The experience of poverty and oppression is for the liberation exegete as important a text as the text of Scripture itself. The poor are blessed because they can read Scripture from a perspective different from most of the rich and find in it a message which can so easily elude those of us who are not poor. The God who identified with slaves in Egypt and promised that he would be found among the poor, sick and suffering demands that there is another text to be read as well as that contained between the covers of the Bible: God's word is to be found in the literary memory of the people of God. But that is a continuing story, and is to be heard and discerned in the contemporary world, among those people with whom God has chosen to be identified.

The biblical text is therefore not a strange world which can come alive only by recreating the circumstances of the past. The situation of the people of God reflected in many of its pages is the situation of the poor. What such biblical interpretation dramatically reminds us is that the pressing issues for any critical exegesis must be the rigorous analysis of the complex production of meaning, the contexts in which that production takes place, and the social and economic interests which an interpretation is serving. There must be a continuous dialogue between that present story told by the poor of oppression and injustice, and the ancient stories they read in the Bible. Indeed, the knowledge of that past story is an important antidote to the kind of unrestrained fantasy which then binds the text as firmly to the world of the immediate present and its context in the same way that historical-critical exegesis bound it to the ancient world. That twofold aspect is well brought out by Carlos Mesters:

> the emphasis is not placed on the text's meaning in itself but rather on the meaning the text has for the people reading it. At the start the people tend to draw any and every sort of meaning, however well or ill founded, from the text . . . the common people are also eliminating the alleged 'neutrality' of scholarly exegesis . . . the common people are putting the Bible in its proper place, the place where God intended it to be. They are putting it in second place. Life takes first place! In so doing, the people are showing us the enormous importance of the Bible, and at the same time, its relative value – relative to life.[11]

This understanding of theology as a second-order task (viz., one of critical reflection on life and practice) is not new to Christian theology. That subtle dialectic between the 'text' of life, viewed in the light of the recognition and non-acceptance of unjust social arrangements, and the other 'text' of Scripture and tradition is the kernel of a lively theological, or for that matter any, interpretative enterprise.[12] The world of the poor, as well as their imagination, provides shafts of light which can often throw into the sharpest possible relief the poverty of much First World interpretation.

A similar point is made about the contribution of liberation theology by Charles Elliott in his 1985 Heslington Lecture:

> Liberation theology is about a fundamental change in the way in which persons, personal relationships and therefore political relationships are conceived and structured . . . Why is liberation theology so important intellectually? . . . Firstly, it is true to elements . . . of the biblical tradition which were long neglected by the colonialist church . . . Neither a colonialist church nor an established church can bear to think that the biblical tradition is actually about challenging power: but if you see the essence of the nature of God as being to free the oppressed from their oppression, then you are necessarily engaged in a challenge to power . . . Secondly it marks a quite different theological method . . . what liberation theologians are saying is . . . the only way you will derive theological truth

is by starting where people are, because it is where poor and particularly oppressed people are that you will find God. Now that stands on its head sixteen hundred years of philosophical tradition in Christendom. From the third century, Christians have thought the way to establish theological truth has been to try to derive consistent propositions, that is to say propositions that are consistent with the facts of the tradition as revealed primarily in the Bible . . . What the liberation theologians are saying . . . is that this will not do as a way of doing theology. If you want to do theology, you have to start where people are, particularly the people that the Bible is primarily concerned with, who are the dispossessed, the widow, the orphan, the stranger, the prostitute, the pimp and the tax-collector. Find out what they are saying, thinking and feeling, and that is the stuff out of which the glimpses of God will emerge. Thirdly . . . this method of thinking about God solves the problem of verification . . . It has always been a puzzle to theologians to know how you test for truth any proposition you want to make about God. The fundamentalist Protestants still say 'It's fine. The Bible will tell you whether it is true or not' . . . The sophisticated liberal theologian will say 'Test it against the tradition, against the mind of the church, against other propositions and see if it is coherent with those' . . . The liberation theologians will say very simply 'the test for truth is the effect it has on people's lives. Is this proposition . . . actually liberating people or enslaving them?'[13]

(i) A NEW WAY OF DOING THEOLOGY?   Most exegetes who are influenced by liberation theology would not want to claim that they have *the* hermeneutical key to the reading of Scripture (though there *are* some who think the perspective of the poor is *the* criterion for a true reading of Scripture). They are insistent that the immediacy of the relationship between the biblical narratives and the situation and experiences of the poor has enabled them to glimpse interpretative insights which have so often eluded the sophisticated, cerebral approach of First World biblical exegesis.

The evangelical and popular roots of liberation theology need to be recognized. It is known in this country as a result of the translations which have been made of many of the writings of the leading liberation theologians from Latin America. The Boff brothers from Brazil, Sobrino from El Salvador, Pixley from Mexico and Nicaragua, Segundo from Uruguay and Miguez Bonino from Argentina have become leading spirits of that theology.[14] The form which liberation theology takes is normally not unfamiliar to the sophisticated theological readership of the First World. Often buttressed with footnotes, and demonstrating a wide knowledge of the philosophical and cultural tradition of European thought, these books seem to offer an alternative (but no less sophisticated) approach to the theological task which uses the familiar language of conventional theological discourse. It is a façade which needs to be pierced in order to understand more clearly what precisely energizes these writers.

At the heart of the theology of liberation is the twofold belief that in the experience of oppression, poverty, hunger and death God is speaking to all people today and that God's presence among the millions unknown and unloved by humanity but blessed in the eyes of God is confirmed by the witness of the Christian tradition, particularly the Scriptures themselves.[15] It is this dual conviction, nurtured by the thousands of Basic Christian Communities, which is the dynamic behind liberation theology. Liberation theology would not exist in any meaningful sense without it and the corresponding preferential option for the poor. It is, as Derek Winter has remarked, 'theological reflection that arises at sundown, after the heat of the day when Christians have dirtied their hands and their reputations in the struggle of the poor for justice, for land, for bread, for very survival'.[16]

Liberation theologians have themselves drunk deep at the well of European biblical scholarship, and are grateful for it. Nevertheless, their method of work differs from what is customary in this country. Many spend a significant part of each week working with grassroots communities in the shanty towns on the periphery of large cities or in rural communities. As part of their pastoral work they listen to the poor and facilitate the process of reflection on the Bible which is going on in the grassroots communities. Unlike many European and North American theologians, their writing has not taken place in the context of academic institutions which have rendered them immune from the personal and social pressures of the countries in which they live. Thus Leonardo and Clodovis Boff are closely identified with grassroots activities

among the poor and marginalized in various parts of Brazil. Jon
Sobrino has known what it is like to be a target of death squads in
El Salvador and to have seen his dear friend Archbishop Oscar
Romero assassinated. It is that experience of identification with
the poor and involvement in the injustices of their environment
which is the motivating force driving the liberation theologians'
theology and the spirit which fills an apparently European edifice
with insight and power.

Thus those involved in liberation theology stress the importance of the wisdom and insight of the poor as the focal point of
theology. They gain insights from listening to the poor, as they
read and use Scripture in the whole process of development and
social change. The exegetes find that this process of listening and
learning has given them a stimulus to their exegesis and, more
importantly, has opened up new vistas and questions in the
interpretative enterprise. This grassroots biblical interpretation
provides a basis for the more sophisticated theological edifices the
liberation theologians wish to build. Yet it is clear that the
different experiences and the world-view of the poor offer an
unusually direct connection with the biblical text. This approach,
whatever its shortcomings in terms of exegetical refinement, has
proved enormously fruitful as far as the life of the Christian
Church is concerned. The liberation theologians are what
Antonio Gramsci, the distinguished Italian Marxist theoretician,
described as 'organic intellectuals',[17] something that is brought
out in this description of the theological task by Leonardo Boff:

Obviously this recapturing of the original import of Christianity entails a break with hegemonic religious traditions.
Normally it is up to the *intellectual of the religious organism* to
sew a new seam when the rupture takes place. On the one side,
through their links with the oppressed classes these intellectuals help them to perceive, systematize, and express their
great yearnings for liberation. On the other side, they take up
these aspirations within a religious (theological) project, pointing up their coherence with the fundamental ideas of Jesus and
the apostles. Thanks to this breaking of the ice, important
segments of the ecclesiastical institution can ally themselves
with the oppressed classes and make possible the emergence of
a people's church with characteristics of the common people.[18]

Rooted in the Basic Christian Communities, an agenda is being set for liberation theology which is firmly based in the struggles of millions for recognition and justice. The text becomes a catalyst in the exploration of pressing contemporary issues relevant to the community; it offers a language so that the voice of the voiceless may be heard. There is an immediacy in the way in which the text is used because resonances are found with the experiences set out in the stories of biblical characters which seem remote from the world of affluent Europe and North America.

The Bible offers a typology which can be identified with and at the same time be a means by which the present difficulties can be shown to be surmountable in the life of faith and community commitment. To enable the poor to read the Bible has involved a programme of education which teaches the contents of the biblical material so that it can be a resource for thousands who are illiterate. In such programmes the value of the primary text, experience of life, is fully recognized. Therefore, the poor are shown that they have riches in plenty to equip them for exegesis. This is balanced with the basic need to communicate solid information about the stories within the Bible themselves, of which many remain ignorant.

So when we talk of the theology of liberation we are not just speaking of the works of the theologians but of a theological approach which gains its inspiration from the activities of the Basic Christian Communities in many countries in Latin America. The Bible is being used as part of the reflection by the poor on their circumstances as they seek to work out appropriate forms of response and action. In that process the reading of Scripture is often by-passing the dominant methods of the First World. To those of us brought up on the historical-critical method the interpretations can often appear cavalier. They frequently have little regard for the historical circumstances of the text, its writer and its characters. There is often a direct identification by the poor with biblical characters and their circumstances, with little concern for the hermeneutical niceties which are invoked in applying the text to their own circumstances. In their use of Scripture the resources of the text are used from their perspective of poverty and oppression, and a variety of meanings are conjured up in a way reminiscent of early Christian and ancient Jewish exegesis.

The perspective of the poor and the marginalized offers another story, an alternative to that told by the wielders of economic power whose story becomes the 'normal' account. The story of Latin America is a story of conquest. It is *Latin America*, a continent whose story begins only with the arrival of the Europeans. The quest for Mayan and Aztec cultures in Central America and the much more recent attempts to uncover the buried story of the hidden millions of Nicaragua since 1979 are examples of a necessary challenge to the normal story which is portrayed as a European one. Liberation theology has its contribution to make to these projects. Of course, its complicity as part of the ideology imposed on the indigenous peoples of the sub-continent as the European conquerors swept previous cultures aside puts Christianity, in however progressive a form, in a rather difficult position. Yet its encouragement of the study of popular religion, whether Christian, Indian or Afro-American, must be part of its project to enable the story of the 'little people' of the sub-continent to be heard. In addition, it has championed the recovery of the religion of those within the Christian tradition who resisted the practice of conquest and despoliation, like Bartolomé de las Casas and Antonio Valdivieso, whose prophetic ministry stands alongside those whom the conquerors would prefer to forget. The familiar story of the wars of kings and princes, which all too easily becomes the staple fare of a normal view of life, is challenged as the horizons are expanded by attention to the voices drowned out by the noise of the mighty. It is part of the task suggested in Walter Benjamin's words: 'In every era the attempt must be made anew to wrest tradition away from a conformism that is about to overpower it.'[19] Those who have suffered humiliation and persecution of a kind which must never be repeated should resist the temptation to use the power they obtain to play the part of the oppressor.

(ii) THE HERMENEUTICAL KEY: GOD SIDES WITH THE POOR   The experience of siding with the majority of an oppressed and impoverished region has sent Christian ministers and theologians back to the pages of Scripture to think again about the demand of God. One of the leading figures in the implementation of liberation theology in the pastoral practice of the Brazilian Catholic Church, Helder Camara, explains how the Church arrived at its 'preferential option for the poor':

> We men [sic] of the church have been so preoccupied in maintaining authority and the social order that we didn't suspect that the social order masks a terrible disorder, a stratified disorder. For centuries, we were concerned with a very passive presentation of Christianity. We preached patience, obedience, respect for authority; we finished up by saying (this was the opium of the people!) that the sufferings here on earth are so ephemeral, and eternal happiness so great, that all this would be forgotten in a flash. But gradually it became clear that we couldn't go on preaching Christianity like this. Social injustice was becoming ever more blatant; so much so, that at Medellin in Colombia in 1968, at the conference of Latin American bishops, we denounced the presence in Latin America of an internal colonialism. It's not just foreign colonialists who come to exploit our people, but the privileged of the continent who maintain their wealth at the expense of penury – of millions of their fellow citizens.[20]

The poor are privileged in the eyes of God, and therefore should be the particular concern of those who are committed to the ways of God. While this divine preference is seen in the legal prescriptions of the Torah and in the condemnations of the canonical prophets of Israel's social arrangements, it is affirmed particularly in the life of Jesus of Nazareth, in whom Christians find the key to reading the text of Scripture as well as life:

> Jesus affirms the privilege of the poor, since He proclaims that they are to inherit the Kingdom. God, who undertakes to correct human mistakes, will give the keys of the Kingdom to the poor, for in the Kingdom justice will reign. It is natural that the victims of injustice and exploitation should be the first to receive the privilege of the Kingdom. Moreover, in Jesus we find a model of the way of life of the poor man who is also a 'servant of Yahweh'; he is not resigned to his poverty, but practises the hope which kindles hope in others too.[21]

If one examines the way in which the Beatitudes are treated in the writings of some liberation theologians, we can see that poverty is not glamourized. Indeed, poverty, which means a lack of resources necessary for life, is regarded as evil. Rather, the Beatitudes reveal the character of God, who identifies with the poor and marginalized: 'the kingdom of God comes first and foremost for those who, by virtue of their situation, have most need of it: the poor, the afflicted, the hungry of this world'.[22] God is therefore to be known by virtue of identity with the poor:

> The kingdom . . . comes to change the situation of the poor, to put an end to it. As the first Beatitude tells us, the poor possess the kingdom of God. That is not due to any merit of theirs, much less any value that poverty may have. On the contrary, the kingdom is theirs because of the inhuman nature of their situation as poor people. The kingdom is coming because God is humane, because God cannot tolerate that situation and is coming to make sure that the divine will is done on earth. Poverty must cease to wreak destructive havoc on humanity.[23]

Jesus' identification, whether in his divine self-emptying (Phil. 2.6ff.) or in the character of the relationships he established during his mission, demonstrates solidarity with those on the margins. Theologians like Gutierrez recognize the difference which is to be found between the Lucan ('Blessed are you poor', Luke 6.20) and Matthean ('Blessed are the poor in spirit', Matt. 5.3) Beatitudes. Instead of preferring one to the other, Gutierrez stresses that both reflect the appropriate attitudes. Matthew's emphasis on spiritual poverty depicts an attitude of openness to God. Luke's more material emphasis demands a commitment by which one assumes the conditions of the needy of this world in order to bear witness to the evil which makes most poor and the minority rich.

Another passage which is used as part of the elaboration of the option for the poor is the parable of the sheep and the goats in Matthew 25. Here the Son of Man judges on the basis of practical responses to the poor and outcast. This Son of Man, according to the Gospel of Matthew, is none other than the figure who had nowhere to lay his head, went up to Jerusalem, was executed and rose again. Finally, he is to appear to his disciples as the Danielic Son of Man to whom all power had been given (Matt. 28.18; cf. Dan. 7.14). He promises that he will be with them always. That presence may seem most naturally to be found in the circle of disciples ('where two or three are gathered in my name', Matt.

18.20). But the last judgement makes it clear that the hidden presence of the risen and glorified Son of Man comes in unexpected persons. Not even the righteous were aware that they had met the glorious Son of Man ('Lord when did we see thee hungry', etc.). Liberation theologians would accept Jürgen Moltmann's point, on the basis of Matthew 25.31ff., that the wretched 'are the latent presence of the coming Saviour and Judge in the world, the touchstone which determines salvation and damnation'.[24] The poor are a reminder of that transcendent God in our midst. That is a significant role, and it gives a clue to the important hermeneutical implications which are derived from this conviction. As the poor are particularly close to God in whom one meets the risen Christ, that must be the place from which to view the world and its injustices.

> Oppressed persons are the mediation of God because, first of all, they break down the normal self-interest with which human beings approach other human beings. Merely by being there the oppressed call into question those who approach, challenging their being human, and this radical questioning of what it means to be a human being serves as the historical mediation of our questioning of what 'being God' means. That is why those who approach the oppressed get the real feeling that it is they who are being evangelised and converted rather than those to whom they seek to render service. What we are saying here . . . is what comes across in the famous gospel passage about the Last Judgement: Going to God means going to the poor. The surprise felt by human beings on hearing that the Son of Man was incarnated in the poor is the surprise we must feel to comprehend the divinity of God on the cross.[25]

As we can see, what some of these writers are claiming is that the vantage-point of the poor is particularly and especially the vantage-point of God. As such it acts as a criterion for all theological reflection and exegesis. In addition, it has ecclesiological implications, for, according to Sobrino,[26] the church must 'be formed on the basis of the poor' and 'as the "centre" of the whole':

> [the poor] are therefore structural channels for finding the truth of the Church and the direction and content of its mission.

The Church of the poor is not automatically the agent of truth and grace because the poor are in it; rather the poor in the Church are the structural source that assures the Church of being really the agent of truth and justice. In the final analysis, I am speaking of what Jesus refers to in Matthew 25 as the place where the Lord is to be found.[27]

Sobrino does not suggest that 'the Church of the poor' is going to be something alongside mainstream Christianity. In asserting that the mark of the true Church is going to be its acceptance of the perspective of the poor he is clearly rejecting the claims of opponents of the theology of liberation that it has been attempting to create a parallel 'popular' Church alongside the institution. Sobrino explicitly rejects this:

> When we say that the Church of the poor is the true Church we are not speaking of 'another' Church alongside the Catholic Church or the various Protestant Churches. Nor are we saying that where this Church of the poor exists it exists in a pure form, uncontaminated by sin and error, nor that it is coextensive with the Church of faith. What we are saying is that the Church of the poor is in its structure the true way of being a Church in Jesus; that it provides the structural means of approximating ever more closely to the Church of faith; and that it is more perfectly the historical sacrament of liberation.
>
> If all this is the case and if it is happening in Latin America, it is because Christ has willed to show himself not in any place whatsoever, nor even in the structure, good in principle which he established, but in the poor. We must describe this new phenomenon of the Church of the poor as representing on the one hand a conversion of the historical Church and on the other its resurrection.[28]

In the light of criticism of the so-called 'Popular Church', theologians like Leonardo Boff have been at pains to stress the deep roots of the Basic Christian Communities within the life of the Catholic Church. Certainly they may offer a new perspective and are (in the words of Cardinal Joseph Ratzinger) a sign of hope for the renewal of the Church. But Boff makes it quite plain that he does not conceive of the Basic Christian Communities as comprising an embryonic sect, however much some of their

critics may like to portray them as such. Rather, he argues that
they are the leaven in the lump, a remnant within the people of
God:

> The new church will have to remain faithful to its path. It will
> have to remain loyally disobedient. It will have to seek a
> profound loyalty to the demands of the gospels. Critically
> reflecting upon these questions and convinced of its path it
> must have the courage to be disobedient to the demands of the
> centre, without anger or complaint, in deep adherence to the
> desire to be faithful to the Lord, the gospels, and the Spirit –
> the same desire that is presumed to motivate the institutional
> church.[29]

We note here the repeated emphasis on Jesus and the Gospels as
the central criterion of obedience. The question of selectivity will
be touched on elsewhere, but its place in the understanding of the
option for the poor must be noted here. The idea of a 'canon
within the canon' has always been an important exegetical device
for Christians. Criticism of the selectivity of the liberation
theologians' option for the poor cannot disguise the way in which
other passages and ethical outlooks have been preferred by those
who have construed Christian discipleship in an equally partisan
and controversial manner. What needs to be stressed, of course, is
that the theme of concern for the poor and outcast does not
exhaust all the material related to social ethics in the Bible. The
entry of more and more rich people into the Church led to a rather
more accepting attitude towards the status quo, and to a compromise over wealth and with the society in which ordinary Christians had to live. This point is noted, for example, by Julio de
Santa Ana:

> . . .there are at least two levels at which the community of
> faith responds to the challenge of poverty: while some Chris-
> tians live as ordinary believers and in one way or another come
> to a compromise between the demands of faith and the styles of
> life around them, others attempt a more radical response, with
> no concessions to context, thus trying to maintain the funda-
> mental demands of faith. As a result, we have on the one hand
> 'ordinary' Christians, and, on the other, those who choose a
> monastic life; on the one hand those who believe they could

continue to have property and wealth, and on the other, those who abandon everything in their eagerness to be absolutely faithful to the demands of the gospel. This we believe was the result of the synthesis which took place in the second century between the problem of the presence of the rich in the church, and the challenge presented to it by the poor and poverty. The two extremes came together in a compromise concerning the way in which brotherly charity should be practised.[30]

The point at issue between the liberation theologians and their conservative critics is the meaning of these passages and the question whether in fact the references to the poor in the Jesus tradition can actually bear the weight of the interpretation of the option for the poor which also involves an *active* struggle against injustice. Much will depend on the interpretation of the eschatological material. The argument is widely used that the earliest Christians, including Jesus himself, did not concern themselves with changing society because they believed that God was going to do that in the near future when the Kingdom of God was brought in. Thus it may be possible to repudiate the idea that a tension ever existed between the radical practitioners of the Jesus ethic and those who sought to work out a compromise with the existing order. Recent study, however, suggests that already in the New Testament a tension such as is outlined by de Santa Ana was being felt.[31] They have recalled us to the Jesus of the synoptic Gospels as a crucial hermeneutical key in understanding the heart of the response of Christian discipleship: 'as you did it to one of the least of these my brethren, you did it to me' (Matt. 25.40).

2   THE FORM OF LIBERATION EXEGESIS

The purpose of this section is to look in a general way at the methods of interpretation practised by the theology of liberation. Since the publication in English of Clodovis Boff's *Theology and Praxis*,[32] it has been made abundantly clear that liberation theologians are prepared to reflect critically on their own exegetical work, both by an outline of its main characteristics and by a discussion of its historical context.

Works of exegesis by liberation theologians have been much

more readily appreciated in recent years, and the contribution of liberation theology to our understanding of the biblical texts has been more widely accepted. Few courses of study on the New Testament nowadays, for example, would wish to ignore Fernando Belo's commentary on Mark[33] or José Miranda's commentary on John.[34] At the same time, the nature of the liberation theologian's approach to the text has provoked some important general discussion of exegesis, for instance in the discussion of 'materialist' readings of the Bible.[35]

However, it is still fair to say that there is widespread ignorance of the methods of exegesis employed by liberation theology, and a failure to discuss the place of those methods in Christian tradition. Instead they are often discussed in terms which deliberately present them as alien to that tradition. To describe the theology of liberation, for instance, as making the 'new ideology' of Marxism its hermeneutical starting-point,[36] fails to recognize the extent to which its starting-point is one that has been common to centuries of Christian interpretation.

All too often the theology of liberation is presented in terms of the adage that every heresy is the revenge of a neglected truth. It is suggested that because traditional exegesis has failed to pay attention to the experience of oppressed Christians in Third World countries, a movement has arisen which is exclusively the reflection of such experience. In fact, liberation exegesis is as appropriate to a First World as to a Third World context. It is a method which sets out to awaken the exegete to the context of his or her reading of the Bible, and this by definition applies to all contexts and not simply to the ones within which the theology of liberation initially emerged.[37]

Many criticisms of liberation theology seem to be at least partly attempts to marginalize rather than to understand it. It is accused of having 'Marxist' presuppositions foreign to the mainstream of Christian thinking, and to be significant only where there is large-scale poverty and starvation. However, it can be argued that the theology of liberation and its exegesis is as relevant – in some ways more relevant – to rich nations as to poor ones, and also that it exists within a framework that is recognizable as traditionally Christian. Far from representing the 'new' force of Marxism asserting itself within the Christian fold, the interpretation of Scripture offered by the theology of liberation is more consistent with traditional methods of exegesis than many people imagine.

The starting-point chosen here for looking at liberation theology's methods of interpretation is Clodovis Boff's *Theology and Praxis*, and in particular his discussion of two different ways of reading the Bible. These two approaches to exegesis, labelled by Boff the 'correspondence of terms' and the 'correspondence of relationships', are not of equal value. The 'correspondence of terms' approach, which represents what many take to be the form of liberation exegesis, is heavily criticized and rejected. The 'correspondence of relationships' approach, on the other hand, which Boff claims to be the proper approach to the text for the liberation theologian, is shown to be consistent not only with aspects of traditional Christian interpretation but also with the methods of exegesis practised by the biblical writers themselves.

Theology and Praxis represents a major contribution to the attempt to erect what the book itself calls the 'methodological scaffolding' of liberation theology. It therefore provides a useful entry-point for our discussion of the way in which the theology of liberation understands the Bible. By examining Boff's definitions of exegesis closely, we shall be able to develop further the arguments so far merely outlined concerning the biblical and traditional character of liberationist exegesis.

(i) THE CORRESPONDENCE OF TERMS   The task of hermeneutics today, according to the 'correspondence of terms' approach, is a very simple one. On the basis of a simple historical examination, it believes that Christian communities today – or at least some Christian communities – live in a world which is similar to, if not identical with, the world in which Jesus himself lived. Hence the Christian community today can be related to its contemporary political context in exactly the same way that Jesus was related to his political context. The task of hermeneutics then becomes analogous to that of producing the same play in modern dress and with characters drawn from the contemporary world. In the twentieth century the part of Sadducees is played by the dependent bourgeoisie, that of the Zealots by revolutionaries, that of Roman power by modern imperialism, and so on.

At least some aspects of the 'correspondence of terms' approach can be highlighted from *The Gospel in Solentiname*, a collection of commentaries by Nicaraguan peasants living in the small Christian community of Solentiname in Lake Nicaragua.[38] When the community worshipped together at mass, the traditional homily on the gospel was replaced by a dialogue about it. The ideas of the *campesinos* expressed in these dialogues were gathered together by one of the founders of the community, Ernesto Cardenal, a priest who after the revolution of 1979 became Minister of Culture in the Nicaraguan government.

Extracts from *The Gospel in Solentiname* have been put together with paintings done in 1981 and 1982 by peasants returning there after the revolution, and have been published in a book edited by Philip and Sally Scharper.[39] Fresh in the minds of the painters was the destruction of the community in 1977 by forces of the dictator Somoza, and his subsequent overthrow in the revolution two years later. The pictures, which illustrate scenes from the Gospels, do so in a way that plainly identifies the leading characters in the events narrated by the biblical text with leading figures in the events leading up to the revolution in Nicaragua.

For example, in a painting illustrating the massacre of the innocents (Matt. 2.16), we see soldiers in the uniform of Somoza's National Guard. They carry automatic weapons, not swords. In another picture, opposite the story of Salome's dance before Herod (Mark 6.14–29), we again encounter a scene from contemporary Nicaragua. Not only are the furnishings and the dress of the characters modern, but set out on the table as part of the refreshments are bottles of Coca-Cola. The bottles point to the all-pervasive influence of the United States, just as in the New Testament period the coinage pointed to the all-embracing power of imperial Rome. In representing the story of the entry into Jerusalem (Matt. 21.1–11), the crowds are portrayed entering a Central American city, bearing placards welcoming the Messiah as 'Liberator'. Corresponding to Pilate's question to the crowd: 'Whom do you want me to release for you?' (Matt. 27.17), is a picture of the crowd bearing placards reading 'Vivo Somoza'.

According to the method of 'correspondence of terms' described above, the gospel story is reproduced in a contemporary context, with twentieth-century figures related to one another in the same way that the characters in the gospel story were related. Boff represents the model in mathematical terms thus:

$$\frac{\text{Jesus}}{\text{His Political Context}} = \frac{\text{Christian Community}}{\text{Its Political Context}}$$

In the Nicaraguan paintings which we have described, the reader is called upon to identify a clear correspondence between the biblical story and contemporary history. Events in Nicaragua, dictated from without by the United States in the North, correspond to events in first-century Palestine, dictated from without by Rome. Powerful local families, like the Herod dynasty in the first century or the Somoza dynasty in the twentieth, act as semi-autonomous dictators under the ultimate authority of an external imperial power. They act brutally to protect their interests, Herod with his soldiers and Somoza with the National Guard. Those whom they oppress are prevented from organizing against them. But popular movements of resistance make headway none the less.

The presumption of the illustrations is that the conditions of contemporary Central America bear a similarity in crucial respects to those of first-century Palestine, and that for precisely this reason the artistic freedom to represent biblical characters in modern form is justified.

Take for instance the following commentary upon the flight into Egypt described in Matthew 2.13–15:

> There are many campesino families that have had to leave their homes in many parts of Central America, fleeing from misery and hunger, or because they have been driven off their lands, or because the National Guard is killing the campesino leaders, burning farmhouses, raping women, jailing whole families, torturing. And the picture of all these families fleeing, mothers carrying their children in their arms, is the same as the flight to Egypt.[40]

The argument is that a community with experience of persecution, exile and torture is justified in representing the biblical story in terms of its own environment precisely because of a historical correspondence between its own life and that of the Jesus movement in its early days.

Few would doubt the truth of this presumption. Certainly the perception of the gospel events will be quite different to a community whose current way of life involves an experience of persecution of which few in contemporary Britain have any first-hand experience. The way in which the gospel comes to life for those who read it from the perspective of certain circumstances in their own life expresses the fundamental insistence of liberation theology that the *Sitz im Leben* of the interpreter is of crucial importance to the work of exegesis. At the same time, it would be wrong to think that the liberation theologian believes in a naive equivalence between the situation in ancient Palestine and that, for instance, in contemporary Nicaragua. Indeed a naive confidence in such an equivalence is something that Cardenal, in his enabling role in the dialogue, seeks to modify in *The Gospel in Solentiname*.

Boff is not content with the 'correspondence of terms' approach. He specifically claims that he wishes 'to raise certain questions with respect to this model, with the objective of preparing to propose an alternative'.[41] Among the questions which he raises are the following:

Have the historical, cultural, political, ideological, and especially religious conditions (for example, the influence of apocalypticism) influencing Jesus been respected?[42]

Has due consideration been accorded the extreme complexity of our society, and the degree of development of political awareness to which we have attained, on the level of analysis and on the level of ideology, during the twenty centuries which separate us from the gospel events?

Can our political contexts be so closely identified, thematically, with the political context of the Bible that resemble them, that we should read 'oppression' for 'Egypt', 'liberation' for 'exodus', and 'political assassination' for 'cross'?

For Boff, there may be parallels between, for instance, first-century Palestine and twentieth-century Nicaragua, but there are also important differences. Where, for instance, is the parallel in the twentieth century to the apocalyptic expectation that characterized the world in which Jesus lived?[43]

Other differences concern Boff too. What, for instance, of the general developments in political awareness that have taken place over the last two millennia, and which even in the Third World

are bound to exercise considerable influence today? Boff criticizes
the lack of sophistication which draws out one or two parallels
between the first and the twentieth centuries, only to assume from
then on that there are no important points of divergence. Sandino
suffering political assassination can then be substituted for Jesus
suffering crucifixion, Somoza can be substituted for Herod, a
United States President for a Roman Emperor, and so on. The
process of using the Bible in the modern day becomes no more
demanding than the act of reproducing the same dramatic text in
modern language and using contemporary characters. Almost
anyone would concede that the task of hermeneutics is more
complicated than that.

Such a model is undoubtedly naive. It presupposes that history
simply repeats itself, a view which could never be acceptable to
the Marxist tradition which is clearly important to the theology of
liberation. It could indeed be said that Boff has a thoroughly
Marxist appreciation of the differences between the ancient world
and modern capitalism, and therefore sees in the 'correspondence
of terms' approach a static view of history, which presumes that
the same conditions can somehow apply in the twentieth century
as applied in the first.

It is also unclear what are the assumptions of the 'correspondence of terms' approach concerning the historical accuracy of the
text. Is it treating passages of the Bible like the infancy narratives
simply as straightforward historical accounts of events in first-
century Palestine? If so, it is clearly unable to come to terms with
the nature of the process by which the text itself was formed, and
with the way in which texts were primarily a response to the needs
of the communities for whom they were composed. Important
questions concerning the historicity of Scripture are raised here,
and will be considered in depth when we look at the second of
Boff's two models.

The Gospel in Solentiname illustrates that the 'correspondence of
terms' approach provides an important challenge to the idea that
the gospel is simply a historical narrative about the past. It rightly
bases its interpretation upon the need to understand the biblical
tradition in the context of current events. However, important
questions are raised about the approach by Boff. First, it appears
to assume that we know more about the past than we do or can,
and that there is a closer relationship between past and present

than history itself can allow. Second, it is unclear what the assumptions of the 'correspondence of terms' method are concerning the limitations of the historical-critical method. These criticisms will be examined further when we move on to Boff's second approach.

(ii) THE CORRESPONDENCE OF RELATIONSHIPS   This represents the approach favoured by Boff himself. It can be represented by the following simple equation:

$$\frac{\text{Scripture}}{\text{Its Context}} \quad \frac{\text{Ourselves (a theology of the political)}}{\text{Our Context}}$$

To explain the definition we can consider each 'side' of the equation in turn.

Where the left side is concerned, it should be noted that whereas the 'correspondence of terms' approach (p. 85) referred to Jesus and his political context, the 'correspondence of relationships' approach refers to Scripture and its political context. The latter approach recognizes that our access to Jesus (and to much of what we can learn about his social and political environment) is mediated through the Bible, and that in the light of biblical criticism we have to face up to the problems raised by that mediation. In Boff's words: 'The work of the *Formgeschichte* and the *Redaktionsgeschichte* schools has taught us that the biblical writings, in their final form, are the result of the superimposition of successive redactional layers – a fact that introduces a distance between the texts as actually presented and the *ipsissima verba Jesu* . . .'[44]

In the light of modern biblical criticism (and indeed not only modern criticism, despite the views of certain modern critics), it cannot be assumed that the words attributed to Jesus in the Gospels are the words which he actually spoke, or that the circumstances of his life and death depicted in the biblical texts are those which actually occurred. Such an assumption would nowadays be limited to the margins of critical scholarship, perhaps only to its 'fundamentalist' or 'evangelical' edges. While most scholars would agree that there is a historical core or ground to what the texts say, they would argue that the purpose of the New Testament was not simply to relate a series of past events.

In line with modern biblical criticism, Boff takes the view that

the Christian communities of the first two centuries interpreted
Jesus' words and deeds not verbatim but in the light of a 'creative
fidelity'. Modern critical scholarship, he argues, has not demon-
strated that the New Testament is an inaccurate rather than an
accurate historical record of events and sayings in Jesus' life.
Rather, it has demonstrated that the text was not intended to be
such a record. Had, indeed, the historical intention been the
primary one, then the New Testament writers would have been
engaged purely in antiquarian research, and would not in consequence have a continuing significance in the present. On lines
that strongly recall the approach of Bultmann, Boff argues that
the primary intention of the biblical writers was to awaken a
commitment of faith from their readers, not simply to inform
them of events that had taken place. He quotes José Comblin to
make the point: 'The object of theology is not simply the
reconstitution of the published words of Jesus. Theology per-
forms its entire task only when it seeks to comprehend the words
of the Spirit, who applies Jesus' words at a determinate time.'[45]

Although Boff stands firmly within a tradition that accepts the
results of critical scholarship, he sees the impact of that scholarship in a particular light. Modern criticism, he believes, is in no
position to accuse the authors of the New Testament of being
'bad' historians, any more than the theology of liberation is
entitled to assume that they were 'good' historians. He sees the
biblical writers neither as 'bad' historians nor as 'pre-historians'
suffering from a 'primitive' world-view that was unable to antici-
pate the subtle practices of the historical-critical method. He sees
them as witnesses to Christ whose primary task is not to be
historians at all. Indeed, although he makes only passing reference to Bultmann in the context of espousing a 'presentistic'
conception of hermeneutics, the closeness of their approaches is
evident.[46]

The point of the 'correspondence of relationships' approach is
not only to describe the intentions of the biblical writers themselves, but to relate that intention to the way in which the
scriptural texts have been understood in the tradition of the
Church, much of whose exegesis has been unjustly neglected by
those commentators who prefer to reject or marginalize any
interpretation that precedes the rise of the historical-critical
method.[47] Indeed, viewed in Boff's terms Scripture is itself very

much a development of church tradition. It represents the response of the early Christian communities to the challenges of their day, one which could speak to their present reality only through a 'creative fidelity' to the words and works of Jesus.[48]

The right-hand side of the equation representing Boff's preferred 'correspondence of relationships' method now falls into place. The theology of liberation must be – and is – part of that church tradition which has always been concerned primarily with awakening a faithful commitment in the present rather than in researching the past. Thus Boff can say that the task today is 'to re-effectuate the biblical act, the act that gave birth to the Bible itself as a text'.[49] By applying the text in the 'creative' way that it does in the twentieth century, the theology of liberation is not 'misusing', 'mishandling' or 'distorting' Scripture. On the contrary, it is acting precisely in accordance with the manner in which the text itself was written, and with the traditions of Jewish and, later, Christian exegesis within which it was born and cultivated.

If the 'correspondence of terms' model suggests that liberation theology is in danger of a naive pre-critical literalism in its approach to the text, the implication of the 'correspondence of relationships' model is quite different. Far from being threatened by modern criticism, this approach requires it in order to justify its own methodology. If the liberation theologian is to justify the way in which what Boff calls 'the theology of the political' interprets reality today, then he or she has to demonstrate continuity with the way in which the early Christian communities interpreted reality through the formation of the Bible. If this continuity can be shown, then it will be possible to place liberation exegesis within a respected tradition of biblical interpretation.

Boff cites Gerhard von Rad as one who 'has shown that the Old Testament was constituted by way of a constant renewal of old traditions in view of new situations'.[50] Although he cites von Rad's monumental *Old Testament Theology*, his point is perhaps most clearly made in von Rad's revision of material from that work in *The Message of the Prophets*, where he discusses the different ways in which scholars have understood prophecy, and makes the following important point about the renewal of tradition:

The way in which tradition mounts and grows can be closely followed in the prophetic writings. Exegesis must be less ready than at present to look on this infusion of new blood into the prophetic tradition as 'spurious' or an unhappy distortion of the original. The process is in reality a sign of the living force with which the old message was handed on and adapted to new situations.[51]

Moreover, this is a principle which can be applied as clearly to the New Testament as to the Old. Von Rad's own examples of 'adaptation', for instance, include not only that of making the prophecy of Balaam apply to the Greeks (Num. 24.24), but also the use of messianic prophecy from Amos in Acts 15.16–17, and Paul's use of prophecy from Isaiah in Romans 15.12.[52] The point about renewing old traditions in view of new situations applies as much to Christian as to Jewish sacred writings.

Boff seeks to make use of von Rad – by no means himself identified with the theology of liberation – in order to demonstrate that the exegesis practised by the liberation theologians in the present is consistent with the forms of exegesis practised by the authors of the Old and New Testaments. He sets out to show that the approach of the liberation theologian is a truly biblical approach, since it was one practised by the biblical writers themselves!

By way of illustration, we may consider the controversial Christian doctrine of the virgin birth. This doctrine is based upon references in two of the four Gospels, Matthew and Luke, and in Matthew's version (Matt. 1.22–3) it is said that the manner of Jesus' birth fulfils a prophecy in Isaiah: 'Behold, a virgin shall conceive and bear a son, and his name shall be called Emmanuel' (Matt. 1.23; cf.Isa.7.14). It is often pointed out that the Hebrew word used in the Old Testament should not be translated 'virgin' but rather 'young woman', or more precisely an adult woman who is still young enough to bear children – but not necessarily a virgin at all. During the last three centuries or so before Christ, Greek-speaking Jews of the Diaspora made a Greek translation of the Old Testament for their own purposes, a translation which came to be known as the Septuagint. The Septuagint used the Greek word *parthenos*, meaning virgin, in its version of Isaiah 7.14, and from this some commentators have concluded that the story of Jesus' virgin birth is somehow derived from a 'mistaken' translation.

This attitude to the birth story is part of a general approach to the 'fulfilment' of the Old Testament in the New. It is pointed out, for instance, that few of Matthew's quotations from the Old Testament are 'accurate', that the text is constantly 'distorted' to suit the interests of the evangelist, and the conclusion is reached that Christianity simply engages in a specious twisting of the Old Testament texts in order to suit the concerns of the New. At the very best, the New Testament authors can be said to have been mistaken, as in the rendering of Isaiah 7.14 to refer to a virgin rather than simply a young woman of an age where it is possible to give birth.

It would be fair to say that this approach to prophecy and fulfilment, which labels Matthew's method a distorting one, is not that of modern scholarship. It is important, however, to note the reason why it is unacceptable. The reason lies in the fact that none of the biblical writers, Jewish or Christian, would have found it inappropriate, to recall the discussion of von Rad's theology, to 'renew old traditions in view of new situations'. There is no need to suppose that the author of Matthew's Gospel was somehow misled by the Septuagint into believing that Isaiah referred to a virgin rather than a young woman. For he could quite simply have applied a text which referred to a woman of child-bearing age to the situation of a virgin in his own day. In the same way, there is no need for the renowned scholar C. K. Barrett to say that 'The Old Testament passages adduced in the New are of varying degrees of cogency,' and to continue: 'It is not easy, for example, to believe that Rachel's weeping for her children (Jer. 31:15) had much to do with Herod's massacre of the innocents.'[53]

What does Barrett mean by 'varying degrees of cogency' or 'much to do with'? It is important not to think that the fulfilment of prophecy, the renewal of old traditions in view of new situations, is a matter of the sort of 'fulfilment' that occurs when a predicted historical event actually takes place. Indeed, it is difficult to think why, apart from the most literalistic understanding of prophecy and fulfilment, one should not think it highly appropriate to recall the tradition of Rachel weeping for her children in the context of the massacre of the innocents. If we recognize, with von Rad, that prophets like Isaiah and Jeremiah 'regarded themselves as the spokesmen of old and well-known sacral traditions which they reinterpreted for their own day and age',[54] then we shall be better able to understand both the use which they themselves make of such traditions, and the use which is made of their own traditions by later writers such as the authors of the New Testament. We shall also be able to understand the exegetical methods of the theology of liberation, which themselves face precisely the same criticisms concerning their 'cogency' that we have found levelled here, for instance, at Matthew's use of Jeremiah.

When, for example, the theology of liberation applies the tradition of the exodus from Egypt to the situation of oppressed peoples seeking freedom from persecution in poor countries of the world today, one can imagine the same 'Barrett-like' reservations being expounded. Did the escape of the Israelites from bondage in Pharaoh's Egypt really 'have much to do with' the situation of Nicaragua overthrowing Somoza in 1979? One response which we may now make is that Somoza's overthrow had as much to do with the exodus as had the baptism of the earliest Christians, which St Paul was quite prepared to connect with the journey of the Israelites out of Egypt:

> You should understand, my brothers, that our ancestors were all under the pillar of cloud, and all of them passed through the Red Sea; and so they all received baptism into the fellowship of Moses in cloud and sea. They all ate the same supernatural food, and all drank the same supernatural drink; I mean, they all drank from the supernatural rock that accompanied their travels – and that rock was Christ. (1 Cor. 10.1–4, NEB)

The primary justification for the methodological approach adopted by the theology of liberation is that it claims to be related to the way in which the biblical writers themselves interpreted their own earlier traditions. We see it related to the method of exegesis employed by Paul, both before and after his conversion, to interpret his own Jewish tradition. It is related similarly to the method of exegesis employed by the author of Matthew's Gospel, as we have seen from the example of Isaiah 7.14. Matthew applied a text which he knew perfectly well referred to a young woman in Isaiah to a virgin in his own *Sitz im Leben*. In the same way, he applied a text (the book of Jonah) which spoke of a man living three days and three nights in the belly of a whale to the three days spent in the heart of the earth by the Son of Man (Matt. 12.39–40).

Boff's preferred model supposes that the theology of liberation adopts a method of interpretation which is related to that employed by those who first reflected upon the life and death of Jesus, and therefore is related to the method adopted by Scripture itself. To the charge that the theology of liberation adopts an approach to the text whose 'creative fidelity' is merely a cover for distortion and manipulation, the 'correspondence of relation-ships' allows Boff to respond by claiming that it is a truly biblical approach.

(iii) LIBERATION EXEGESIS AND FIDELITY TO THE TEXT   Our discussion of the 'correspondence of relationships' highlights one of the ironies of a familiar understanding of Scripture that represents one kind of approach from a Protestant perspective. On the one hand, such an approach is deeply committed to the supreme authority of the Bible for Christian faith. On the other hand, its approach to exegesis has tended to be deeply hostile to allegorical forms of interpretation and to the Catholic notion of a *sensus plenior*, when it can be amply demon-strated that these represent a hermeneutic adopted by the scriptu-ral writers themselves (e.g. Gal. 4:21–31) and perhaps even by Jesus himself (e.g. Mark 4.3–20; 12.1–9). The form of liberation exegesis suggests that it can be aligned with these forms of interpretation, and it is noticeable that one important critic of liberation theology writing from an Evangelical viewpoint, Andrew Kirk, makes precisely this connection, arguing that liberation exegesis 'has a certain analogy with the Catholic understanding of the relationship between Scripture and tradi-tion'.[55]

Kirk, however, insists that what he calls the 'classical way of doing biblical exegesis' moves in quite the opposite direction to the theology of liberation, moving 'from the biblical texts to the writer's theological intentions and then to external referents', whereas liberation theology is accused of 'reversing' this order and 'moving from the external referents to the biblical text'.[56] In fact, however we are to make sense of Kirk's description, it is the theology of liberation which has more claim to being a 'classical' way of exegesis, if by classical is meant a way of exegesis commonly practised by the biblical writers themselves.

Whatever its claims may be, the form of exegesis defended by Kirk in terms of an 'alternative hermeneutic' to liberation theology, based upon the Reformation principle *sola scriptura*, is arguably less determined by fidelity to Scripture than by fidelity to a form of historicism which is of much more recent origin. Indeed much of what passes for the 'historical-critical' method, while it is presented as a tool for extracting 'the meaning' of the text, in effect distances the contemporary reader from the very world of the biblical writers which it is intended to uncover, and certainly fails to understand their own intentions. In the Anglo-Saxon world, it tends to produce two diametrically opposite and equally inappropriate schools of thought. On the one hand, a naively literalistic 'fundamentalist' wing of scholarship pronounces the scriptural writers 'good' historians, telling the story of Jesus 'as it happened'. On the other hand, the other and more mainstream wing of scholarship pronounces them 'bad' historians, and offers to 'correct' their insights in the light of modern 'objective' methods. Both wings omit to make themselves critically self-conscious of the 'historical-critical' method as such, and of its limitations as a hermeneutical tool. In this context we can understand the importance of Boff's concern to distance the theology of liberation from the 'correspondence of terms' approach which he understands to be similarly limited by historical assumptions.

If we apply to the theology of liberation the principle which has been applied by von Rad to the biblical writers themselves, that of 'renewing' old traditions in view of new situations, then we naturally have to consider what are the constraints upon interpretation admitted by the liberation theologian. How does liberation exegesis interpret ideas of truth and falsity in the understanding of texts? Or does its embrace of the idea of renewing old traditions in new situations mean in reality that the text can be given any meaning whatsoever, as some critics of liberation theology insist?

Boff helps to answer these questions by his discussion of what he sees as two pitfalls in interpretation. One, which he describes as 'semantic (or textual) positivism', can clearly be associated with the historical approaches whose limitations we have tried to set out. 'Semantic positivism' is an approach to interpretation of the Bible which exploits the need for scholarly research when investigating Christian sources in order to locate and capture the meaning of the text for all time. It claims that the meaning can be fixed eternally and then stored away, able to be brought out again and used in its pristine condition in all subsequent generations. Such an approach rejects the idea that a text which once referred to a young woman can subsequently be applied to a virgin. The understanding of the text must always be the same, fixed in granite in terms of 'the original intention of the author' or 'the meaning' of the text.

The second pitfall in interpretation outlined by Boff is, however, equally important. This he calls 'hermeneutic improvisation', and is an approach that takes from Scripture only what serves the interests of the reader. Passages of the Bible are used as 'proofs' for pre-established theological attitudes. The Christian corpus becomes 'a kind of cafeteria, where everyone can find something or other to suit his or her particular tastes'.[57] It is this second pitfall which is often identified with the theology of liberation by its critics.

But Boff insists that the second pitfall is profoundly interconnected with the first. Underlying both approaches, he claims, is the same failing, namely a desire to manipulate and control the text in such a way that dialogue between text and reader is effectively excluded. Instead of dialogue, both the 'pitfall' approaches demonstrate the reader 'wanting something from' the text, and determined to extract it whether the text 'likes it' or not! This sort of language may seem quaint, virtually personifying the text – but that is just the point. It needs to be recognized that the text has a capacity to 'answer back', and that in the process of interpretation the interpreters are themselves interpreted.

Hermeneutics must be dialectical, a shifting connection between reader and text. This is possible only if neither is permitted to deny the other. The reader denies the text in the fallacy of subjectivism. All that is allowed to be of significance is the pre-established position of the interpreter. The opposite fault is that of essentialism, the fault of much 'historical' scholarship. Here all that is permitted to be of importance is the text, whose meaning is supposedly established for all time quite independently of any reader. One position makes the text irrelevant to the reader's preconceptions; the other approach makes the reader irrelevant to the meaning of the text.

Boff seeks to identify a connection, then, between an approach which is guilty of imposing the preconceptions of the reader upon the text and an approach which seeks to extract the 'original meaning' of the text as 'true for all time'. Each denies the dialogue between interpreter and text, but they do so from opposite directions. One seeks to remove the text from the dialogue; the other seeks to remove the reader from the dialogue. But from their different starting-points they both have the effect of denying the dialectical character of interpretation.

In consequence, the liberation theologians find their opponents guilty of the 'crime' of which they themselves are accused, namely that of seeking to manipulate the text. They would argue that attempting to fix our understanding of the text for all time by means of claims concerning its 'original meaning' is as much an exercise in manipulation as is the 'fallacy of subjectivism' which extracts only what serves the interests of the reader. In both cases the interpreter seeks to control rather than to be controlled by the Word of God.

The theology of liberation practises a method of exegesis which claims to be consistent with traditional approaches to Scripture. If it represents a break with the past, then it is primarily with the relatively recent past that has been dominated by the so-called historical-critical method. Much of Boff's hermeneutical critique, indeed, is clearly indebted to the criticisms of the historical-critical method that came earlier this century from the giant figures of Karl Barth and Rudolf Bultmann. It is a critique deeply aware of the ways in which the interpreter attempts to slide out from under the text which might challenge the ways in which he or she lives or the values which he or she holds. The historical-critical method allows my reading of the text to be a judgement on the past but in no way a judgement upon me – a criticism which could as easily come from Bultmann as from the theology of liberation. It is a method which expresses the human understanding trying to control and master the text rather than to be controlled by it – or by the Word speaking through it – a criticism which is as much Barth as Boff. Moreover, if the theology of liberation appears in many cases to be deeply critical of 'academic scholarship' and the detached nature of the academic, it would be quite wrong to represent this as if it were somehow a view at odds with two millennia of 'objective' Christian thinking. On the contrary, the theology of liberation arguably has a greater claim to a traditional view of the unity of thought and practice in Christianity than the view of many of those who treat it as an unheard-of break with the canons of true theological scholarship.

The renewal of old traditions in the light of new situations, the heart of liberation exegesis, has nothing to do with a desire to manipulate the text. It has to do with a willingness on the part of the interpreter to allow himself or herself to be manipulated by the text, to allow the *Sitz im Leben* of the reader to be criticized and judged by the Word of God. It is a form of exegesis that is willing to make the reader vulnerable to the scriptural content, to make room for what Karl Barth called 'an act of the content itself'.[58]

(iv) LIBERATION EXEGESIS AND THE LEGACY OF BULT-MANN   A section on Rudolf Bultmann's approach to exegesis may seem out of place in this book, but two reasons might be offered to justify its inclusion. In the first place, there are important parallels between existentialist and liberation approaches to exegesis, and these would seem to justify some relevant observations about the most important theologian who has offered an existentialist approach to the Bible. Indeed the parallels have been brought out by a number of works of liberation theology, among which we might specifically mention Dorothee Sölle's *Political Theology*, which she perceived as a dialogue with Bultmann.[59]

In the second place, liberation theology is all too easily perceived as an aberration, a temporary exegetical phenomenon representing either a capitulation to current secular fashion or a response to specific social and political realities of our day. We have tried to respond to this criticism by setting the theology of liberation within an established tradition of exegesis. For that reason, we think it important to draw attention to those forms of twentieth-century interpretation which can be understood as standing in close relation to liberation theology, and even as sharing or anticipating a number of its methods. Existentialist approaches to Scripture, deeply significant as they are for biblical exegesis (what introduction to the study of the New Testament does not include Bultmann's essay 'New Testament and Myth-ology'?[60]), represent one such form of twentieth-century interpre-tation, and our discussion is intended further to bring out its links to the theology of liberation.

It should also be said that both approaches have come under fire from similar directions. Both face criticism from supporters of the historical-critical method who accuse them of 'subjecti-vism', 'relativism', and lack of respect for the author's intentions (the former two need always to be placed in inverted commas and defined carefully). While the existentialist and liberation 'schools' represent different approaches to the text, they have had to face what is in many respects a broadly similar challenge. It therefore seems appropriate to spend some time discussing the relationship between the two.

Bultmann recognized that by asking what the Bible meant for a people who lived two millennia ago (a question which the authors of the biblical texts themselves would never have accepted as a definition of the task of exegesis!), we avoid the crucial question of what it means for us today. It is that crucial question which the theology of liberation seeks to ask, and although its tools may be different from those employed by Bultmann, there is an obvious link between their approaches. Bultmann may have asked what the text of Scripture means to us by employing the existentialist language of Heidegger; the theology of liberation may use categories drawn from a tradition of socio-political thought owing more to Karl Marx. Yet both have a common approach to interpretation which recognizes that the point of exegesis is to address questions in the reader's life now – whatever their different views as to how that life is to be analysed.

Dorothee Sölle recognizes the importance of Bultmann's per-ception in 'Is Exegesis Without Presuppositions Possible?' that presuppositionless exegesis is an impossibility.[61] She perceives in the programme of 'demythologization' a process which needs to be applied in every generation, but she charges Bultmann with an 'individualist constriction' in his approach to the text.[62] Because he reduced the question of meaning to that of individual exist-ence, Bultmann failed to recognize the political intention inherent in the cosmological images used by the biblical narrative. He recognized in the 'myths' of the first century a primitive science but not a primitive politics. He excluded the political dimension of myth. His concentration on the scientific immaturity of the writers blinded him to what Ernst Bloch called the 'rebellious-eschatological' character of myth, 'a form of slave-language for men who cannot openly express their hopes'.[63]

Bultmann approached the task of re-presenting the kerygma in a 'scientific' age, an age used to 'washing-machines and aeroplanes' and conscious of the all-embracing nexus of causal law taken for granted by modern science.[64] However, Sölle points out, he failed to see that the kerygma must also be re-presented in a politically and economically – as well as scientifically – very different environment from that of the New Testament writers. He considered the extent to which human beings in the modern world have achieved a scientific mastery, but not the extent to which they have achieved political mystery. He recognized that they no longer, for instance, view light and darkness as beyond their control, but did not consider whether they hold starvation and hunger, or inflation and unemployment, as beyond their control. He appreciated the way in which modern society has acquired the means to control the natural environment, while neglecting the struggle to determine the political and economic environment.

Sölle claims to be completing, in a 'political theology', what Bultmann began. She writes: 'More and more it appears to me that the move from existentialist theology to political theology is itself a consequence of the Bultmannian position.'[65]

Bultmann insisted that the interpreter is not a blank slate upon which the text writes its message, but that the interpreter approaches the text with certain questions in mind that themselves constrain the way in which he or she will understand it. But Sölle seeks to develop this argument by pointing out that these constraints concern not only the scientific but also the political environment of the interpreter. The 'mythological' character of New Testament writings like the book of Revelation has to be understood not only in terms of a particular scientific but also a particular political *Sitz im Leben*, which has in turn to be related to the political context of the reader – a programme which contemporary liberation exegesis has attempted to follow through.[66]

Bultmann's programme of demythologization was expressed in the context of rejecting the idea of 'presuppositionless exegesis'.

It was also expressed in the context of recognizing that the point of exegesis is to awaken faith through an act of commitment by the reader. He was profoundly concerned with the problem of how men and women in a modern 'scientific' age might come to appreciate the demands of the gospel upon them. His understanding of the resurrection, for instance, was not so much that it 'did not happen' as a historical event, but rather that the point of interpreting the Bible is not to study the past but to hear God's Word in the present. Therefore, whatever 'happened' when Jesus emerged from the tomb, the significance of the resurrection lies in the faith which it awakened in the disciples and, moreover, can awaken in us as his disciples today.[67] In Bultmann's own words:

Are we to read the Bible only as an historical document in order to reconstruct an epoch of past history for which the Bible serves as a 'source'? Or is it more than a source? I think our interest is really to hear what the Bible has to say for our actual present, to hear what is the truth about our life and about our soul.[68]

The theology of liberation is profoundly concerned to emphasize, with Bultmann, that 'our interest' as readers of Scripture is to 'hear the truth about our life and about our soul'. But it would claim that this truth has to be recognized not only in the form of an existential transformation of the individual, but also through a political transformation of his or her social environment – indeed the two are inseparable. Its method of exegesis would claim to be adopting Bultmann's approach to interpretation while removing the 'individualist constriction' which it perceives in the particular tools that he advocated. For this reason it is, as Sölle argues, a completion rather than a rebuttal of Bultmannian hermeneutics.

The links between existentialist and liberation exegesis would be clearer still were there not certain ambiguities in Bultmann's own thinking. The key notion of *Entmythologisierung* (demythologization) in his thought must apply to every reader approaching the text in any period of time. As Bultmann himself affirmed, there is demythologization *of* the New Testament because there is demythologization *in* the New Testament – for instance Paul's treatment of death entering the world in Romans 5.12ff.[69] But to see that the biblical writers themselves reinterpret earlier myths, just as we reinterpret the myths inherited from them, entails that every age engages in the work of demythologization. The myths of our own time will be treated in the same way in centuries to come. The traditions of the past, as Boff avers, will be constantly renewed in the light of new situations. Unfortunately, Bultmann did suggest that the Christian message can be interpreted without any element of myth. This view depends upon what is meant by 'myth', an issue on which Bultmann was similarly unclear. At times he used it in a sense close to 'analogy', in order to point to the inevitable limitations of human speech about God. In that sense, myth will survive in any society seeking to reflect about God.[70] At other times he used it to represent a way of thinking according to which human beings believed that the power or powers overlooking and determining their activity were tangible forces derived from this world, for instance good and evil spirits. In the modern world, Bultmann argued, we know that the stars are physical bodies 'whose motions are controlled by the laws of the universe', and not 'daemonic beings which enslave mankind to their service', so such 'mythological' ideas can be firmly disposed of.[71]

Whether or not we agree with Sölle that Bultmann failed to recognize the political dimension to belief in 'good and evil spirits' and 'daemonic powers', it is possible to see that in the second sense of 'myth' the task of the interpreter in a scientific age might be considered a purely negative one. That is to say, he or she will be 'demythologizing' rather than 'remythologizing', undressing the body to reveal the naked truth rather than re-expressing the Christian message in the myths appropriate to the situation of humanity today. This is the sense of 'myth' which has been happily adopted by those scholars who see Bultmann as someone who offers them another weapon in the armoury of the historical-critical method, and who believe that 'demythologization' represents a means of reaching back to the 'original meaning' of the text behind the layers of mythical encrustation.

In fact, few writers could be further from the historical-critical method than Bultmann. He made his position clear in an important essay, 'The Problem of Hermeneutics', published originally in 1950, in which he insisted that 'every interpretation incorporates a particular prior understanding (*Vorverstandnis*) – namely, that which arises out of the context of living experience to which the subject belongs'. Without such a prior understanding, he argued, and 'the questions initiated by it, the texts are mute'. And he continued:

> In such a view the answer is also found to the dubious question *whether objectivity in the knowledge of historical phenomena, objectivity in interpretation, is attainable* . . . For facts of the past only become historical phenomena when they become significant for a subject which itself stands in history and is involved in it . . .[72]

In other words, an accurate reconstruction of the past by an act of detached self-effacement on the part of the interpreter is impossible. The past cannot 'speak for itself'. It will always be read, understood, questioned and constructed in the light of the *Sitz im Leben* of the historian. Facts of the past are fashioned into 'historical phenomena' according to the style of the age which is fashioning them. For this reason 'The demand that the interpreter must silence his subjectivity and extinguish his individuality, in order to attain to an objective knowledge, is therefore the most absurd one that can be imagined.'[73]

As Bultmann pointed out in the later essay 'Is Exegesis Without Presuppositions Possible?', to which we referred earlier, the interpreter cannot be considered a blank slate on which the text writes its pure message, but always has an active rather than passive role in understanding, approaching the biblical writings with 'a specific way of raising questions',[74] a pre-understanding. It is the reality of this pre-understanding that is so important to the understanding of exegesis, for it introduces the interpreter and his or her *Sitz im Leben* into the hermeneutical process. Studying the *Sitz im Leben* of the reader becomes as important a part of that process as the investigation of the *Sitz im Leben* of the writer. The task of understanding is seen to be a 'fusion of horizons', that of the interpreter and that of the text, rather than the detached academic's view of one horizon only.[75]

(v) LIBERATION EXEGESIS AND CONTEMPORARY APPROACHES TO BIBLICAL CRITICISM   The 'fusion of horizons' between text and interpreter has implications that are clearly recognized by the theology of liberation. Juan Luis Segundo spells them out in *The Liberation of Theology*:

> Thus the fundamental difference between the traditional academic theologian and the liberation theologian is that the latter

feels compelled at every step to combine the disciplines that open up the past with the disciplines that help to explain the present. And he or she feels this necessity precisely in the task of working out and elaborating theology, that is to say, in the task of interpreting the Word of God as it is addressed to us here and now.[76]

The exegete must work not only in the traditional disciplines, such as history and archaeology, which primarily study the past, but also in those, like social theory, which primarily study the present. The traditional methods with which the biblical student is so familiar – source, form and redaction criticism – concentrate exclusively on the *Sitz im Leben* of the biblical writer. What sources did the writer use? What was his intention in 'editing' material before him into a Gospel or a letter? What current religious traditions influenced the arrangement of his material? Segundo recognizes the need to ask questions about the interpreter of the text as well. It is important, for instance, to understand the social and economic world within which the Bible is read, as well as that within which it was written, if we are to understand how it is to be interpreted. The traditions and sources drawn upon by those who read the texts now are as significant as the traditions employed by those who composed them. And alongside a study of the redactional intentions and 'interests' of the authors, it is necessary to examine the purposes of, and contemporary influences on, the interpreter.

This broader understanding of the hermeneutical process is now widely accepted, and is evident in a variety of different exegetical 'schools'. Liberation theology could only be counted as one of many such schools. However, it exists in a close relationship to most of the others, drawing on them and in turn influencing them. The insights of structuralist hermeneutics have had a clear influence on liberation exegesis, for instance in the importance of Roland Barthes' work for Fernando Belo's interpretation of Mark's Gospel.[77] Feminist writing, in its searching examination of the influence exercised by a predominantly male Christian Church on the formation and the interpretation of the Bible, has also been closely linked to liberation theology.[78] The employment of 'critical theory' across a wide range of disciplines, particularly by the Frankfurt School, has had a profound influence on biblical hermeneutics too.[79] It is certainly no longer possible to consider liberation theology's approach to problems of biblical interpretation without some understanding of the sociology of knowledge and the writings of Paul Ricoeur and Jürgen Habermas.[80]

Much of what the theology of liberation has drawn from these other schools of thought has concerned what we have seen Segundo describe as the disciplines which open up the present. These, as much as those which open up the past, form an integral part of the exegetical process. They make it impossible to study the *Sitz im Leben* of the writer without at the same time examining that of the reader. Liberation exegesis adopts what Habermas has called an 'ideological suspicion' in order to consider the connection between knowledge and human interests in the interpreter[81] – a process which academic theology has been happy to apply to the biblical writers themselves for more than a century. Hence the feminist theologian approaches the text acutely aware that previous commentators have been predominantly male; the liberation theologian approaches the text acutely aware that previous commentators have been predominantly from Western Europe rather than the 'Third World'. It would probably be fair to say that the validity of this approach, concentrating on the context of the interpreter as part of the work of exegesis, has now become quite widely accepted. But, as Duncan Ferguson has observed, 'There is a fear, justified I think, on the part of liberation theologians that traditional American and European theology contains ideological elements which sustain bourgeois society, the class structure, and the misery of the proletariat.'[82] Such elements have, however, created rather more than a 'justified fear' on the part of liberation theologians. They have occasioned a systematic analysis of the ways in which the social and cultural world of the interpreter contributes to the nature of contemporary biblical exegesis.

Much of the 'new hermeneutic' was engaged in the process of describing in different ways the nature of the interpreter's involvement in exegesis. It was as if the establishment of the idea that no exegesis was without presuppositions had opened the floodgates to theories of what those presuppositions actually were. Some understood them primarily in terms of language itself, as in Ernst Fuchs' 'Speech-Events' and Gerhard Ebeling's 'Word-Events'.[83] Others went a stage further back still, and perceiving, in Walter Wink's words, that the brain was the 'uninvited guest' at all cultural phenomena,[84] looked to structural anthropology to uncover the impact on exegesis of the patterns of thinking adopted by the human brain.

Literary criticism of the Bible is connected to structural and linguistic approaches. It has developed its own critique of forms of interpretation which have presumed that in the Bible they are looking for an inventory of doctrines or a set of moral home-truths, rather than a narrative whose moral or theological significance cannot be set out in the form of a set of definitions.[85] Literary criticism exposes not only the literalist presuppositions of many interpreters but also the manner in which their pre-understanding makes the Bible unreadable in the modern world.

It is not possible in this introduction to do more than mention these other forms of exegesis, all of which have more or less close links with the theology of liberation. We have tried to examine them from the perspective that explores the implications of refusing to detach the interpreter from the process of interpretation. It cannot be said that liberation exegesis is the only form of interpretation aware of this perspective, or that it alone can provide a complete account of the perspective from which the Bible is currently read and understood. What can be said is that alongside, and in a close interrelation with, other contemporary methods of interpretation, the theology of liberation approaches the Bible in a way that draws on traditional approaches to the text and on new insights into the process by which the canon of Scripture was formed. It has too close a connection with the way in which hermeneutics has developed generally in the twentieth century to be regarded as a mere aberration, a stray egg dropped by a Marxist cuckoo into the Christian nest.

(vi) CONCLUSION   In his *Theology and the Church*, a response to the Vatican document published in September 1984, *Instruction on certain aspects of the Theology of Liberation*, Juan Luis Segundo declares that 'a theology of liberation correctly understood constitutes an invitation to theologians to deepen certain essential biblical themes with a concern for the grave and urgent questions which the contemporary yearning for liberation and those movements which more or less faithfully echo it pose for the church.[86] In the course of the next few chapters we shall outline some of those 'grave and urgent questions', not only in a Third World but also in a British context. Using the 'correspondence of relationships' approach outlined by Boff, we shall look at the way in which a political theology addresses itself to our situation. It will not be a simple 'updating' of the presumed situation and conflicts of Jesus' own life, as set out in the 'correspondence of terms' approach. No one can claim to be interpreting the text in a liberationist way who simply says: 'For Herod read Somoza or Thatcher.' Rather, it will be a form of interpretation that relates its concern for the 'grave and urgent questions' of today to the way in which the biblical texts themselves represented a concern for the grave and urgent questions that arose during the period of their long gestation.

The exegetical approach of the liberation theologian maintains the dialectic between text and interpreter. It neither allows the interpreter free rein at the expense of the text, with a licence to make of it what he or she wants, nor the text free rein at the expense of the interpreter, as in those 'objectivist' approaches which think that the situation of the reader is irrelevant to the exegetical task. It is an approach which seeks to be faithful to the long hermeneutical process by which, within the Judeo-Christian tradition itself, the texts themselves emerged as commentary upon the changing political situation of their own times.

In a profound study of the sociology of knowledge, *Knowledge and Human Interests*, Jürgen Habermas wrote as follows:

> Whether dealing with contemporary objectivations or historical traditions, the interpreter cannot abstractly free himself from his hermeneutic point of departure. He cannot simply jump over the open horizon of his own life activity . . . An interpretation can only grasp its object and penetrate it in a relation in which the interpreter reflects on the object and himself at the same time as moments of an objective structure that likewise encompasses both and makes them possible.[87]

The fact that the interpreter cannot jump out of his or her cognitive skin is not a denial of objectivity. It does not mean drowning truth in a bath of relativism. It means understanding that the possibility of objectivity exists only in the relation between object and interpreter, as Habermas argues here. Concepts of truth and objectivity are not made redundant by the approach which, in common with others, liberation theology makes to the text, aware of the crucial significance of the present horizon of the interpreter to exegesis. But, as Habermas says, the 'objective structure' which is employed here must encompass both object and subject. The truth of which liberation exegesis speaks as much as any other method of exegesis must be recognized as dialectical. It is a dialogue between past and present, in which neither can displace the other. If there is a danger of the past being displaced by liberation theologians who adopt the Bible as an additional weapon with which to mount a pre-determined campaign, there is a danger of the present being displaced in the approach to the text of much academic scholarship. It may therefore be that liberation exegesis has an important contribution to make to biblical interpretation. In the following chapters we shall offer some examples of its work.

NOTES

1 On the problems of the historical-critical method, see, for example, W. Wink, *Transforming Bible Study* (London: SCM Press, 1981), ch. 7, and (in more detail), *The Bible in Human Transformation: Toward a New Paradigm for Biblical Study* (Philadelphia: Fortress Press, 1973), ch. 1. On the relations between First and Third World exegesis, see C. E. Gudorf, 'Liberation Theology's Use of Scripture: A Response to First World Critics', *Interpretation* 41 (1987), pp. 5–18, but note also the robust defence of the First World approach in J. Barr, *Holy Scripture: Canon, Authority, Criticism, The Sprunt Lectures 1982* (Oxford: Oxford University Press, 1983) and J. Barton, *People of the Book?: The Authority of the Bible in Christianity. The Bampton Lectures 1988* (London: SPCK, 1988).

2 See, for example, J. D. G. Dunn's inaugural lecture, 'Testing the Foundations: Current Trends in New Testament Study' (University of Durham, 1984), p. 23.

3 cf. M. Kahler, *The So-Called Historical Jesus and the Historic Biblical Christ* (Philadelphia: Fortress Press, 1984).

4 F. Jameson, *The Political Unconscious: Narrative as a Socially Symbolic Act* (London: Methuen, 1981), p. 35.

5 See, for example, G. Theissen, *The First Followers of Jesus: A Sociological Analysis of the Earliest Christianity* (London: SCM Press, 1978), W. Meeks, *The First Urban Christians: The Social World of the Apostle Paul* (New Haven/London: Yale University Press, 1983) and the concise survey in D. Tidball, *An Introduction to the Sociology of the New Testament* (Exeter: Paternoster Press, 1983).

6 See W. Meeks, *The Moral World of the First Christians* (London:

SPCK, 1987) and J. Stambaugh and D. Balch, *The Social World of the First Christians* (London: SPCK, 1986).

7 C. Mesters, 'Como se faz Teologia hoje no Brasil?', *Estudos Biblicos* 1 (1985), pp. 1ff.

8 ibid., p. 10.

9 See C. Mesters' comments in his essay 'The Use of the Bible in Christian Comments of the Common People' in N. K. Gottwald (ed.), *The Bible and Liberation: Political and Social Hermeneutics* (Maryknoll, NY: Orbis Books, 1984) and 'The Use of the Bible in Christian Communities of the Common People' in S. Torres and J. Eagleson (eds), *The Challenge of Basic Christian Communities: Papers from the International Ecumenical Congress of Theology 1980* (Maryknoll, NY: Orbis Books, 1984), pp. 197–210.

10 Such a reminder is continually offered by Ernesto Cardenal in his contributions to *The Gospel in Solentiname*, where a historical perspective is injected into the contemporary discussion by the *campesinos*; see E. Cardenal (ed.), *The Gospel in Solentiname*, 4 vols (Maryknoll, NY: Orbis Books, 1977–84).

11 Mesters, 'Use of The Bible', Gottwald (ed.), *Bible and Liberation*, p. 122.

12 See J. Libanio's succinct summary in his contribution to D. Winter (ed.), *Putting Theology to Work* (London: British Council of Churches, 1981), pp. 77ff.

13 C. Elliott, 'Is There a Liberation Theology for the UK?', Heslington Lecture, the University of York, 1985, p. 11.

14 There are useful introductions to the thought of the leading proponents of liberation theology in P. Berryman, *Liberation Theology: Essential Facts About the Revolutionary Movement in Latin America and Beyond* (London: I. B. Tauris, 1987), C. and L. Boff, *Introducing Liberation Theology* (London: Burns & Oates, 1988) and T. Witvliet, *A Place in the Sun: An Introduction to Liberation Theology in the Third World* (London: SCM Press, 1985).

15 A point well made in G. Gutierrez, *The Power of the Poor in History* (London: SCM Press, 1983), pp. 65–6.

16 Quoted from his study pack on Basic Christian Communities published by Christian Aid, 1988.

17 This was the way in which Frei Betto, a Brazilian Dominican, described the work of the liberation theologian in a lecture delivered in Cambridge in December 1987. For Gramsci's ideas, see Q. Hoare and G. N. Smith (eds), *Selections from the Prison Notebooks* (Lawrence and Wishart, London 1971), pp. 10ff, 60, 330ff.

18 L. Boff, 'Theological Characteristics of a Grassroots Church', in Torres and Eagleson (eds), *Challenge of Basic Christian Communities*, p. 133.

19 Walter Benjamin, *Illuminations*, H. Arendt (ed.), (New York: Schocken 1978), p. 255.

20 Quoted in Derek Winter's study pack on Basic Christian Communities published by Christian Aid, 1988.

21 J. de Santa Ana, *Good News to the Poor: The Challenge of the Poor in the History of the Church* (Maryknoll, NY: Orbis Books, 1979), p. 95. See further J. Parr, 'Jesus and the Salvation of the Poor. The Use of the Bible in Latin American Liberation Theology', unpublished PhD thesis, Sheffield University, 1989. We are indebted to John Parr for help with this section.

22 J. L. Segundo, *Jesus of Nazareth Yesterday and Today, vol. 2: The Historical Jesus of the Synoptics* (London: Sheed & Ward, 1985), p. 62.

23 G. Gutierrez, *A Theology of Liberation* (London: SCM Press, 1974), p. 107.

24 J. Moltmann, *The Church in the Power of the Spirit: A Contribution to Messianic Ecclesiology* (London: SCM Press, 1977), p. 127.

25 J. Sobrino, *The True Church and the Church of the Poor* (London: SCM Press, 1985), p. 222.

26 ibid., p. 93.

27 ibid., p. 95.

28 ibid., pp. 123–4.

29 L. Boff, *Ecclesiogenesis: The Base Communities Reinvent the Church* (Maryknoll, NY: Orbis Books/London: Collins Flame, 1986), p. 63.

30 de Santa Ana, *Good News*, p. 62.

31 See, for example, Theissen, *First Followers*.

32 C. Boff, *Theology and Praxis: Epistemological Foundations* (Maryknoll, NY: Orbis Books, 1987).

33 F. Belo, *A Materialist Reading of the Gospel of Mark* (Maryknoll, NY: Orbis Books, 1981).

34 J. P. Miranda, *Being and the Messiah: The Message of St John* (Maryknoll, NY: Orbis Books, 1977).

35 For an introduction by Belo to the 'materialist' approach later put into practice in his commentary on Mark, see his article 'Why a Materialist Reading?' in H. Kung and J. Moltmann (eds), 'Conflicting Ways of Interpreting the Bible', *Concilium* 138 (1980), pp. 17–23. See also M. Clevenot, *Materialist Approaches to the Bible* (Maryknoll, NY: Orbis Books, 1985) and below pp. 94ff.

36 As does Duncan Ferguson in his *Biblical Hermeneutics: An Introduction* (London: SCM Press, 1986), p. 177.

37 This point is developed more fully below in Part Five.

38 Cardenal (ed.), *Gospel in Solentiname*.

39 P. and S. Scharper (eds), *Gospel in Art*.

40 ibid., p. 16.

41 Boff, *Theology and Praxis*, p. 145.

42 ibid., pp. 145–6.

43 This question was asked by Wolfhart Pannenberg in his *Jesus – God and Man* (London: SCM Press, 1968), p. 242: 'The imminent expectation of the Kingdom of God, which determined the activity and the life of Jesus, is no longer a live option for us in its original sense. Even holding to it literally would no longer succeed in repeating the attitude of Jesus and his first disciples. The two

thousand years that lie between him and us make that impossible. The mere process of historical time makes every attitude that can be assumed today different from Jesus' imminent expectation.'

44 Boff, *Theology and Praxis*, pp. 146–7.

45 ibid., p. 303 (n. 85).

46 ibid., p. 297 (n. 33).

47 Classically to be seen in W. G. Kummel's *The New Testament: The History of the Investigation of its Problems* (London: SCM Press, 1973). Kummel gives almost no attention whatsoever to the investigation which preceded the Reformation period, and very little to what preceded the rise of the historical-critical method. There is no justification for neglecting fifteen hundred years of exegesis beyond the bias of rejecting whatever preceded (as also whatever follows!) that method.

48 This suggestive phrase, 'creative fidelity', is for Boff the *only* faithful approach to Scripture – the only way of reading *kata graphas*. See Boff, *Theology and Praxis*, p. 151.

49 ibid., p. 296 (n. 26).

50 ibid., p. 302 (n. 77).

51 G. von Rad, *The Message of the Prophets* (London: SCM Press, 1968), p. 27.

52 ibid., p. 27.

53 C. K. Barrett, 'The Interpretation of the Old Testament in the New' in P. R. Ackroyd and C. F. Evans (eds), *The Cambridge History of the Bible, vol. 1: From the Beginnings to Jerome* (Cambridge: Cambridge University Press, 1970), pp. 377–411. The quotation comes from p. 401.

54 von Rad, *Message*, p. 144.

55 J. A. Kirk, *Liberation Theology: An Evangelical View from the Third World* (Basingstoke: Marshall, Morgan & Scott, 1979), p. 186.

56 ibid., p. 186.

57 Boff, *Theology and Praxis*, p. 152.

58 See Karl Barth's essay, 'The Strange New World Within the Bible', in *The Word of God and the Word of Man* (London: Hodder & Stoughton, 1928), pp. 28–50.

59 D. Sölle, *Political Theology* (Philadelphia: Fortress Press, 1974), which is aptly subtitled 'A Conversation with Rudolf Bultmann'.

60 R. Bultmann, 'New Testament and Mythology', in H. W. Bartsch (ed.), *Kerygma and Myth: A Theological Debate* (London: SPCK, 1960), pp. 1–44.

61 See R. Bultmann, 'Is Exegesis Without Presuppositions Possible?' in S. M. Ogden (ed.), *Existence and Faith: Shorter Writings of Rudolf Bultmann* (London: Hodder & Stoughton, 1961), pp. 289–96.

62 Sölle, *Political Theology*, p. 48.

63 E. Bloch, *The Principle of Hope* (Cambridge, Massachusetts: MIT Press, 1986).

64 See Bultmann, 'New Testament and Mythology' in H. W. Bartsch (ed.) *Kerygma and Myth* (London: SPCK, 1960) pp. 1–44.

65   Sölle, *Political Theology*, p. 2.
66   See, for instance, E. Schussler Fiorenza, *The Book of Revelation: Justice and Judgment* (Philadelphia: Fortress Press, 1985).
67   Bultmann, 'New Testament and Mythology', pp. 38–43.
68   R. Bultmann, 'The Problem of Hermeneutics' *Essays Philosophical and Theological* (London: SCM Press, 1955), pp. 241–2.
69   R. Bultmann, *The Theology of the New Testament* (London: SCM Press, 1952), vol. I, pp. 258–9.
70   A great deal of the debate is merely a matter of definition, as Bultmann himself concedes: 'There certainly are [surviving traces of mythology] for those who regard all language about an act of God . . . as mythological. But this is not mythology in the traditional sense, not the kind of mythology that has become antiquated with the decay of the mythical world view.' ('New Testament and Mythology', p. 43.) This is just the point. Are we talking about mythological language as such, or about a 'kind of mythology', i.e. a particular sort of mythology that, as Bultmann says, has become antiquated?
71   Bultmann, 'New Testament and Mythology', pp. 9–16.
72   Bultmann, 'The Problem of Hermeneutics', p. 254 (his italics).
73   ibid., p.255.
74   See Bultmann, 'Is Exegesis Without Presuppositions Possible?', p. 289.
75   The idea of a 'fusion of horizons' (*Horizontverschmelzung*), derived from Hans-Georg Gadamer's *Truth and Method* (London: Sheed & Ward, 1975), is analysed in A. C. Thiselton, *The Two Horizons: New Testament Hermeneutics and Philosophical Description with Special Reference to Heidegger, Bultmann, Gadamer and Wittgenstein* (Exeter: Paternoster Press, 1980).
76   J. L. Segundo, *The Liberation of Theology* (Maryknoll, NY: Orbis Books, 1976), p. 8.
77   In the introduction to his *Materialist Reading*, p. 6, F. Belo, besides pointing out the influence of Marx on his thought, 'renders homage' to Roland Barthes' book *S/Z* (Paris: Editions de Seuil, 1970).
78   This is not to deny the autonomy of feminist theology as a movement, but it does have in common with liberation theology a concern for the *Sitz im Leben* of the (predominantly male) interpreter. See, for instance, the discussion entitled 'Biblical Criticism, Christian Woman and the Church' in Mary Hayter's *The New Eve in Christ* (London: SPCK, 1987), pp. 146–68.
79   See R. Geuss, *The Idea of a Critical Theory: Habermas and the Frankfurt School* (Cambridge: Cambridge University Press, 1981); P. Ricoeur, *Hermeneutics and the Social Sciences* (Cambridge: Cambridge University Press, 1981).
80   See J. B. Thompson, *Critical Hermeneutics: A Study of the Thought of Paul Ricoeur and Jürgen Habermas* (Cambridge: Cambridge University Press, 1981) for an introduction to their writings.
81   J. Habermas, *Knowledge and Human Interests* (London: Heinemann, 1972).

82 Ferguson, *Biblical Hermeneutics*, p. 177.
83 E. Fuchs, 'The Hermeneutical Problem' in J. M. Robinson (ed.), *The Future of Our Religious Past: Essays in Honour of Rudolf Bultmann* (London: SCM Press, 1971), pp. 267–78; G. Ebeling, *Introduction to a Theological Theory of Language* (London: Collins, 1973).
84 Wink, *Bible in Human Transformation*.
85 T. R. Wright, *Theology and Literature* (Oxford: Basil Blackwell, 1988). See especially the section 'Literalism: The Common Enemy' on pp. 13–20.
86 J. L. Segundo, *Theology and the Church: A Response to Cardinal Ratzinger and a Warning to the Whole Church* (London: Geoffrey Chapman, 1985), p. 172.
87 Habermas, *Knowledge and Human Interests*, p. 181

3

Exploring the Implications of a Liberation Exegesis in a First World Context 1: The Political Gospel

1   LIBERATION EXEGESIS: CONCERNS AND EMPHASES

The twin focus of liberation theology on the synoptic Gospels and on the coming of the reign of God reflects the preoccupations and emphases of Bible study in the Basic Christian Communities. Of course, the preoccupation with Jesus and the Kingdom is not particularly distinctive. It is hard to imagine a lecture on Jesus or on the Church and politics in Europe which does not resort to that particular theme. It is easy to see how the concern of Jesus with the poor and the outcast, his challenge to the authorities of his day and his persecution by them together offer an attractive paradigm for those who are themselves engaged in a struggle with authority and facing up to the reality of persecution and death.

As many of the liberation theologians have themselves received their graduate education in Europe and North America, it is hardly surprising that they should in large part reflect the interpretative concerns of that tradition whose investment is in the rediscovery of the biblical world and the search for the original meaning of the text. Consequently the theologians of liberation have taken up the quest for the historical Jesus as a means of criticizing a preoccupation with the superhuman, remote Christ of ecclesiastical confession. In the Christologies of Sobrino and Boff,[1] for example, there is a stress on the importance of the historical Jesus as a central criterion by which the theology of the Church, particularly its dogmatic explication of Jesus' significance, can be judged. A historical person wrestling with the specific social and political problems posed by his context offers liberation theology an Archimedean point in its demand that the specific contexts of theologians should be taken more fully into account. Thus Sobrino writes:

> The subjective starting point of Christology is faith as a lived experience . . .
>
> Looking for an objective starting point means looking for that aspect of the total and totalizing reality of Christ that will better enable us to find access to the total Christ. Here I propose the historical Jesus as our starting point. By that I mean the person, proclamation, activity, attitudes, and death by crucifixion of Jesus of Nazareth insofar as all of this can be gathered from the New Testament texts – with due respect for all the precautions imposed by critical exegesis . . .
>
> It can be historically verified that the various interpretations of liberation theology in Latin America seem to agree on one point: If a Christology disregards the historical Jesus, it turns into an abstract Christology that is historically alienating and open to manipulation. What typifies Jesus as a historical reality is the fact that he is situated and personally involved in a situation that displays structural similarities to that of present-day Latin America. At least we can detect a similar yearning for liberation and a similar situation of deep-rooted sinfulness. It is the historical Jesus who brings out clearly and unmistakably the need for achieving liberation, the meaning of liberation, and the way to attain it.[2]

Of course, the problem with such an important place being given to the historical Jesus is the fact that such portraits are themselves inevitably subject to the vicissitudes of historical research. The Jesus of history is the construct of the academic élite of the First World academies. That construction may prove to be an attractive one and a potent norm by which to judge theologies which have not themselves always been socially engaged. The Latin American theologians find themselves in a vulnerable position, however. The quest for the historical Jesus is a product of the European Enlightenment, and its export to Latin America along with the other dominant ideologies of Western culture renders the Latin American theological task parasitic upon the agenda set in Europe. Just as easily, the reaction against that quest can lead to the undermining of the biblical foundation of some liberation theology. The Jesus of history who can challenge the teaching of the Christian Church may readily be seen to be a chimera, more symptomatic of the minds which created him than the world of Second Temple Judaism, as Albert Schweitzer potently argued.[3]

Another popular book with peasants and the poor is the book of Revelation. This is because it speaks in graphic terms about the kinds of conflicts which are so real to the poor and oppressed.[4] Conflict is a word which seems to be frequently on the lips of many poor people. The experience of the state as an oppressor and the enormous concentration of wealth in the hands of the powerful make the imagery of Revelation 13 and Revelation 17–18 particularly apposite. In these passages the depiction of the state's diabolical role and the injustices of a society that has grown rich on the basis of oppression and exploitation chimes in with the experience of millions of poor. Those who have protested have frequently paid the price with their lives. When martyrs like Oscar Romero, the Archbishop of San Salvador,[5] can die because of their stand for justice, the promise of hope to those who hold fast to the testimony of Jesus is a living word in the midst of 'the great tribulation'. In the continuing struggles of the poor for basic facilities, of *campesinos* in rural areas to hold on to their land in the face of the ever-expanding arm of agro-business and multinational development, suffering and death are a reality of life. Revelation helps those in the struggle to hold on to hope. The view of history from its underside challenges the 'normal' common-sense approach to life where the rescheduling of debts, 'surgical' strikes against subversives, economic growth and the like are seen for what they always are: other ways of oppressing those who have no voice. As Wayne Meeks has graphically put it: 'The vision of the Apocalypse shreds and rips away that common sense [i.e. the taken-for-granted consensus about the way things are] with as much violence as that with which John sees the sky itself removed.'[6]

Of course, liberation exegesis can lay itself open to the charge that it uses a 'canon within the canon', a specific set of texts or passages which one can then use to make sense of the whole of the Bible. That is, however, an essential part of all biblical exegesis, for it is impossible to make sense of that disparate collection of material without doing that. Thus the Christian reading of the

Hebrew Scriptures starts from the assumption that these find
their fulfilment in Jesus the Messiah.

Clearly liberation exegesis is less comfortable with the Pauline
epistles, with their more conservative social ethics. Liberation
theologians stress the contextual nature of the biblical material.
They would argue that what we have, say, in Paul's injunctions
about the state in Romans 13 are not absolute demands laid upon
Christians to obey the government but conditions laid down for
the Christians in Rome in the mid-fifties AD which may not have
been appropriate for the Roman Christians ten years later at the
height of the Neronian pogrom. Some understanding of the
liberationist approach taken to this controversial passage may be
gleaned from the discussion of it in *The Kairos Document*.[7]

The critique of state theology in *The Kairos Document* concentrates on an analysis made of Romans 13, Paul's famous injunction urging the Roman Christians to be 'subject to the powers that
be'. It rejects the idea that Paul presents an absolute doctrine
about the state, and argues that the text must be interpreted in its
context. That context was a situation in which Christians felt that
they were exonerated from obeying the state because Christ alone
was their king and with Christ's reign all secular authority was to
be rejected. Paul, it is argued, insists on the necessity of some
kind of state, but that does not mean that all that the state does is
approved of by God. When a state does not obey the law of God
and becomes a servant of Satan, it is passages like Revelation 13 to
which one should turn instead.

That process of relativization whereby the specific context of
ethical injunctions is considered is one that is deeply rooted in
contemporary Pauline scholarship. It demands that we take
seriously precisely what is being asserted about the 'powers that
be', namely, that there are always going to be such powers,
whether in Church or state, until the Kingdom of God comes.
Acceptance of the necessity of government is not the same as the
acceptance of any and every government. That Paul is dealing
with such a theme seems to be suggested by the description of the
powers as the enforcers of good and the barrier to evil. Such terms
must be viewed in the light of God's standard of righteousness,
not that which is good in the eyes of the state.[8] In so far as most
states do not uphold the goodness of God in its entirety, they can
never demand unqualified allegiance from those committed to the

Kingdom of God whose goodness and values usually differ quite drastically from those of the powerful of the world.

From the perspective of the synoptic Gospels and the book of Revelation, we can see the major themes of Pauline theology in a new light: the hope for the liberation of our bodies in the midst of a world which is longing for the birth of a new age agrees with the larger version of the book of Revelation and reminds us of the eschatological focus which governs the whole of New Testament theology.

2 THE POLITICAL READING OF THE SYNOPTIC GOSPELS

The New Testament scholar Anthony Harvey was one of the leading theologians on the Archbishop's Commission which produced *Faith in the City*, a report on inner-city poverty in Britain.[9] Harvey also published *Jesus and the Constraints of History*, a major study of Jesus which appeared a few years before.[10] Occasionally the kind of sentiments in *Faith in the City* emerge there too. Thus he can write: 'the whole tenor of Jesus' work and character as conveyed by the gospels is in total contradiction to any ideology which involved violence or forceful political action. Jesus cannot credibly be described as one whose teaching was situated within the context of revolution and political reform'.[11]

Few would dissent from Harvey's view that Jesus was not a revolutionary (assuming, that is, that a person who proposed to overthrow the existing order by force of arms is meant here) – though questions may be raised as to whether Jesus' option specific to its own socio-political context remains decisive in this respect for Christians in other situations. Nevertheless there are other places where Harvey rightly concludes that in Jesus we find a figure whose activity is deeply disturbing within the political context of first-century Judaism. Although 'the prophet does not physically change things by his actions . . . his actions may represent the change which God wills to bring about and which the prophet is charged to proclaim'. Such prophetic activity and convictions challenged the status quo:

a person who assumed the right, even by a symbolic gesture, to pass judgment on any temple institution was thereby claiming

the authority of the prophet . . . Therefore an essential element
on any real advance towards the reign of God and a new age would
have to be some radical change in economic circumstances.

Such a person 'must be obeyed and followed. If not, he must be
eliminated,' for 'a man who said such things [as Jesus did] was
deserving of death if a dangerous and unwelcome popular movement was to be avoided'.[12]

This indicates that Harvey is of the opinion that Jesus' person
and activity were such that they were perceived to be a threat to
political stability. The question then is: Why can this not be
regarded as an indication that Jesus' teaching can be set in the
context of political reform and revolution? There is clear evidence
in the Gospels to justify the use of the term 'political' to describe
Jesus' activity. What Harvey describes is a very revolutionary
figure engaged in a project which was going to revolutionize the
understanding of the present responsibility of the people of God.

Whether or not Jesus may legitimately be described as a social
reformer is a moot point. One of the problems with such a
category is that it arises out of our modern situation. For us a
social reformer is a person involved in a secular project which has
little, if any, 'religious' component. As such Jesus can hardly be
termed a social reformer, for Jesus' activity was shot through with
the vision of the Bible for the ordering of the life of the people of
God. What is more, Jesus was not in the business of reform of the
Temple or of the institutions of the old order. Rather, according
to the synoptic narrative, by the end of his life he predicted the
end of the old order of society and the beginning of a new one.

Nor can we suppose that Jesus was involved in any formal sense
in the political processes of his day. He was not as far as we know
a member of the Sanhedrin or a local elder. But such a lack of
involvement in the 'official' organs of political power should not
lead us to suppose either that Jesus was not in the business of
political change or that he did not exercise political power. It was
the power of the charismatic leader who attracts a following, the
kind of leader who is at the edge of conventional life and whose
political thrust consists in the position of marginality which
makes an alternative political culture, however embryonic its
form, a possibility. As Clodovis Boff has put it:

Jesus was not, historically, a militant in the strict political sense, understanding politics as the superstructure encasing everything else, invested with the exercise of authority over the whole of society. He did not strive to do away with all authority, after the manner of an anarchist, or to inaugurate a new authority in a rough and brutal manner. Rather he accepted established authority critically . . . If we take the word 'revolution' in its broader acceptation, as denoting any radical change or structural transformation, then we should have to say that Jesus was revolutionary . . .[13]

Discussion of the mission of Jesus raises another question which has dogged the relationship between the New Testament and contemporary social ethics throughout this century: eschatology. Few would deny the central importance of eschatology both in Jesus' proclamation of the reign of God and as a dynamic system of beliefs which undergirded the outlook of the New Testament writers. That common ground is in itself part of the problem. There is an underlying assumption that the eschatological horizon of early Christian existence made first-century believers uninterested in the political realities of their context as they looked forward to the imminent end of this world and the coming of the new world of God's Kingdom. Since Johannes Weiss' seminal study *Jesus' Proclamation of the Kingdom of God*[14] appeared in 1892 (though the roots of his position lie much deeper in Christian theology), many scholars have maintained that there is a sharp distinction between God's eschatological Kingdom and the kingdoms of this world. Thus Jesus did not come to preach a this-worldly Kingdom at all: 'my kingdom is not of this world' (John 18:36, AV). We are frequently told that God's Kingdom is not something to be brought about by human initiative, for it is God's business alone. God's Kingdom cannot be contained within present history; it is entirely transcendent. So any attempt to see the Kingdom in terms of specific social and political programmes has departed from what Jesus wanted to say about the reign of God.

These points are succinctly made in *God in Strength*,[15] an influential study of Jesus' teaching on the Kingdom by Bruce Chilton:

At every point, Jesus' announcement directs our attention to God; the effects of the kingdom cannot be worked up into an entity separable from him. To do so results in a stereotyped scheme which can only by complicated exegesis be fitted into the flexible diction of Jesus' preaching. Attempts to see the kingdom as an apocalyptic régime, as a political movement, as a programme for social improvements, i.e., as anything other than the revelation of God, also run the risk of putting ideology in the place of faith. Such attempts are not only problematic as exegesis, they also ill accord with Jesus' refusal of self-will in favour of openness to a personal God. The basic stance of Jesus as well as his diction constrain us to do what we in so many ways resist: to apprehend God revealed in consummating strength.[16]

The thrust of these comments is that eschatology and history have little in common, and that what Jesus and the first Christians were talking about was a world-denying religion in which the hope for the future had only a marginal impact on the present form of this age, which was thought to be passing away. The fundamental problem with this thesis, pervasive as it is in contemporary New Testament study, is that it accepts the view of eschatology as set out by Weiss, that the future reign of God has little or nothing to do with this world. Hope for the future is to be grounded in the transcendent God and in God's Kingdom. Whatever the theological merits of maintaining God's transcendence over against creation,[17] there is little to suggest that the Jews of Jesus' day believed that the future reign of God would take place in any other world than this, nor is there any evidence to suggest that Jesus and his followers dissented from this view. Thus the earliest Christian eschatologies fairly consistently down to the time of Irenaeus in the second century looked for the consummation of all things in this world, when Christ would reign.[18]

Liberation theology has questioned whether a world-denying eschatology really does justice to the biblical tradition, and has placed Jesus' struggles within the context of the specific political situation of his day and demanded that the horizon of hope be given a this-worldly dimension. It is the implications of this approach that we shall be examining in the following sections, first by examining the kind of interpretation of the narrative of Jesus' mission which is current among some liberation exegetes and then by exploring the issue of the relationship between history and eschatology.

3   THE POLITICAL MARK

The fascination of liberation theology with the historical Jesus has involved a concentration on the particularities of Jesus' political project and the dynamics of the conflict that he engendered with the powerful. An example of this kind of understanding, which states the position in a succinct form, is to be found in the view of George Pixley. Jesus the wandering preacher preached the egalitarian beliefs of the reign of God. These ideas were deeply rooted in the tribal past of Israel but obscured by the exclusively oligarchic political projects of the Temple and the monarchy. In the face of opposition to his egalitarian message Jesus determined to go to Jerusalem to confront the system of oppression, the Temple. By means of the trade and the taxes collected in the Temple, Pixley argues, the priests extracted the surplus labour of the peasants. So, by attacking the banking and commercial aspects of the Temple Jesus was not attacking a minor sideshow. The economic base of the Temple's domination was challenged by Jesus.[19]

With the death of Jesus there was an abrupt terminus to this egalitarian project, and the messianic movement internationalized and 'there arose a universal, spiritual, and individualistic religion that offers inner salvation to oppressed men and women within various class systems',[20] Marx's opium of the people. But the significant thing about Pixley's interpretative project is his conviction that the biblical tradition is not a homogeneous means of offering that opiate, but that it contains within it a very different set of attitudes to the status quo. Some of those themes within Mark's Gospel we need to explore.

What we find in Pixley's work is an approach that is familiar to most First World exegetes: a process of historical reconstruction, albeit one which concentrates on the class struggle endemic within Second Temple Judaism. There is little overt concern here with the present meaning of the text, yet the relevance of Pixley's reading for those struggling against powerful vested social and economic interests in the Third World is quite apparent. In his view mainstream Christianity seems to offer little hope as it has followed the path of compromise and acceptance of Caesar. What he seeks to demonstrate, however, are the strands of the gospel narrative which can easily be submerged.

This process of retrieval is what is apparent in a much more difficult and unconventional reading of the Gospel of Mark, where the political character of that narrative is brought home dramatically, even if sometimes in a rather convoluted manner.

(i) A MATERIALIST READING OF THE GOSPEL OF MARK   An interesting development in some recent liberation exegesis has been the recognition that an approach which is more sensitive to the fabric and detail of the text and the responses it provokes is necessary. There is a recognition that the New Testament texts are themselves social products. So-called materialist interpretation forcibly reminds us that writing is itself part of a complex process of production in which the product and the producer are themselves part of complex economic systems.[21] We know so little about the production of the original biblical books and the social circumstances of their writers that we are not in a good position to say much about the productive processes of which they were a part and of which their literary product is a complex expression. The material of the text, however, is capable of laying bare some of the secrets of another story to be told of the writer's world of oppression and struggles for power, of the suppression of the ideas of the weak and insignificant, and the dominance of the ideology of the powerful. As the monuments to the ideological struggles of the ancient world, the biblical texts can offer the modern reader some glimpse of both that other story now lost from our direct gaze and of a fuller understanding of life which embraces the struggle for social and economic power. Materialist interpretation drawing upon a long tradition of Marxist literary criticism has sought to reconstruct the social formation which gave birth to the biblical texts and, by understanding the economic systems of which they were a part and their place in them, to throw light on ancient struggles and eclipsed movements for change.[22]

Fernando Belo, followed by Michel Clevenot, has used contemporary literary criticism as well as Marxism in his search for an analysis of the text of Mark as a social product.[23] As far as both

Belo and Clevenot are concerned, the Gospel of Mark is a product of the social formation of its day, and the text needs to be examined in this light. Belo is not primarily interested in getting behind the text of Mark to what really happened either in the life of Jesus or in the life of the Marcan community. Questions of the historicity or otherwise of the events described are of relatively little interest, though the wider historical setting of the narrative and the evidence of the text as a social product which seeks at the aesthetic level to resolve and compensate for the dislocations of social reality is his major concern. He is concerned to work out a form of structural analysis of the text which will enable him to lay bare the social conflicts that are in some way covered up by the particular literary and aesthetic moment. Belo refuses to follow the path of conventional New Testament exegesis, or for that matter previous interpretations in the Marxist tradition which have tended to look for the social and economic character of early Christianity rather than concentrate on the texts as social products. In his view the text is a complex whole in which different types of textual material (myth, parable, discourse, narrative) are juxtaposed and play different functions within the narrative. This involves him in an elaborate analysis of the different codes (ideas relating to geographical location, culture, economic life, etc.) and the strategies of different actors in the unfolding narrative. In this he is indebted to the literary critical work of the distinguished French writer Roland Barthes.[24]

Belo argues that there are two distinct systems represented in the Torah, one based on Leviticus (what he calls the pollution system), and one based on Deuteronomy (the debt system, which is specifically concerned with social equality). The fact that there are two systems is indicative of previous class conflict within Judaism. The Levitical system, centred as it is on the cult and the privileges of the priests, contrasts with the Deuteronomic system, which promoted social justice and cohesion rather than division based on caste and ritual purity. In the canon of the Old Testament it is the Levitical system which occupies a more prominent position, because it was the ideology which triumphed. According to Belo, the priestly caste was responsible for the final form of the canon and thus gave their class power a solid foundation in the biblical story and laws. It may be wondered why the opposing system should have been included at all. This is an issue which does not detain Belo, but it may be noted that part of the strategy of dominant ideologies is frequently to *include* rather than reject, and so incorporate the oppositional ideas into their own belief system.[25]

The distinction between the two systems has a prominent role to play in Belo's interpretation of Mark's Gospel, for it is with a radicalized version of the system based on Deuteronomy that Belo considers that Jesus sides over against the system promoted by the cult, the Temple in Jerusalem. The Temple is singled out as the central focus in the ideological field, for the Temple was what sustained the economic power of a priestly and aristocratic élite and enabled them to maintain their position of political dominance in Jerusalem.[26]

Jesus' emphasis on the egalitarianism of Deuteronomy is found in the distance he seems to put between himself and money throughout Mark's Gospel. It is most graphically illustrated by the dialogue between Jesus and his disciples during the first feeding of the multitude (Mark 6.30–44): The interpretation offered here is in the simplified version of Belo's position written by Michel Clévenot.

> . . . the disciples suggest sending the people 'to *buy* themselves something to eat' (6.36) and speak of 'two hundred denarii' (6.37). Jesus replies: 'How many loaves have you?' (6.38), '*Give* them something to eat' (6.37). The bread is distributed; the crowd is filled. The movement indicated by the text is clear; it is the opposition of buying with money to giving what they have. What the text exalts is not the multiplying of the loaves but rather the merchant system that governs exchange by money and the promotion of the system of the gift in which everything belongs to everyone. In a social organization dominated by those who have in their hands the economic, political, and ideological apparatus, we can have bread only for money. To affirm that we must share wealth is obviously to introduce a subversion of the system of classes. It is not surprising that the rich find that message saddening (10.1–22).[27]

So in the narrative Jesus is presented as one who subverts the prevailing ideological consensus, particularly the system based on Leviticus.

In the early part of the Gospel there is gradually articulated a division between Jesus and the disciples on the one hand and the crowds on the other. Jesus' strategy is to avoid the towns, which are the centres of the crowds and the authorities, and when he cannot escape, to create a space for himself and his disciples. As the narrative unfolds, the ability to understand the strategy of Jesus not only as a messianic practice but also as one that is different from the Zealots' is a matter of importance. In this the parables play an important role. The parable of the sower, for example, offers a way of understanding the narrative of Jesus. Belo contrasts the first soils which speak of the various forms of rejection of the gospel and the last soil, which refers to the consequences in the lives of those who break entirely with the contemporary order. The problem with the authorities is that their presuppositions prevent them from understanding the true character of Jesus' mission. Indeed, eventually they understand Jesus' life not as a messianic practice but as one diametrically opposed to the ways of God, a way of violence which threatens the entire political and ideological system upon which their power is based.

Belo's reading of Mark's Gospel seems very strange, because it plays down a feature which has been dominant in most Marcan study, the cross. The conclusion of Belo's reading is that the strategy of Jesus was to proclaim the Kingdom and by his mighty works convince his disciples that he was the Messiah. The problem with the crowds is that their understanding of messianism is dominated by the Zealot strategy which seeks to find a military leader to fight the Romans and into which mould they seek to fit Jesus. The orders given to those cured to remain silent is a way of preventing the precipitation of a messianic movement of the Zealot type. After the recognition by Peter, Jesus' strategy alters, first to an articulation of the character of his Messiahship over against the view of the Zealots, and second to a journey to Jerusalem as a prelude to the extension of his message to the pagan world. Belo and Clevenot repeat the opinion of many scholars that Jesus was not a Zealot; his goal, they claim, was not a revolution which would completely abolish the existing economic order but a rebellion which would restore it to its pristine form:

. . . the Messiah presented by Jesus was prophetic and

anti-royal . . . Mark did not want to present Jesus as a Zealot Messiah. But that does not mean, as the traditional idealist exegesis claims, that Mark made him a spiritual Messiah, abandoning the temporal domain to the jurisdiction of Caesar. Our materialist reading enables us to see here a strategy that might be called 'communist, nonrevolutionary, and internationalist.' It was communist because . . . it aimed at reestablishing sharing, the value of use against the value of exchange. It was nonrevolutionary because the economic and political conditions of the Jewish . . . system integrated into a slaveholding Roman imperial system did not permit a revolutionary transformation of the relationships of production. It was internationalist because the narrative constantly crossed the borders of Palestine and ended by bursting out towards Galilee in the direction of pagan countries . . . Having created a prophetic-messianic counterfield anatagonistic to the Jewish field, Jesus set out on the road to confront that field on its own ground, the Temple.[28]

Belo argues that Jesus did not go up to Jerusalem to die. Indeed, he notes the way in which Jesus seeks to escape from the crowds and the risk of arrest (Mark 11.11ff.). He comes to Jerusalem to preach in the Temple, to proclaim that in the light of the rejection that was taking place the 'vineyard' (Mark 12.1ff.) would be given to others, and then to move on to the Gentiles. It is only the transfer of Judas back from the circle of disciples to the circle of the dominant class that enables the latter to put an end to Jesus' strategy, which is thus interrupted and therefore incomplete, though just before he dies he predicts his absence and asks the disciples to focus themselves on shared bread rather than his own person (Mark 14.22). Jesus challenges the current conceptions of the family, wealth, the centrality of the Temple and the hegemony of the priests, and rejects the conventional master/servant relationship. His message is nonviolent communism. Belo says that there was only one way in which Jesus' non-violent communism could have been practised in a situation where the Roman economic and political system was so powerful (other than by marginalization in a community like that of the Essenes), and that was by means of opening up the gospel to the nations. The resurrection narrative indicates that Jesus' story did not end with his death: the mission to the pagans was renewed by way of Galilee (Mark 16.7).

A major feature of Belo's interpretation is his view that in Mark we have the juxtaposition of a messianic narrative, centred on the miracles and the radical teaching, and a theological discourse which permeates the second half of the Gospel and offers an explanation of Jesus' death. He contrasts the two, suggesting that the former (the pre-paschal narrative) is not dominated by the cross and the divine necessity of Jesus' suffering, whereas the latter (the post-paschal discourse) is. Belo suggests that in Mark the post-paschal elements have begun to erase the central importance of the messianic narrative based on praxis. He considers that a liberation exegesis must seek to restore the priority of that praxis from a text where the very act of narration has tended to subordinate the messianic narrative to theological reflection. In so doing the narrator changed the execution of Jesus, which was originally devoid of doctrinal significance, into a death with profound theological meaning. Thus he gave the narrative of the execution of Jesus for subversion a significant push in the direction of the dominance of a theological discourse in which the political character of Jesus' death is gradually evacuated of its content. This is the first step on the road to a Christianity in which the theological as opposed to the practical becomes dominant.

The reason for this development is to be traced to the political powerlessness of the emerging Christian communities in the face of Rome. Charity as practice will soon become subordinate to and a consequence of doctrinal orthodoxy. This stands in marked contrast to the major thrust of Mark's messianic narrative: the practice of power in relation to the bodies of those afflicted with uncleanness; the practice of teaching (i.e. of understanding the practice of power); the practice of the subversion of the Israelite symbolic field and a strategy for dealing with the crowds and authorities. The messianic practice is a process of transforming a given raw material (economic, political and ideological relations) into a product (a new *ecclēsia*; in the circle of the disciples), a transformation which is effected by human labour. The messianic practice of Jesus represents a radicalization of the system based on Deuteronomy and the prophets and a rejection of the system based on Leviticus. In this emphasis on the practice of Jesus and the detection of the shift towards the primacy of the theological rather than the practical in the account of Jesus' life one can detect a distinctive emphasis of the theology of liberation (the priority of practice) applied to a particular problem in the Marcan account of Jesus' life.

So Belo's reading of Mark exposes the way in which the text of Mark is itself a story of radical change in the first part of the Gospel, particularly the account of Jesus' *deeds*. This is interrupted by an emerging preoccupation with theological reflection on the significance of Jesus' death. The execution of a subversive messianic claimant is thus on the way to becoming an unhistorical and other-worldly myth which involves an escape from issues of justice. Jesus' bloody execution by the Romans as a martyr[29] for the Kingdom is uprooted from its historical context and made into a timeless abstraction. That process is a product of a situation of political powerlessness in which the living out of a subversive, radical story is compensated for by the construction of theological reflection. The interruption of the subversive story of Jesus is a reflection of the political powerlessness of the first Christians who found no adequate outlet for their messianic enthusiasm. The political structures offered little space for change. Telling the story of Jesus in this form accurately represents the frustration of those who seek to live out the way of the Messiah in a hostile environment.

The tendency to juxtapose passion and miraculous activity in Mark's Gospel has already been alluded to. For a time these themes became the focus of an influential pattern of interpretations in mainstream exegesis which extended beyond Mark's Gospel to include consideration of the theology of Paul as well. Exponents of this view hold that what is being opposed in Mark's Gospel is the view that Jesus is a *theios anèr*, a charismatically gifted individual whose divine approbation is signalled by his miraculous powers. This meant that discipleship involved the replication of such charismatic activity in the present by the performance of deeds which would establish the credentials of the followers. It is argued that Mark's Gospel was written to counteract such exaggerated claims by dwelling on the passion of Jesus as the true mark of his claim to be Son of God rather than access to supernatural power to perform spectacular deeds. Also, it has been suggested that Paul was counteracting similar tendencies when he wrote 2 Corinthians and like the author of the Gospel of Mark placed emphasis on suffering and death, rather than external attestation, as marks of apostolicity.[30]

In an age in which the attraction of Pentecostalism has been great, particularly (but not only) in the Third World – with a resulting tendency to avoid the consequences of the Kingdom in the form of Jesus' suffering and death – such exegetical emphases are entirely understandable. One wonders, however, whether the stark juxtaposition of the powerlessness of the suffering Messiah and the triumphalism of his Spirit-filled followers found in some contemporary exegesis on Mark owes as much to the prevailing pessimism in mainstream ecclesiastical circles as to the realities of first-century Christianity. After all, neither Mark nor Paul seems to deny or even play down the importance of the mighty deeds. Quite the reverse seems to have been the case (2 Cor. 12.12). What the modern commentators who stress the suffering and death seem to want to guard against is an unrestrained optimism that action will surely lead to the desired results, which fails to take seriously the way in which the rejection and suffering symbolized by the cross seems to stand over every utopian drive. What some modern scholarly attempts to unearth pre-Marcan miracle collections about a powerful divine man are doing is reaffirming the point made by Belo: the Marcan messianic narrative is overlaid with the theological reflection of suffering and death, a veritable demonstration of human powerlessness and frank recognition of the limitations posed by the social formations of the present. To the extent that contemporary exegesis on Mark has dwelt so much on the passion of Jesus it shares with the text of Mark that feeling of powerlessness. The cross becomes an ideological device which justifies the socio-economic realities and warns against naive idealism. Indeed, it is a mark of much exegesis that there is a clear dislike for the utopian drive to change the world which the messianic activity might seem to inculcate. When the cross becomes a fetish which excludes other aspects of the tradition or, better, subtly erases their significance, the question has to be asked about its function within the struggles for power.[31]

(ii) EXPLORING THE IMPLICATIONS OF A MATERIALIST READING   Belo's reading of Mark raises a host of questions for more conventional approaches. Even if one wants to part company over details of his interpretation, the suggestiveness of his method demands we pay attention to the twists and form of the narrative. Above all, the questions he raises about the whole process of production of meaning provide a telling reminder that the socio-economic circumstances of the original writer and readers, just as much as our own, pervade the meaning we produce. We are driven back to this dramatic and powerful story with fresh perspectives and a very different textual horizon.

Conflict is at the heart of the Gospel of Mark.[32] Jesus comes as the one full of God's Spirit, with a message of the Kingdom of God which challenges the teaching of the scribes (Mark 1.15, 22). It is a conflict of rival ideologies, convictions and strategies: the ideology of the Kingdom versus that of the scribes and, particularly towards the latter half of the Gospel, the Temple. The supra-human ideologies are exposed in the light of the demonstration of the nearness of God's reign. This aspect of Jesus' activity is to be understood if a reader of the synoptic Gospels is to understand what is at stake. The prevailing ideology led not to integration but to separation, between pure and impure, sane and demon-possessed. There is in Jesus' ministry a fundamental challenge to all that maintained the contemporary culture, including its 'inner' superhuman forces. Jesus the bearer of the Spirit comes on the scenes on the margins of his world: at the Jordan, in the desert, by the sea, in the mountains, not in Jerusalem or the towns. The place of religious authority and power is the centre of opposition which ultimately leads to his death.

At the very start of his ministry Jesus is tempted by the devil and launches into a struggle with the demonic world. This struggle is not merely confined to the 'spiritual' realm (as if it were possible to separate it from the material in the world-view of the biblical writers). Opponents of Jesus are human beings and are agents of the forces opposed to the reign of God. Whereas in Luke (and Matthew?) the temptation of Jesus is told in such a way that the conquest of the representative of the powers opposed to God paves the way for an unhindered activity (at least in the short term – Luke 4.13), such a view of the temptation which regards it as a self-contained entity is by no means apparent in Mark. The temptation is but the beginning of a struggle.

In Mark, therefore, the narrative moves on two levels: the spirits/demons and the opponents. The conquest of the powers of evil and the recognition by the demons of the opponent is a theme which runs throughout the early part of the Gospel. The relationship between the two can be seen in Mark 12.13ff. Jesus recognizes the temptation which is going on (manifest in the use of the same word, *peirazo*, as is used in the temptation story). Jesus is being tempted by the Pharisees and Herodians just as he had been tempted in the wilderness by Satan. The opponents of Jesus are not curious inquirers interested in academic debate. Their question is rooted in their suspicion of Jesus for his challenge to all that maintains the old order. Their apparent sanity (in contrast to the outlandish behaviour of those possessed by unclean spirits) should not allow the reader to suppose that they are neutrals in this struggle. Jesus' opposition to them is rooted in the ideological struggle which underpins their own world-view. What we have, therefore, is a man taking on not merely the religious establishment but the whole ideological edifice manifest in material form in the Temple. While it might be tempting to see this in purely religious terms as the reformation by Jesus of Jewish religion, the implied distinction between religion and politics is difficult to maintain within Judaism.

Mark's Gospel narrates the actions of Jesus in healings and in expelling the impure spirits: signs that the strong man is being bound and the powers of darkness overcome. Jesus' message of the Kingdom of God was about a new order in which the powers of darkness were to be (and were already being) overthrown: 'If I by the finger of God cast out demons, then you know that the kingdom of God has come upon you' (Luke 11.20, authors' translation). He is struggling against the forces of evil, whether in the dislocation of individuals, who embody the fragmentation of a divided community, or in those who question his messianic authority and outlook. Angelic and supernatural powers are part and parcel of the way in which the world is viewed. It is important to recognize that in speaking of such powers there is frequently a specific individual or social dimension to their activity. We are not talking about disembodied spirits free from the affairs of men and women. The powers are an indication of a supra-individual dimension to the problems of life. It is not just the case that there are individuals who need dealing with, for what confront Jesus are not merely disturbed individuals but persons who are taken over by a power whose characteristics are manifest in disruptive behaviour and social dislocation. They are, as it were, indicators of the distortion of the world, whose distance from 'normal' people is itself a sign that the latter allow those designated abnormal or possessed by unclean spirits to carry the burden of a wider social dislocation:

> The problem revealed by the exorcisms is . . . a general social problem, the break-down in interpersonal communication, a profound alienation in social relations . . . In a society which expresses its problems in mythical language groups under pressure may interpret their situation as threats from demons . . . If these symptoms are accepted as expressions of insoluble conflicts and the possibility of solving the problems so expressed is offered through exorcism, they may become a public language successfully used by man.[33]

Thus what Jesus is struggling with in the so-called exorcism stories is much bigger than the demon-possession of individuals. He challenges the ethos of an order which is inadequate. The very presence of a lack of harmony and social cohesion points beyond itself to hope for a time of integration and wholeness, the Kingdom of God.

In Mark's Gospel the spirits confronted by Jesus are frequently designated 'unclean spirits' (e.g. Mark 1.23; 3.11). That uncleanness is according to criteria set by those in power which result in certain individuals being driven to the margins because of their behaviour or some other 'abnormal' characteristic. The paradox is that it is the unclean who recognize the Messiah and provoke action on Jesus' part. Yet that recognition is not a glad response of those longing for liberation but the angry reaction of those who prefer to maintain the status quo, however inadequate, in the face of the disturbance following action by the Messiah. The unclean spirits want to be left alone because they are the 'spiritual' or ideological ethos and support of the present age of separation and division. But it is not only those possessed by demons who prefer no change. In a sense, the 'normal' are in an even worse position, because their normality is shown for what it is in their stubborn refusal to do anything other than blaspheme the messianic spirit (Mark 3.22ff.) and thereby reveal their abnormality. We find that the first two chapters of Mark describe Jesus in conflict with the scribes and others over the interpretation of the law and the character of his practice, leading to deep hostility. Later, when he arrives in Jerusalem, a similar sequence of conflict stories is to be found. There lies behind the conflicts with human beings a superhuman struggle with all those forces of injustice which maintain the old order.

The story of the healing of the Gerasene demoniac is indicative of the importance attached to the attack on the powerful world of those forces opposed to God. The demoniac is possessed by a devil called Legion, the name given to those military forces occuping the country:

> The allusion to the Roman occupation is unmistakable. The hostility towards the Roman occupiers is made clear when the demons clearly express their wish to be allowed to remain in the country (5.10). This is precisely what the Romans also want. They are not concerned with forcing particular individuals into submission, but with controlling the whole country. The story symbolically satisfies the desire to drive them into the sea like pigs. It becomes clear why the successful exorcist is sent away: his presence is a real threat to social peace. This is not to say that this miracle story contains a deliberately encoded political message. Within the society of this time political and religious factors did not exist separately. The two were intertwined from the beginning. The struggle was carried out in both spheres. Roman domination, like any foreign rule, had from the outset a religious aspect: with the foreigners came their gods. Judaism could see in them only idols and demons . . . The presence of a foreign political power was always the presence of a threatening numinous power, a pollution of the land. Roman rule could thus be interpreted as a threat from a demonic power – for all the Romans' tolerance in religion and politics. This made the activity of the exorcist a 'sign' of future liberation.[34]

The demoniac is a living embodiment of the Roman occupation and oppression. It is not just the fractured lives of individuals that are being mended but those suprahuman forces which have produced dislocation of God's order and which are embodied in those who are most sensitive to that oppression that are being tamed. The unclean spirits named with a word linked with the forces of occupation are sent into the unclean animals and eventually perish in the sea. The Roman occupying forces are symbolically destroyed in the sea, just as the beast and the false prophet are destroyed in the lake of fire at the climax of the demonstration of divine justice in the book of Revelation (Rev. 19.20).

Jesus' struggle with the powers of darkness manifest in the contemporary society is one which is continued from the moment of the wilderness experience right the way through the ministry. Reconciliation with the forces opposed to Jesus is hardly ever countenanced in the gospel stories. The forces opposed to Jesus are not to be accepted as ordained by God as permanent parts of the divine order of things. Whether they be the political powers or the supra-individual powers whose demonic character is embodied in corrupt social systems which enslave men and women, they have to be removed to pave the way for the coming of the reign of God. Jesus' powerful deeds indicated the nearness of the end of this present evil age dominated by the powers of darkness: 'No one can enter a strong man's house and plunder his goods, unless he first binds the strong man; then indeed he may plunder his house' (Mark 3.27). That is not to deny that integration, wholeness and forgiveness and reconciliation are important. The situation of the Gerasene demoniac after the exorcism is a paradigm of what the coming of the Messiah means (Mark 5.15). Such a present demonstration of the eschatological wholeness or *shalom* overcoming the contradictions in the old order cannot be taken as an indication of reconciliation with the old order. The Kingdom offers reconciliation and the overcoming of those distortions which are inherent in the world as it is. It is only when it is present in all its fullness that God will be all in all (1 Cor. 15.28). Present signs of what is to come cannot mean that reconciliation with the world-as-it-is is demanded; that would be to accept that God and Belial do actually have communion with one another (cf. 2 Cor. 6.15). Reconciliation is the consequence of the process of struggle which is still not complete.

That pattern of conflict, so often recognized as a dominant theme within the synoptic Gospels, is often related to the 'spiritual' sphere. The persistence of the acceptance of such a separation is testimony enough to the pervasiveness of the dualism in contemporary theology.[35] No happier hunting ground for that separation between sacred and secular, spiritual and material has been found than in the discussion about the tribute money (Mark 12: 13–17). Here, surely, there is a passage which indicates that Jesus was not prepared to disturb the existing order? This view is buttressed both by contemporary attempts to separate the Kingdom of God from the human kingdoms, rooted in Augustine's and Luther's emphatic separation of the human and divine realms[36] and by the way this passage has been read both by Matthew and Paul. Matthew's identification of the coin as the coin designated for the tribute and Paul's unequivocal support for the payment of taxes indicate that Jesus' reply *was* taken as an injunction to pay taxes to Caesar and recognize the demands of the state as legitimate (Rom. 13.6–7). Paul's setting, particularly the situation of the Roman Christians, left little room for manoeuvre. Whereas Jesus was not part of the Roman jurisdiction for much of his life, the Christians in Rome had little alternative except to pay their taxes, unless they wanted to court imprisonment and death.

Four ways of interpreting this passage have been canvassed which allow that Jesus was giving Caesar a valid role in the political life of his day.[37] The conventional assumption is that Jesus is allowing a limited autonomy to Caesar, provided that this does not infringe the demands of God. Second, there is the view that what Jesus is recommending in this passage is a complete separation of spheres of influence under God between the spiritual and the temporal, between religion and politics. Third, there is the view that the kings of the earth received their sovereignty by divine permission and accordingly the saying means that by giving Caesar what is Caesar's the Jews would be giving God what was God's.[38] A fourth approach asserts that the second half of Jesus' reply, 'Render . . . to God the things that are God's', is to be understood as undermining the obligation to Caesar completely by subordinating it to obligation to God. The land of Israel belongs to God alone (Lev. 25.23), and no part of it was to be handed over to a pagan ruler.

With regard to the second view, it is most unlikely that Jesus' words involved an acceptance of a separation between the sacred and secular spheres. That kind of separation between the sacred and the secular which has become such a feature of our Western Christianity was certainly not typical of the Judaism of Jesus' day. Jews regarded God as the creator of the world. The whole universe was regarded as God's domain, and no earthly ruler had any absolute right of possession or authority. Thus, giving God what was God's due meant offering to the supreme ruler of the whole world all that belonged to God.

But why did Jesus not say this? A simple answer is that the context in which the question was asked demanded circumspection. Jesus was not here offering a definitive ruling on relations between his followers and the state but a clever, if ambiguous, answer, given in a situation where he had been put in a tight corner by his opponents. It is not sufficient to suppose that if Jesus had meant this it was expressed so cryptically that the point might well have been missed.[39] Ambiguity was an essential part of a response in a situation where there were those who were seeking to trap him in his speech. Luke, who was probably drawing on a version of the passion narrative that was independent of Mark, indicates that the issue of the tribute *was* a factor in the accusation before Pilate (Luke 23.2). The fact that it was included as part of the basis for the case against Jesus before the Roman prefect should make us pause before assuming that the meaning of the saying is entirely transparent.

Jesus' prophetic role and radical preaching could conceivably have comprised a programme for radical change and a short-term acceptance of the reality of Rome pending its demise in the face of the divine sovereignty. This must not be understood as an acceptance of the earthly city as anything other than a temporary phenomenon, however. It would then arise from the politico-religious strategy of one whose primary challenge was to the Jewish nation, its institutions and life as God's means of offering a light to the nations. The focus of attention on Rome would have distracted attention from the inadequacies of the Jewish polity as a reflection of the organization which God required.[40] We may compare the ministry of Jeremiah in this respect. Jeremiah had warned his hearers that Babylon was God's servant and that their immediate well-being lay in submission (Jer. 27.4ff. and 38.17ff.). He also directed their attention to the inadequacies of their response to divine justice. Preoccupation with an external enemy can so easily detract from the need to attend to the impoverishment of the internal polity of Israel. Lack of evidence of Jesus' concern with Rome should not be interpreted as a separation between the religious and the political but between the primary and secondary spheres of political concern for Jewish prophets.

The context of the saying is one where Jesus is being put to the test. Among his questioners are the Herodians, the supporters of the puppet-king in the area from which Jesus himself came, Galilee, and a person who had shown (probably suspicious) interest in Jesus (Mark 6.14; Luke 13.31). It should not surprise us if Jesus were to give an answer which was ambiguous and would not have implicated himself either with the rejection of Roman power by the Jewish freedom-fighters or with those collaborators who had come to some accommodation with the occupying power. Jesus has little to say about Rome, because according to the synoptic Gospels he visited Jerusalem during his prophetic career only once. He seems to have spent most of his time in Galilee, which was not under Roman jurisdiction but was ruled by Herod Antipas, for whom Jesus seems to have had little regard. Concern for Rome and its power was of secondary concern to the internal justice of the people of God, particularly in those areas which were outside Roman jurisdiction.

The discussion takes an interesting turn when Jesus makes his opponents show him a coin. He diverts the question from mere theory to the reality of the means of exchange whereby the tribute was expected to be paid. The discussion of the issue, therefore, is not left in the realm of abstraction. Whether we can place great weight on the fact that he himself does not appear to possess a coin is uncertain, but it is not without significance. It may be another indication that Jesus is here dealing with a jurisdiction and a set of issues which were both unfamiliar to a Galilean and incompatible with the style of life which he had been leading. After being presented with a coin bearing the image of the Roman emperor he asks whose image and superscription it is. The reason for this is not immediately obvious. Is it in order to indicate rights and duties to the one whose image is before him? Or does he wish to point out that the possession of the coin by Jews is evidence that the possessors are contaminated by an alien ideology which in direct contradiction to Jewish law allowed images of human beings to be engraved? Those who possess such objects of an alien system might expect, therefore, to have to abide by the rules of that system; as Bruce comments, 'whatever else belongs to God, a coin which by its very form and appearance contravenes God's Law cannot be regarded as his'.[41] In the context of Jewish repudiation of idolatry a distancing of oneself from the marks of idolatry would be entirely comprehensible. Jesus' response, therefore, may indicate that participants in the Roman economic system were bound to pay the tax, but those who recognized the supremacy of God over the universe were bound to maintain their distance from Rome and its exploitative and idolatrous practices. This is well brought out in Robert Eisler's perceptive treatment of the incident which merits quoting at length:

> Jesus has not a single denarius . . . Jesus has no money because he *will* have none of it . . . Jesus who carries no money . . . thus acts . . . like the Essenes, among whom 'there is no commerce' . . . and they have no private property among them' (Ant. xv.373ff). He further expressly forbade his disciples to carry any money . . . Jesus, the wandering carpenter . . . rejects money on principle both for himself and his disciples. He postulates the gratuitous gift of all services to one's neighbour as a free act of love. Thus only the discourse on the tribute money becomes intelligible. The 'lovers of money' who carry about with them and possess the Roman emperor's money, and with it the image of the 'lord of this world', the enemy of God who claims worship for himself, owe 'his money', the poll tax, to that lord. They have fallen away from God and so have irretrievably incurred servitude and the payment of tribute to the emperor. But he, who, like Jesus and his disciples, disdains Caesar's money and the whole monetary system of the empire, and who enjoys with his brethren the loving communion of all possessions of the 'saints', such a one has renounced the service of idols and is no longer indebted to Caesar but merely to God, to whom he owes body, soul, thoughts, words and works – in short, everything. 'Render unto Caesar the things that are Caesar's' really means: 'Throw Caesar's, i.e. Satan's, money down his throat, so that you may then be free to devote yourselves wholly to the service of God' . . . Far from sanctioning the payment of tribute to Caesar, Jesus is wholly on the side of Judas of Galilee, but goes far beyond him in that he requires his disciples, the citizens of the coming kingdom of God, to renounce not only their service of Caesar, but also, and above all, their service of mammon. He who no longer possesses money, uses money, or wishes to use money, need pay no more taxes to Caesar. He who continues

and wishes to continue in the service of that enemy of God, the demon mammon, must also bear Caesar's yoke; he is unworthy of the kingdom of freedom, of the New Israel which acknowledges no master but God.[42]

In the Gospel of Mark there is a progressive separation of those who discern Jesus's ministry in different ways.[43] The growing opposition and division leads into Mark 4, the first stretch of teaching in Mark's Gospel, which consists of the parable of the sower and its interpretation, and two other seed parables, and which climaxes in the stilling of the storm. The setting for Jesus' teaching is in the open air by the sea, away from the normal arenas of religious teaching like the synagogue and the Temple. The teaching itself takes the form of story-telling rather than the pronouncement of precise dogmas and laws. It is directed to the crowd and uses familiar features of everyday life. In using this illustrative method Jesus relies on his hearers to use their own imagination to come to an understanding about himself and his work. The hearers are expected to listen carefully, not because the answers to their questions are going to be given to them on a plate but because they themselves have to understand and own the significance of what is confronting them.

Immediately after the parable of the sower there is an enigmatic discussion about the mystery of the Kingdom and the function of parables in which Jesus seems to suggest that parables are told to *provoke* incomprehension (Mark 4.12). The earliest interpreters of Mark, Matthew and Luke found problems with this and softened Mark's harsh wording to make the incomprehension appear to be a consequence of unperceptive hearing rather than the result of the teaching method of Jesus. But there is a sense in which the use of illustration after illustration not only leads to further bewilderment but also contributes to incomprehension. The parabolic method demands an assent from the hearer in order to participate in the process of coming to new understanding. The hearer has to want to make connections between the story and the issue being explained. In a situation where there is hostility and division, that consent which is necessary in order to assist the educative process is often not there. To persist in the use of parables, therefore, will only *lead* to further incomprehension and hostility. Why Jesus chose to continue to use this teaching method is unclear. Perhaps it reflects the conviction that the understanding of God's reign must involve the hearer in a transformation of his or her own mind; therefore, to retreat from that method of teaching represented a retreat from taking seriously the maturity and integrity of the hearers as men and women created in God's image.

In the parable of the sower Jesus contrasts different kinds of responses and in the face of growing opposition stresses the importance of distancing oneself from the clamour of the dominant ideology (which is beginning to reject Jesus). An everyday occurrence is used as the basis for a significant reflection on the character of the reign of God and the opposition and division it has provoked. It consists of two parts, the simple story and then an interpretation offered to an inner circle of disciples. From the interpretation Jesus helps his disciples to understand the varied fortunes of the proclamation of the reign of God. It is far from being an unqualified success. Indeed, most of the time it seems to be a failure. Even in those instances where there is a response, that can be short-lived. But appearances are in fact deceptive, and the fruit of the reign of God will not be manifest until the future. The interpretation reflects on the varied, and often poor, response to the proclamation of the reign of God and illustrates the cost of taking it seriously. There is a price to be paid for discipleship (Mark 4.18–19) which the disciples will have to hear more about in the future (Mark 10.29ff., 39ff.). For those who respond the resource will be given to persist in their discipleship. Precisely because they have responded they will be given more. Those who have not allowed the seed to dwell in them and grow so that their patterns of existence are transformed cannot hope to be true disciples. The other parables in the chapter pick up themes from the sower. Both the seed parables promise a future recognition of the present hidden character of God's reign. It is a small and almost imperceptible beginning in the life of Jesus and his circle which will extend over the whole of creation in the future. That point is made in the parable about the light in Mark 4.21–2: things which are at present hidden will be made manifest.

The disciples are only dimly aware of the change that is needed. Yet the reader is presented with starkly contrasting assessments of Jesus' activity by the various parts of the story (agent of the Kingdom, etc., in Mark 1.15, 22, or agent of Beelzebub in Mark

3.22). So the ability to discern becomes critical. There is the need to replace the defective ideology of the old order. The most telling moment of discernment comes when the pagan centurion confesses Jesus as Son of God (Mark 15.39). The reader understands that the moment when he makes this confession is a significant one. In the desolation of an execution a man sees another extinguished by his opponents yet confesses him Son of God. The moment when the opponents thought they had won is in fact the moment of their defeat.[44] The whole edifice of their ideology, centred in the Temple, has been destroyed. The Temple, with its separation of its holy place from outsiders and the holy of holies from all but the high priest, is shown to be empty, a sham. At the heart of the Temple was its most holy part, where God's presence was believed to dwell, undergirding the action which went on around it and the belief which gave it its importance. Everything was geared to the maintenance of a view of God which focused on that building. When that had been destroyed the whole edifice of stone and doctrine was revealed as a ramshackle shell with no *raison d'être*. The opponents of Jesus were supporting an obsolete system, for its destruction was promised (Mark 13.2). God was to be found in the struggle against that institution, not in it. The centurion recognized this fact. The prophet Ezekiel had witnessed the demystification of the power of the Temple and had spoken of it as the departure of the divine glory (Ezek. 10). That was the prelude to its destruction. It could no longer be regarded as anything special in the divine economy. In Mark's Gospel the focus of divine activity is to be found not in a wonderful building but in a dead man and his way. He was executed both for his challenge to the prevailing ideology and for his unwillingness to back down for making that challenge.

The opponents of Jesus upheld an ideology which allowed the marginalization of people and the dominance of the economic and cultic system. The struggle against the spirits is the challenge to that dominant order. Unlike the system of his opponents, Jesus offers the promise of acceptance and integration, the overthrow of the realm of the powers. The opponents support accommodation with Rome, the immorality of the Herodian court and the distorting centrality of the Temple. In their system the impure spirit is incarnate. Its rejection is a mark of its demise. Indeed, a key to understanding Mark's Gospel is the mark of doom set upon the Temple. Jesus' way is set against the whole cultic apparatus. That view of Mark is widely held, though its political and ideological significance is not sufficiently stressed. Too much emphasis is placed on the 'religious' aspect of the challenge, without recognizing the importance of ideology in the whole fabric of Jewish society. So what we find in Mark's Gospel is an account of conflict: between on the one hand the reign of God and the action of the eschatological salvation outside the Temple and on the other hand the firm view of the opponents that the prevailing culture, concerned as it is with the support of a society which divides, marginalizes, justifies wealth and makes economic gain out of theological virtue, is inimical to the radically new.

4   THE PROBLEM OF HISTORY AND ESCHATOLOGY

A prominent theme thrown up by liberation theology and its reading of Scripture is the historical character of God's eschatological activity. In much liberation theology we find evidence of a move away from a notion of the Kingdom of God as an other-worldly entity that has little or no direct contact with the present world.[45] In some respects this marks a reaction not only against a view of Christian hope which concentrates on this other-worldly character but also against the received wisdom of New Testament exegesis that Jesus' proclamation of the Kingdom of God concerned a transcendent entity.[46] In the case of this latter belief the part played by Augustine in forming not only a Christian understanding of the state but also attitudes towards eschatology is enormous.[47] Drawing upon his distinctive interpretation of the messianic kingdom in Revelation 20 as a description of the era of the Church, Augustine argues that the Church now on earth is both the Kingdom of Christ and the kingdom of heaven (*City of God* xx.9) Thus the City of God is quite clearly a transcendent, heavenly reality.

To be fair to Augustine, however, we need to recognize the peculiar circumstances in which his major contribution to political theology, *The City of God*, was written. In it he seeks to combat the view that the sack of Rome was the result of the traditional divinities' anger at the abandonment of Roman religion and the decline into Christianity. What is set forth by Augustine is a radical

questioning of simplistic attempts to read off from the complex-
ities of the historical process evidence of the hand of God in the
affairs of men and women. He does this by espousing a sharp
division between the earthly city and the City of God. The former
is always characterized by corruption and violence and can never
be identified in its entirety with the City of God. All that can be
hoped for is a modicum of peace and justice to ensure some kind
of stability and harmony:

> Secular politics is taken seriously by Augustine, but relentlessly
> excluded from the sphere of the sacred. He refuses to assimilate
> the two cities to one another, and judges that even a Christian
> civil government is no more than a temporary and relative
> expedient. Politics requires to be nourished and challenged by
> the gospel; only in its relationship to the City of God is it
> possible to understand the earthly city aright as either a band of
> robbers being drawn by their lust for power and riches towards
> perdition, or a fellowship of pilgrims lovingly seeking the city
> whose builder and maker is God.[48]

There is a very important contribution made by Augustine's
version of the relativizing of politics by eschatology: the Church is
placed as a witness to the Kingdom and thus as the organ whereby
the injustices of the present age can be exposed. The Church can
never be identified with the City of God, for it is also to varying
degrees corrupt because of its participation in the values of the old
order. The Church can only point in the direction of the City of
God. Yet this task, complicated and beset with problems as it is,
is its essential ministry of opposition and critical reflection on
fallible human arrangements.

The legacy of Augustine's Concept of the City of God has been
so pervasive in Christian history that the alternative view of a
this-worldly hope has either been interpreted in other terms or
pushed to the margins of the Christian tradition as a doctrinal
experiment which, like some forms of early Christology, was
found to be inadequate. Mixing the future hope and history is
seen as a symptom of that naive optimism and unrealistic activism
which can lead only to disaster. Such a view has seemed to receive
explicit confirmation by the main thrust of New Testament
exegesis since Weiss and Schweitzer. Typical of much of this is
the following statement from the work of Joachim Jeremias: 'In

the sayings of Jesus, the conception of the *basileia* is *stripped* not only of all nationalistic features but also of all *materialistic features*. There is no elaboration of the conditions of the end time, say, the fertility of the new earth or the joy of heaven.'[49]

What emerges in this statement is a clear attempt to put some distance between Jesus and the contemporary eschatological ideas in Judaism by reducing them of their historically specific content and nationalist sentiments. While we cannot doubt that the tradition of Jesus' words as it has reached us is fairly reticent about the precise details of the eschatological hope, such an absence serves only to point to the importance attached to present responsibilities rather than the offer of a refuge in millennial dreams. E.P. Sanders[50] is right when he speaks of the absence of specific political blueprints from the Jesus tradition (though in this respect the Gospels are little different from most other Jewish eschatological texts in the paucity of utopian detail). Where he seems to me to be mistaken is in supposing that the lack of such detail indicates that Jesus was basically apolitical. Jesus was not involved in the formal political processes of his day, but his activity not only had a clear relationship to that process as it was conceived at the time but also to a large extent challenged it by standing apart from it.

Enough has been said to indicate that the Gospels demand a much greater recognition of the extent to which eschatological beliefs are intertwined with specific political projects in the life of Jesus. Cardinal Joseph Ratzinger[51] has rightly perceived the importance of this issue for liberation theology, and perceptively suggests that what we have in it is a return to chiliastic views (i.e. the belief that the future reign of God will be part of human history). These he thinks were firmly rejected by mainstream Christianity from the Scriptures onwards. In his view, chiliasm acknowledges the possibility of the fulfilment of an eschatological hope within the confines of the historical process:

> . . . in this world too God's goal with man and history must be achieved . . . there must be . . . a final age within history in which everything will be as it really should. This means that the categories of that which is within history and that which transcends history are combined. That which is within history is awaited in forms that in themselves do not belong to

historical thinking; that which transcends history becomes miraculous by being expected as a form of history.[52]

Ratzinger then offers examples of the way in which biblical exemplars reject the chiliastic and espouse a different strategy based on a rational assessment of the limited political options open in the situation rather than on the fantastic hope of divine intervention. He considers that Jeremiah sees himself faced 'with theopolitical behaviour that he wishes to replace with national politics for reasons of theological responsibility'.[53]

This means that Jeremiah's opponents were convinced of an absolute guarantee on the part of God for the safety of the Temple, Jerusalem, and the continuance of the house of David. They considered this guarantee as a factor in the political process even though there was little to indicate this kind of security. Jeremiah in contrast demanded rational politics which in conduct towards Babylon would be guided by the actual conditions of power and the possibilities that followed from these realities. That, according to Ratzinger, was what Jeremiah saw as an expression of faith in God. He sees Jesus' position as akin to that of Jeremiah. Jesus predicts that such a fusion of faith and politics will lead to the final destruction of Jerusalem. His failure corresponds in this way exactly to the failure of the prophets.

Ratzinger rejects chiliasm's synthesis of eschatology and politics as not being 'a possibility in the fundamental decision of Christianity'. The real target of his criticism is manifest when he states:

the fanatical theological expectations that we encountered in the War Scroll of Qumran can be found again in an astonishing way in the literature of liberation theology . . . the sole contribution of liberation theology consists of linking irrational aims and reasons with political argumentation in such a way that what emerges is political action that is exactly planned in detail but as a whole is profoundly irrational. There is no real connection between the promise and its means; individual sensible projects can thus arise but one will have to label the whole as leading astray.[54]

He seeks to distance himself from the historical eschatology of Joachim of Fiore, which he rightly perceives:

opened up the path to Hegel and Marx: history is a process that pushes forward in which man [sic] is actively at work building his salvation which in its turn is not to be recognized from the mere logic of the present but is guaranteed by the logic of history.

In Ratzinger's view, Joachim made a 'fateful link' between monastic utopianism and chiliasm,[55] so that God as Trinity was understood as the principle of progress in history. In saying this Ratzinger argues that there is a historicizing of a utopian strand within Christianity which had its origins in Platonism. Whereas 'the Platonic utopia developed as a means of regulating the political reason, in chiliastic politics faith and reason are blended in a manner injurious to both sides'. The synthesis of Platonic utopianism and theology 'does not relate this realisation to the world as such and its political corporations but to the charismatic non-world which arises from the *voluntary* flight from the world'.[56]

Ratzinger minimizes the centrality of the historical character of the eschatological expectation in the earliest period down to the time of Justin and Irenaeus by suggesting that the political element is lacking and that in Irenaeus' work 'the idea is merely a postulate of his christology and concept of God'.[57] In saying this Ratzinger is following the contours of the subjugation of eschatology which took place in the Hellenistic Church as it departed from the Judeo-Christian pattern of hope. In the earliest period chiliasm is no aberration, but is at the heart of early Christian eschatology and owes its final marginalization to the reinterpretation of its doctrine by Augustine (who was himself dependent on the Donatist writer Tyconius).

Ratzinger's distinction between the theopolitical views of the false prophets and the 'rational politics' of Jeremiah seems more a product of hindsight as viewed from the perspective of *realpolitik*. Jeremiah does not in any way offer a common-sense view akin to the perspective of one who considers politics 'the art of the possible'. Indeed, the world-view of the theocratic tradition that is offered by his opponents motivates Jeremiah as well. Jeremiah, however, gives an alternative and disconcerting theopolitical solution which is offered not as 'rational politics' in any conventional sense of that term but which is the product of Jeremiah's conviction that he has access to the counsels of God. Unlike the wise men of the court, whose observations of the world led to the production of maxims to govern the right ordering of the world, Jeremiah's insight is based on prophetic insight which has the air of 'irrationality' when viewed from the perspective of the tradition which governed the outlook of his contemporaries. Jeremiah's challenge incorporates the view that his nation was to be subject to Babylon. That was to be accepted; there was no escape from that fate, given the iniquities of the nation. This assessment arises from the prophet's conviction that he has insight into the mystery of God and the divine purposes for the times and seasons of the nations of the world, similar to what we find in the apocalyptic tradition. It is wrong to suggest as Ratzinger does that the theopolitical attitudes of the false prophets 'led to the catastrophe of Jerusalem and the premature end of Jewish political independence'.[58] That end, according to Jeremiah, was guaranteed by God, and by God's purposes in history as a judgement on Israel's sins. Thus it is not justifiable to polarize the canonical prophet's solution from that of his opponents in the form of a contrast between rational common sense and theological fantasy cut off from reality.

The same is true of Jesus' attitude to the political realities of the Jerusalem of his day. The destruction of Jerusalem is predicted within the context of Jesus' proclamation of the reign of God and the rejection of his prophetic claim by the rulers of the Temple and of Jerusalem. Jesus' predictions are not merely 'rational politics'. 'The things that make for peace' which are rejected by the leaders when they reject his claim to be Messiah are in fact Jesus' eschatological programme and claim. Jesus does not reject the fusion of faith and politics, for he himself offers an example of that fusion in his assertion that the eschatological reign is already at the doors and is evident in the ruins of the old age. His is the supreme example of the chiliastic mentality.[59]

What Ratzinger seems to be outlining under the guise of the inbreaking of the transcendent into history is at the heart of what traditional theology asserts about the resurrection of Jesus and the experience of the Spirit. In other words, the intertwining of history and eschatology is at the heart of what is distinctive about the first Christians' interpretation of the Jewish tradition and their attachment to the story of Jesus. The modern tendency to polarize history and eschatology, the transcendent and the material, God and humanity, ignores the stubborn refusal of the Bible to draw such hard and fast lines between them. The expression of the Christian hope in the form of the tension between the now and the not yet refuses to push eschatology and the transcendent into some other realm but demands that the present is seen as a time of eschatological significance.

It is apparent from this that Ratzinger wants to drive a wedge between faith and politics, utopia and the real world. Yet he is faced with the problem that the monks seemed to be in the business of realizing utopia in the real world, or (in terms of Ratzinger's definition of chiliasm) mixing faith and politics in the same injurious way as chiliasm. He gets round this problem by arguing that the world where their utopia became a reality was the non-world, i.e. the wilderness. The inadequacy of his argument here reveals the difficulty he finds himself in because of his attempt to create an artificial divide between monasticism and chiliastic ideas. Ratzinger's breadth of vision and theological knowledge is flawed, however, by his deep-rooted hostility to the chiliastic/millenarian tradition. As a result, connections which might easily be made are denied, even when in his terms developments which are in the mainstream of Catholic teaching seem to come close to the position which he is wanting to reject.

Ratzinger's statement on the affinities between the outlook of the War Scroll from Qumran and contemporary liberation theology leaves a reader of that material at a loss as to how to react. Nothing which has been produced by the leading proponents of liberation theology remotely corresponds to the caricature offered by Ratzinger. Indeed, there is a consistent renunciation of fantastic projects which are unrelated to political circumstances. There is nothing whatever in the bulk of liberation theology to link it with the minute preparations of a group whose links with society at large were in fact so tenuous that such a fantasy of a winnable holy war could be nurtured without restraint. Most liberation theologians and those with whom they work are engaged in costly small-scale protests and programmes at the grassroots which offer a glimpse of God's eschatological Kingdom amidst the injustices of the old order. It is true that some liberation theologians would want to question Ratzinger's view of the relationship between history and eschatology, in particular the consequent diminution of human agency within the eschatological process. The centrality of the portrait of the synoptic Jesus in the theology of liberation places a clear constraint on the fantastic and unreal, and it demands of those who believe that the Kingdom impinges on the life of the present the recognition that such commitment usually ends up with a cross rather than the millennium. The journey of Jesus to Jerusalem (and, for that matter, of Paul, if Acts 21.10ff. is anything to go by) hardly illustrates the rational politics Ratzinger favours, but rather they find their origin in the chiliastic tradition from which he wants to distance himself. When Paul stresses that human common sense or wisdom is foolishness to God he is only putting in a hyperbolic way the uncomfortable fact that the centre of the Christian religion is not conventional rationality but the career of a messianic pretender who failed. A concept of rationality and political judgement is introduced by Ratzinger into the biblical prophetic model which hardly does justice to the biblical narrative.

Underlying many of the suspicions about chiliastic ideas are the disruptive effects that these have had in Christian history. Something of that unease may be glimpsed in Ratzinger's desire to distance chiliasm's 'theopolitical' programme (as he terms it) from the mainstream biblical emphasis which, he asserts, steadfastly refuses to confuse the historical with the eschatological. The problem posed by such a mingling of the future age of absolute perfection with the mundane history where things carry on as before is grasped by Karl Mannheim. Mannheim's theoretical outline of what he terms 'the chiliastic mentality' offers a paradigm which is particularly apposite. He speaks of the conviction that the present moment is one of critical significance within the whole gamut of salvation-history: action is necessary, for it is no ordinary moment but one pregnant with opportunity for fulfilling the destiny of humankind. Thus the future hope is not merely a regulative ideal which acts as a stimulus to action and a norm by which one can judge the present state of affairs. Mannheim suggests that the present offers the possibility of realizing the millennium: 'For the real Chiliast, the present becomes the breach through which what was previously inward bursts out suddenly, takes hold of the outer world and transforms it.'[60] The absolute perfection of the millennium ceases to be a matter of speculation and becomes a pressing necessity for active implementation. The reason is that the *kairos*, or propitious moment, has arrived. As a result the chiliastic mentality has no sense for the process of becoming; it was sensitive only to the abrupt moment, 'the present pregnant with meaning'. For those gripped by this conviction the divine breaks into human history and is active through those who respond to the call to inaugurate the millennium. In this the chiliastic mentality contrasts with that strategy which sees the enlightened élite as a 'leaven in the lump of society'.

With the conviction that the age of perfection can become a reality here and now there is an inevitable distancing from the present age of imperfection: '[The] Chiliastic mentality severs all relationship with those phases of historical existence which are in daily process of becoming in our midst. It tends at every moment to turn into hostility towards the world, its culture, and all its works and earthly achievements . . .'[61] The responses of those who are convinced that the *kairos* has arrived are various. Violence is one possibility, in which the elect, inspired by the divine impulse, take up the sword in a holy war. But the tradition of peaceful direct non-violent action is another alternative.[62]

What is not sufficiently recognized by Ratzinger is that there are significant strands within the New Testament which exhibit this kind of outlook. The present becomes a moment of opportunity for transforming the imperfect into the perfect; history and eschatology become inextricably intertwined, and the elect stand on the brink of the millennium itself. We can see this in the career of Jesus of Nazareth as he proclaims the present as decisive in God's purposes and himself as the messianic agent for change. Similarly, Paul of Tarsus took upon himself, as the result of his deep-seated convictions, the role of the divine agent by whom the eschatological act of offering the gospel to the nations could be completed. It has been assumed that Jesus' *eschatological* expectation was for an other-worldly Kingdom of God brought in by God alone without any human agency. Humankind, according to this view of the messianic age, comprises merely passive spectators of a vast divine drama which has the cosmos as its stage. In the light of this one can understand why reserve is expressed towards a close alignment with historical projects which take sides in contemporary political struggles.

This prevalent reading retains a clear contrast between history and eschatology, the latter being conceived as something totally *beyond* history. Such ideas have, often unwittingly, helped to bolster consensus or even a conservative attitude towards the status quo in society, academy and Church. But such a dichotomy between history and eschatology is not entirely borne out by the ancient documents themselves. It was certainly a matter of opinion as to whether the promises were near to fulfilment, and we may suppose that this was a basic issue which separated Christians from their Jewish contemporaries. But it is important that we be clear that *this* was the issue rather than the impossibility of seeing the eschatological as part of the historical. Nowhere in the earliest writings (particularly the scriptural tradition) do we find such a distinction being made. Early Christian and Jewish writings offer a this-worldly materialistic hope which did not consist only of a cataclysmic irruption from the world beyond and the destruction of the present world for the manifestation of the divine righteousness. Human agency is always seen as part of the eschatological manifestation. When we recognize that the teaching in the New Testament, particularly that attributed to Jesus, enjoins the ideals applicable to God's reign *on earth*, the New Testament writings can be seen as embodying the struggles of those who looked forward to a new age and recognized the obligation to live in the present *as if* they were living in the age to come. They do seem to correspond to the chiliastic outlook to which Ratzinger and others take exception, and as such liberation theology seems to have pointed in the direction of an important aspect of the tradition in affirming this chiliastic legacy.

There is a wider issue here which has been touched on by recent theology but which has received little attention in discussions of twentieth-century exegesis. There has been a growing criticism of the dualistic notions which undergird post-Enlightenment philosophy and theology. That applies to questions of biblical exegesis also. As we have noted at the beginning of this section, the discussion of eschatology by Weiss makes a clear distinction between God's work and human activity. The Kingdom of God, we are told, is entirely transcendent; it is God's task alone. On this model there is little doubt that there are two histories – salvation-history and secular history – which only partially overlap. This reconstruction of ancient Jewish and early

Christian eschatology took place in an intellectual climate where the contrast between God and the world, the sacred and the secular exercised full sway over the way in which texts were being interpreted. Without diminishing the significance of the application of the Jewish eschatological ideas to the New Testament, we cannot assume that the way in which those ideas were understood by nineteenth-century exegetes necessarily gave us a precise glimpse of the mind-set of Jewish-Christian messianism. In the light of the dominance of certain assumptions about early Christian eschatology it is easy to see why there should have been so little question about the character of New Testament beliefs. The other-worldly imminent expectation has seemed to be an unchallengeable scientific finding of modern critical exegesis. Yet the texts themselves, as well as the attention given to the philosophical context of exegetes in the history of interpretation, demand that we think again. Liberation theologians like Gutierrez have joined with others in rejecting the dualism which subtly distances God from the world and salvation from human liberation and the sacred from the secular. There is one history, and the desire to speak of God in relationship to some special sphere of existence is a product of a philosophical era where such dualism pervades our thought.

Ratzinger's suggestion that liberation theology belongs to a theological tradition which is fundamentally alien to mainstream eschatology and social ethics should be questioned. Of course, there may well be other reasons to question the *appropriateness* of the chiliastic tradition. It is not just institutional self-interest and inertia which manifests itself in suspicion of chiliasm, there are also questions about appropriateness and the criteria for eschatological action at a particular moment. Few would want to justify all aspects of Thomas Müntzer's programme of violence,[63] for example, and many might question the appropriateness of the strategy of those like Camilo Torres[64] who decide that there is no possibility of change except by violent means. It is not only Christian theologians in the mainstream who have expressed reserve. Marx himself expressed considerable reserve towards the more enthusiastic of his followers who felt that it was possible to take short cuts to communism without adequate reflection on the present state of society and the likely success of their action.[65]

This might be seen as a recipe for quietism. If we cannot be sure when the millennium will come (assuming we are convinced that the historical is the arena of the eschatological), we may be tempted to avoid any decisive action. Such reserve is an understandable part of a view which resists the notion that a perfect understanding of reality is available. The typical chiliast, however, has the unwavering conviction that the millennium has arrived and that the frailty of perception does not apply to the chiliast. With the chiliast there is simplicity of approach and clarity of purpose and the paralysing effects of uncertainty do not detain him/her. A reading of both the Old and the New Testaments seems to deny both quietism and complete certainty, however.

The apocalyptic tradition, particularly in the book of Daniel, lays out a scheme of things in God's purposes. The seer is enabled to see the whole course of history, so that premature anticipation of the eschaton is seen to be futile, indeed unhelpful. Until the historical process has come to its fruition the obligation on the elect is to remain faithful to the ways of God and to seek to take upon oneself the yoke of the Kingdom, both individually and corporately, by enabling the will of God to be done on earth as in heaven. Where there is dispute over the readings of the signs of the times and there is a division of opinion over whether the critical moment has arrived, even here there may be room for continued dialogue, provided that the action taken by those convinced that the *kairos* has arrived conforms to the paradigm of the messianic proclamation of the *kairos* in the narrative of Jesus.

In the mature reflections of Paul now contained in the canon we find there stressed the importance of the eschatological reservation: the recognition that the presence of the day of salvation must not exclude the acceptance of the completion of that process in the future. So Paul in Romans 8 can speak of the present as both a time of struggle and groaning as well as one which allows the elect to taste the first-fruits of the glory to come via the eschatological Spirit. He is not sympathetic towards the Corinthian or Thessalonian enthusiasts who seek to behave as if the future perfection has already been achieved.[66]

In 1 Corinthians 4.8 he rebukes the realized eschatology of the Corinthians. In 2 Thessalonians 3.10 he warns those Christians who think that now is the time to give up present responsibilities and wait around for the Kingdom that they misunderstand the difficulty of the task of struggle that lies ahead. The present responsibility is to be active agents in the power of the eschatological Spirit, bearing witness to the Kingdom that is to come. Paul emphatically does not devalue the present as a time of making the most of the limited opportunities for the pursuit of the millennium that may be offered, something which the Thessalonian enthusiasts seem to have ignored in favour of 'leaving it all to God'.

This is no mere debating matter, however. A group of South African ministers and theologians have deemed it right to read the signs of the times and have determined that the moment of truth for their nation has arrived.[67] In this, the necessity of direct, non-violent action, is contemplated and indeed recommended as appropriate patterns of discipleship. The question we feel bound to ask is: How do we know that the *kairos* has come? Could it not be that, like Müntzer, they are making a terrible mistake? It is demanding existential issues like this that make liberation theology and its indebtedness to this significant strand of biblical tradition such a potent force in the contemporary world.

NOTES

1 J. Sobrino, *Christology at the Crossroads: A Latin American Approach* (London: SCM Press, 1978) and L. Boff, *Jesus Christ Liberator: Critical Christology of Our Time* (London: SPCK, 1979).

2 Sobrino, *Christology at the Crossroads*, pp. 351–3.

3 In A. Schweitzer, *The Quest of the Historical Jesus* (London: SCM Press, 1981).

4 Some other hints why this is the case may be seen in A.A. Boesak, *Comfort and Protest: Reflections on the Apocalypse of John of Patmos* (Edinburgh: St Andrew Press, 1987).

5 See J. Sobrino, *Archbishop Romero: Martyr for Liberation* (London: CIIR,[2] 1986), originally *Archbishop Romero: Model of Faith*.

6 W. Meeks, *The Moral World of the First Christians* (London: SPCK, 1987), pp. 145–6.

7 The Kairos Theologians, *The Kairos Document: Challenge to the Church = A Theological Comment on the Political Crisis in South Africa*, introduced by J. W. de Gruchy (Grand Rapids: Wm B. Eerdmans, 1986).

8 cf. Boesak, *Comfort and Protest*, p. 99: 'Paul, in Romans 13, is at pains to make clear that it is expected of government to be an agent of God, a servant of God, "for your good" . . . Because governmental authority should be a servant of God for the good of God's

people, it is inconceivable that a government can use the sword not to establish justice but to maintain injustice . . . and still be an agent of God. When this happens, the power becomes the beast from the sea.'

9 The Archbishop of Canterbury's Commission on Urban Priority Areas, *Faith in the City: A Call for Action by Church and Nation* (London: Church House Publishing, 1985). The theological foundation of the Commission's work can be found on pp. 47–8.

10 A. E. Harvey, *Jesus and the Constraints of History: The Bampton Lectures, 1980* (London: Duckworth, 1982).

11 ibid., p. 47.

12 ibid., pp. 131, 134, 143, 150.

13 C. Boff, quoted in D. Forrester, *Theology and Politics* (Oxford: Basil Blackwell, 1988), p. 126.

14 J. Weiss, *Jesus' Proclamation of the Kingdom of God*, ed., tr. and introduced by R. H. Hiers and D. L. Holland (London: SCM Press, 1971).

15 B. D. Chilton, *God in Strength* (Linz: Plochl, 1979). See also B. D. Chilton (ed.), *The Kingdom of God in the Teaching of Jesus* (Philadelphia: Fortress Press/London: SPCK, 1984), pp. 1–26, 121–32.

16 Chilton (ed.), *The Kingdom of God*, p. 126.

17 See further, N. Lash, *Easter in Ordinary: Reflections on Human Experience and the Knowledge of God* (London: SCM Press, 1988).

18 See the article 'Chiliasmus' in *Reallexikon für Antike und Christentum* ii, pp. 1073ff.

19 See G. Pixley, *God's Kingdom: A Guide for Biblical Study* (London: SCM Press, 1981), pp. 72–82

20 ibid., p. 93.

21 For a useful introduction see K. Fussel, 'The Materialist Reading of the Bible' in N. K. Gottwald (ed.), *The Bible and Liberation: Political and Social Hermeneutics* (Maryknoll, NY: Orbis Books, 1984).

22 On Marxist literary criticism, see R. Williams, *Marxism and Literature* (Oxford: Oxford University Press, 1977), T. Eagleton, *Criticism and Ideology* (London: Verso, 1976) and F. Jameson, *The Political Unconscious: Narrative as a Socially Symbolic Act* (London: Methuen, 1981).

23 See F. Belo, *A Materialist Reading of the Gospel of Mark* (Maryknoll, NY: Orbis Books, 1981) and M. Clevenot, *Materialist Approaches to the Bible* (Maryknoll, NY: Orbis Books, 1985). For an assessment of the importance of Belo's work, see C. Rowland, 'The Theology of Liberation and its Gift to Exegesis', *New Blackfriars* 65 (1984), pp. 157ff.

24 He uses Barthes' analysis of Balzac's novel *Sarrasine* in R. Barthes, *S/Z* (Paris: Editions de Seuil, 1970). On Barthes, see J. Culler, *Barthes* (London: Fontana, 1983).

25 Discussed in Jameson, *Political Unconscious*, pp. 85ff.

26 Some of these issues are touched on briefly in G. E. M. de Ste Croix, *The Class Struggle in the Ancient Greek World* (London: Duckworth, 1983), pp. 400ff. For parallel attempts to discern struggles in

post-exilic Judaism, see O. Ploger, *Theocracy and Eschatology* (Oxford: Basil Blackwell, 1968), P. D. Hanson, *The Dawn of Apocalyptic* (Philadelphia: Fortress Press, 1975) and M. Barker, *The Older Testament* (London: SPCK, 1988).

27 Clevenot, *Materialist Approaches*, p.78.

28 ibid., p. 93.

29 For some suggestive comments on this see L. Boff, 'Martyrdom: An Attempt at Systematic Reflection' in J.-B. Metz and E. Schillebeeckx (eds), 'Martyrdom Today', *Concilium* 163 (1983), pp. 12–17.

30 There is a concise discussion of this approach in H. Koester and J. M. Robinson, *Trajectories Through Early Christianity* (Philadelphia: Fortress Press,² 1979), pp. 187–98; see also the critical comments of M. Hooker in *The Message of Mark* (London: Epworth, 1983), pp. 34ff.

31 See P. L. West, 'Christology as "Ideology"', *Theology* 88 (1985), pp. 428–36.

32 See J. M. Robinson, *The Problem of History in Mark and other Marcan Studies* (Philadelphia: Fortress Press, 1982).

33 G. Theissen, *The Miracle Stories of the Early Christian Tradition* (Edinburgh: T. & T. Clark, 1983), pp. 249–50; see also W. Wink, *The Powers, vol. 1. Naming the Powers: The Language of Power in the New Testament* (Philadelphia: Fortress Press, 1984) and *The Powers, vol. 2. Unmasking the Powers* (Philadelphia: Fortress Press, 1986).

34 Theissen, *Miracle Stories*, see also C. Myers, p. 255. *Binding the Strong Man* (New York: Orbis, 1989).

35 See Lash, *Easter in Ordinary* and F. Kerr, *Theology After Wittgenstein* (Oxford: Basil Blackwell, 1986), concisely expressed by R. McAffee Brown, *Spirituality and Liberation* (London: Hodder & Stoughton, 1988).

36 See Q. Skinner, *The Foundations of Modern Political Thought* (Cambridge: Cambridge University Press, 1978), vol. 2, Part 1, pp. 3ff.

37 There is a survey of research in F. F. Bruce's article 'Render to Caesar' in E. Bammel and C. F. D. Moule (eds), *Jesus and the Politics of His Day* (Cambridge: Cambridge University Press, 1984), pp. 249–63.

38 J. D. M. Derrett, *Law in the New Testament* (London: Darton, Longman & Todd, 1970), pp. 335–6.

39 Bruce, 'Render to Caesar', p. 259.

40 See further, M. Borg, *Conflict, Holiness and Politics in the Teaching of Jesus* (Studies in the Bible and Early Christianity 5 (New York: Edward Mellen Press, 1984) and G. B. Caird, *Jesus and the Jewish Nation* (London: Athlone Press, 1965).

41 Bruce, 'Render to Caesar', p. 260.

42 R. Eisler, *The Messiah Jesus and John the Baptist* (London, Methuen, 1931), pp. 332ff.; cf. Bammel, *Jesus and the Politics of his Day*, pp. 32ff.

43 See Belo, *Materialist Reading*, p. 187.
44 cf. G. Aulen, *Christus Victor: An Historical Study of the Three Main Types of the Idea of the Atonement* (London: SPCK, [3] 1937) and J. A. T. Robinson, *The Body: A Study in Pauline Theology* (London: SCM Press, 1957), pp. 42ff.
45 See, for example, G. Gutierrez, *A Theology of Liberation* (London: SCM Press, 1974), pp.160ff.
46 So Weiss, *Jesus' Proclamation*, p. 114.
47 On Augustine's *City of God*, see the discussion of the interaction between theology and politics in R. A. Markus, *Saeculum: History and Society in the Theology of St Augustine* (Cambridge: Cambridge University Press, [2] 1988). See also G. Lohfink, *Jesus and Community: The Social Dimensions of Christian Faith* (Philadelphia: Fortress Press/New York: Paulist Press, 1984), pp. 181–5 on the problems of Augustine's legacy.
48 Forrester, *Theology and Politics*, pp. 25–6.
49 J. Jeremias, *New Testament Theology: The Proclamation of Jesus* (London: SCM Press, 1971), p. 248.
50 E. P. Sanders, *Jesus and Judaism* (London: SCM Press, 1985), pp. 228ff. See further, C. Rowland, 'Sanders' Jesus', *New Blackfriars* 66 (1985), pp. 412ff.
51 J. Ratzinger, 'Eschatology and Utopia' in *Church, Ecumenism and Politics* (Slough: St Paul, 1988), pp. 237ff.
52 ibid., p. 240.
53 ibid., p. 241.
54 ibid., p. 244.
55 On the millenarian character of monasticism, see J. Mohler, *The Heresy of Monasticism* (Staten Island: Alba, 1971).
56 Ratzinger, 'Eschatology and Utopia', p. 250.
57 ibid., p. 244.
58 ibid., p. 242.
59 See K. Mannheim, *Ideology and Utopia: An Introduction to the Sociology of Knowledge* (London: Routledge & Kegan Paul, 1936), pp. 190ff.
60 ibid., p. 193.
61 ibid., p. 198.
62 For the role of non-violence in the Latin American struggle, see the Peace Pledge Union's pamphlet *Non-Violence and Liberation. Central and South American Experience* (1987).
63 See T. Scott, *Thomas Müntzer: Theology and Revolution in the German Reformation* (London: Macmillan, 1989) and the evidence of this thinking in Peter Matheson (ed.), *The Collected Works of Thomas Müntzer* (Edinburgh: T. & T. Clark, 1988).
64 On the parallels between Camilo Torres and earlier radicals, see Andrew Bradstock, 'A Christian Contribution to Revolutionary Praxis? An examination of the significance of religious belief for the political philosophies of Gerrard Winstanley and Camilo Torres', unpublished dissertation, University of Kent, 1989.

65 See S. Avineri, *The Social and Political Thought of Karl Marx* (Cambridge: Cambridge University Press, 1968), pp. 252–3.
66 See R. Jewett, *The Thessalonian Correspondence: Pauline Rhetoric and Millenarian Piety* (Philadelphia: Fortress Press, 1986).
67 *The Kairos Document* (see note 7).

4

Exploring the Implications of a Liberation Exegesis in a First World Context 2: The Challenge of the Book of Revelation

1 APOCALYPTIC AND THE HERMENEUTICS OF SUSPICION

One of the most significant features of the historical-critical approach to the Bible is its dissatisfaction with the phenomenon of the text as it stands and the need to get behind it to the struggles which led to its production and the reality of the situation to which it so imperfectly bears witness. This dissatisfaction and need can be seen within the Tübingen school's construction of Christian origins based on a sceptical treatment of the historicity and tendentiousness of the New Testament material.[1] The hermeneutics of suspicion has been the stock in trade of the biblical historical critic for the last hundred years or more and has enabled the critic to throw light on what the biblical world might have been like. Its refusal to accept the text as it stands is based on the conviction that the literary product is itself covering up more than it reveals.

Liberation theology has set great store by the hermeneutics of suspicion. This emphasis manifested itself particularly in the quest for the Jesus of history and the laborious attempt to get behind the dogmatic presentation of the Lord of Christian faith to the real Jesus, however uncomfortable that may have been for Christian orthodoxy. Liberation theology's links with the Marxist critique of ideology and the quest to expose the reality of a situation by the application of 'scientific' methods of textual and social research are themselves features of the positivist environment in which modern theology has developed. It is necessary to identify these links, because what we find in liberation theology's suspicion of the character and conclusions of First World theology is very much derived from the same intellectual climate as First World theology.

Nevertheless, liberation theology has emphasized the central place of a socio-economic context on the function and development of ideas. It is precisely that which is at the heart of its most pungent challenges to theology. Liberation theologians question the use made of certain doctrines and ask in whose interests they have been utilized: for the ruling class or the poor? It is important for them, therefore, to challenge the dominance of the theological agenda set by First World theology when the pressing concerns of the poor in the Third World demand very different priorities. The emphasis on the contextual nature of all theology has led liberation theologians to question the absolute character of theological pronouncements from the past as well as the present and to a theological unmasking of the reality. The task can be exemplified by the following words from Leonardo Boff:

> What is the connection between a particular theological theme and a particular set of historical circumstances? . . . Who is helped by a particular theme or a particular type of Christology? What interests does it represent and what concrete projects does it support? Theologians do not live in clouds. They are social actors with a particular place in society. They produce knowledge, data, and meanings by using instruments that the situation offers them and permits them to utilize . . . The themes and emphases of a given Christology flow from what seems relevant to the theologian on the basis of his or her social standpoint . . . In that sense we must maintain that no Christology is or can be neutral . . . Willingly or unwillingly Christological discourse is voiced in a given social setting with all the conflicting interests that pervade it. That holds true as well for theological discourse that claims to be 'purely' theological, historical, traditional, ecclesial and apolitical. Normally such discourse adopts the position of those who hold power in the existing system. If a different kind of Christology with its own commitments appears on the scene and confronts the older 'apolitical' christology, the latter will soon discover its social locale, forget its 'apolitical' nature, and reveal itself as a religious reinforcement of the existing status quo.[2]

Liberation theology forcibly reminds us that we need to look critically at the way in which theology has come to focus on specific issues. Thus the contemporary theological enterprise cannot escape critical reflection of its assumptions and preferences. This is no theoretical issue only, nor is it merely part of the spirit of the age. Within the Basic Christian Communities such a hermeneutics of suspicion is nurtured by careful attention to the apocalyptic tradition. As we have seen, Revelation is for a variety of reasons the biblical book which enables millions of the poor to work out a different understanding of their reality as compared with what they are usually asked to accept. It offers hope but also stimulates resistance and sees the inevitable suffering of the poor and marginalized as an important component of an active witness to Jesus. The Apocalypse's view of the world, with its dualism and avoidance of consensus, its extravagant symbolism of evil and this-worldly hope, has always been a frightening and threatening part of the canon. As a refuge for enthusiasts and an inspiration for subversive elements, it has disturbed that order which institutions like the Church have so often been ready to promote.[3] Yet its place in the canon has provided resources for those who are suspicious of the attitude that accommodation with the powers that be and the present arrangements of the world can be God's last word on the subject. The Chilean theologian Pablo Richard is not alone in stressing how important this book is for the *campesinos*.[4] Some consideration of the reasons for this can perhaps enable us to see how deeply rooted the hermeneutics of suspicion is within the biblical tradition. Apocalyptic provides a discourse for social criticism.[5]

The first thing to be said about the Apocalypse is that it does not remain content with the phenomena of the world as they appear to 'normal' perception. What it sets out to do is to enable a radical 'unmasking of reality' (to quote Karl Mannheim's suggestive phrase).[6] It is a way of looking at the world which refuses to accept that its dominant powers, whether benign or otherwise, are the ultimate point of reference for the world. By positing another dimension to human existence, whether it be God or a hope for a better world, apocalyptic relativizes present arrangements. The future horizon of hope for a better world 'where sorrow and sighing will flee away' can enable those who reject present arrangements not only to long for but also to work for that era of justice. Of course, the language of hope need not necessarily lead to social engagement. When the hope is individualized and absolutely transcendentalized, then it can readily become a means of escape from the world, a flight from reality. But the way in which the contrasts between heaven and earth, good and evil promote dissatisfaction with the present ought to encourage engagement rather than fatalism. This is particularly so if the conflict between present and future, heaven and earth is expected to be resolved. What the Apocalypse encourages its readers to believe is that this will in fact be the case.[7] Only when there is despair of ever seeing that fulfilment in this world and the denial of historical consummation can questions arise about the futility of real change in the present order. Then one can understand why concentration is placed instead on preparation to live in some transcendent world.

An attraction of the book of Revelation for those whose way of thinking and reflecting is so different from the particularly rational theological discourses of the First World is that its discourse consists of picture and symbol rather than depending on systematic argument. This does not make its message and approach any less rational, but it asks the reader to participate in another way of speaking about God and the world, a way of speaking which refuses to be tied down to the niceties of carefully defined formularies. The parables of Jesus have consistently refused to be tied down to one particular meaning, however much the twentieth-century parable studies have tried to do precisely that. Similarly, the book of Revelation prompts a variety of meanings because of its lack of historical specificity in ways which are tantalizing, open-ended and, of course, highly unpredictable in their effects. Also, the book of Revelation appeals to the imagination, the heart as well as the head. This makes it more readily understood by those whose approach to the world is not primarily via the kind of rationality of the academy (though it needs to be stressed that Revelation *does* have its own rationality). Like the newspaper cartoons which make a political comment more tellingly than any editorial, however skilfully written, the resources of apocalyptic imagery can conjure in the imagination a grasp of reality and offer an instrument to understand reality with the result that the reader is stimulated to change it. It is a mode of discourse which taps deep wells of human responsiveness among those who through the experience of struggle, persecution and death have learnt what it means to wash their robes and to make them white in the blood of the Lamb.

The Apocalypse's dualism challenges the notion that human injustice is the centre of the universe by positing another horizon: at present, heaven. There God is now enthroned and from it the new Jerusalem will descend and then God and humanity will be united in the reign of justice. In Revelation 17–18 the state and public and private greed are thus decentred and indeed viewed with scorn and a sense of tragic contempt. The grandeur of Rome, which seems to be invincible and even divine, is revealed for what it really is. It is a bombastic sham maintained by vicious and diabolical means. This is a stunning critique of the accepted order and received wisdom. It can appeal to those who have suffered from the folly of conventional wisdom and the nonsense of what passes as common sense. They can see the worthlessness of a social structure which condemns millions to poverty, disease and death while a minority enjoy the fruits of the earth. But the view from the underside/outside of history is uncomfortable for those on the top or in the centre.

The hope for a better world is preserved in the apocalyptic tradition. We know from the history of early Christianity that the hope for a messianic kingdom on earth inspired by Revelation 20 was a dominant eschatological belief within the first century of the Church's life. That historical perspective, later kept alive within the alternative circles in the history of the Church, is very much part of many liberation theologians' eschatology. Such a hope gives a positive significance to action for social change, as it refuses to believe that this world will pass away and such efforts will thereby be seen not to be futile as compared with the task of rescuing men and women from an evil age. Liberation theologians would have us note that it is the *form* of this world which is passing away rather than this world itself. As we have already seen, that suspicion of a historical and materialist eschatology which is so characteristic of Western Christianity is a major point of difference between liberation theologians and their more centrally placed colleagues. What the apocalyptic (and for that matter prophetic) tradition reminds us is that the hope for God's reign on earth is not merely the materialist beguiling of a secular philosophy but a recourse to a language of hope which has been buried deep within the Christian tradition.

An acute problem does emerge, however, because of the way in which contemporary persons and events are often 'demonized' within a grassroots interpretation of apocalyptic symbolism. Thus, contemporary personages and systems can readily be identified with the beast of Revelation 13 and the great harlot seated upon the beast in Revelation 17. Such a *contemporary* historicizing of the symbolism is quite repugnant to those of us brought up to treat these texts solely eschatologically (thereby removing them from the historical sphere) and to seek consensus rather than conflict. The dualism of the apocalyptic tradition puts a large question mark against such an eschatological and consensual approach. The problem may be glimpsed in the way in which the institutions of state and Church are treated in *The Kairos Document*.[8]

The Kairos Document starts with the arresting words: 'The time has come' (recalling Jesus' words at the opening of his ministry in Mark 1.15). 'The moment of truth has arrived . . . It is the Kairos or moment of truth not only for apartheid but also for the church.' The document recognizes the splits among the Churches over the issue of apartheid and criticizes 'State Theology' and 'Church Theology' either for support of the government or for being too lukewarm in their criticism. There is a concerted 'unmasking of South African reality', particularly in the use made of the Bible. Christian Churches are taken to task for advocating reconciliation as 'an absolute principle that must be applied in all cases of conflict or dissension', for 'in our situation in South Africa today it would be totally unChristian to plead for reconciliation and peace before the present injustices are removed'. Neutrality is nothing but a means whereby the status quo of oppression can continue.

The Churches are told to pursue God's peace and expose false claims to peace. *The Kairos Document* rejects reformism and the gradualist approach in South Africa as being demonstrably ineffective and an attempt to reconcile the irreconcilable: 'God does not bring his justice through reforms introduced by the Pharaohs of this world'. It also rejects non-violence as an absolute principle and argues that the violence perpetrated by the security forces is as much, if not more, of a problem: 'How can acts of opression, injustice and domination be equated with acts of resistance and self-defence?' Referring to the biblical tradition, it points to the use of violence in the struggle of Israel for liberation and rejects the idea that Jesus said Christians should never use violence in self-defence. In other words, it affirms the just war theory that there *are* circumstances in which limited violence may be legitimately used. As such the writers of the *Kairos Document* feel themselves able to identify a righteous cause which can then be prosecuted by force if necessary.

One can recognize the dangers of this kind of approach where the opposition is so readily regarded as the antichrist (though it is not something that the biblical tradition itself is all that squeamish about, as 1 John 2.20ff. makes plain).[9] The issue is not whether this kind of theologizing should be done. As we have seen, it would involve a complete negation of the apocalyptic theology if use was not made of the dualism which contrasts the reign of God and the institutions of injustice opposed to God. What is more, the exorcisms of the demons and the overcoming of the powers of darkness are such a central part of Jesus' mission that faithfulness to him means understanding what this kind of confrontation and struggle with the powers might be about.[10] Rather, the issue is whether there is a comprehensive enough hermeneutic of suspicion which recognizes that the children of light themselves cannot but be infected with the reign of darkness. The reign of God has not come in all its fullness. To behave as if it had is itself a denial of the reality of evil and the extent of the struggle. Confronting the powers and naming the antichrist necessarily involves the potential, indeed the reality, of the demonic within ourselves. 'Demonizing' one's opponents can be accompanied by a self-righteous attitude which so easily lapses into perfectionism. The children of light can see themselves as the appointed agents of the divine will; matters begin to be sharply defined and the division between good and evil clearly seen. We all know that things *are* more complicated than that. This is what prevents us from what many would deem as a reckless use of Scripture in favour of any particular cause, especially when it means casting those who oppose us as agents of darkness (cf. 2 Cor. 11.13–15).[11]

The value of Augustine's approach to the relationship between history and eschatology, the earthly city and the heavenly city, is that it refuses to sanctify a particular system, but rather asserts that all are flawed. There is no guarantee of clarity this side of the millennium. The difficulty of certainty and the risk involved in committing oneself to a past where greater clarity seems to be found than is actually the case should not prevent us from being ready to act. We must do this in the full knowledge of our fallibility, and with as high a suspicion (if not a higher suspicion) of our own motives as we have of our opponents'. Jeremiah's words about the deceitfulness of the human heart (Jer. 17.9) are particularly apposite for those who espouse righteous causes. The need for a constant eschatological reservation has nowhere been expressed more clearly than in the words of Theodor Adorno:

> The only philosophy which can be responsibly practised in face of despair is the attempt to contemplate all things as they would present themselves from the standpoint of redemption. Knowledge has no light but that shed on the world by redemption: all else is reconstruction, mere technique. Perspectives must be fashioned that displace and estrange the world, reveal it to be, with its rifts and crevices, as indigent and distorted as it will appear one day in the messianic light.[12]

Confronting the powers and the demons in others and in the institutions of Church and state must be accompanied by the co-operative task of confronting them and struggling with them in ourselves. Individual champions of sacred causes who feel the need to leave behind the critical support of the people of God are particularly vulnerable to self-deception. But to be honest about that does not diminish the importance of the task of the Church to confront the powers in line with the ministry of Jesus. The account of that struggle with the forces of darkness within the story of Jesus shows the conflict continuing throughout the ministry (e.g. the temptation, Peter's confession and immediate identification with Satan in Mark 8.29, 33). It is a ready reminder of the careful process which is involved in recognizing the demonic at work in the old aeon.[13]

Another problem with an apocalyptic epistemology is that its quest for revelation can offer an easy answer to unfathomable human problems through divinely bestowed insight. The desire for 'higher wisdom through revelation'[14] is in some circumstances an antidote to a radical pessimism which despairs of ever being able to make sense of the contradictions of human existence. The only way forward in such circumstances can appear to be

complete reliance on the revelation of God to a fallible and inadequate humanity. In general terms we may suppose that something
of this was at work in the apocalyptic culture which flourished in
the second half of the Second Temple period. That should not
surprise us, given the bleak national prospects. Apocalyptic could
breed a mood of acute despair and depreciation of human ability to
make sense of history, which could lead to a rejection of all but the
revealed word that answers all the problems of existence. Of
course, the kinds of answers offered are by no means uniform, and
they indicate that the ancient apocalyptic is itself ambivalent about
the way in which one can come to know the mind of God.

There are apocalypses (or at least parts of them) which use the
concept of revelation to offer a definitive solution to human
problems. So we find in a work like Jubilees, which purports to be
an angelic revelation to Moses on Sinai, a retelling of biblical
history which conforms largely with what is found in Scripture. At
many points, however, there are divergences, and the significance
of these is nowhere greater than when ethical questions emerge.
This is evident when the calendar and Sabbath observance are
discussed. With regard to the former, the revelation makes it quite
clear that the calendar laid down by this angelic revelation (which
affects the days on which major festivals and holy days are celebrated) is not only different from what applies elsewhere, but that
deviation involves a complete repudiation of the law of God. Here
revelation is used to exclude and anathematize opponents and their
behaviour. Such a use of apocalyptic, which in effect denies the
fallibility of the recipient, also removes any possibility of discussion of the subject. Something similar can happen when final,
authoritative interpretations of Scripture are offered by means of
revelation, such as we find, for example, in Daniel 9.23 and in the
biblical interpretation at Qumran (see 1QpHab 8).[15]

Not all apocalypses offer unambiguous and exclusive answers
which seem to brook no dispute. However, all the apocalypses
certainly offer revelation, much of which is in effect what was
traditionally believed. So the horizon of hope is reaffirmed by
revelation and the historical perspective of salvation is supported.
But the form of the revelation is such that it can produce as much
mystification as enlightenment. Not all visions offer an unambiguous answer to questions. Indeed, there is frequently a need for
angelic interpretation of enigmatic dreams and visions, and even

these interpretations are not without their ambiguities. So it proved necessary for revelations coined in one era to be the basis of 'updating' and application in the different political circumstances of another (e.g. Dan. 9.24 on Jer 29.10). Thus the symbolism of the fourth beast in Daniel 7 is given new life in the Roman period, when it ceases to refer to Greece and is instead applied to Rome (a process which continued, as the history of the interpretation of Dan. 7 shows). Examples of this link with Rome may be found in both Revelation 13 and in 4 Ezra 12 which allude to Daniel 7.

Some apocalypses refuse to provide 'answers' through revelation and offer nothing more than the refusal of a complete answer, such being beyond the human mind to grasp. Instead there is an emphasis on the present struggle. This is especially apparent in 4 Ezra. Here issues of theodicy are particularly apparent. The seer wishes to know why Israel has been allowed to suffer and why God seems content to allow the bulk of humanity to perish. The revelation, akin as it is to God's answer in the book of Job, is to stress the puny nature of human understanding in the face of the transcendence of God, to stress the ultimate victory of God's righteousness, and to urge the need for those committed to the ways of God to continue in that narrow way in order to achieve the millennium. It is a realistic, almost anti-utopian, apocalypse in which dreams of the future are subordinated to the reality of present obedience in the face of human injustice. Here there is no solution but struggle. No short cuts can be allowed, whether by the dramatic intervention of God through enlightenment or angelic battles, or by a cheap hope which avoids the demand of a present implementation of divine righteousness.

So, despite their reputation as vehicles of fantastic speculation and naive hope, some apocalypses are on closer inspection far more 'down to earth' and concerned with present responses in the light of the coming Kingdom of God. Thus, setting the Apocalypse's message of hope within the context of the letters to the seven churches prevents that extravagant symbolism from becoming loosened from the moorings of the reality which confronts the churches.

The dominant concern with 'reality' in the writings of liberation theologians demands that the symbolism must always be part of the dialectic which must take place between the story of the people of God and the tradition as a whole. That, of course, means that a historical referent may from time to time be found in the use of the apocalyptic imagery. It should not, however, lead to the view that the particularity of evil and oppression actually exhausts the meaning of that rich symbolism.

The letters to the angels of the seven churches are a necessary grounding of the language of hope. The users of the Apocalypse have to be reminded that the unmasking of the concrete realities of oppression and the consequent defusing of their power and destructive quality offers no escape from the ongoing struggle. The interpretative tools offered by the apocalyptic tradition may enable us to see that the power and bombast of the mighty oppressor is short; but it still has to be resisted.

2   THE APOCALYPSE: THE SUBVERSIVE MEMORY

No one today is going to doubt that texts are a problem, and that they need interpretation in order for their riches to be put to productive use in contemporary life. The legacy of the nineteenth century is too strong for us to shake off the deep-seated suspicion of the appearance and to seek instead to pierce to the 'reality' which is concealed by the text. There are no texts which offer us an exact representation of the reality to which they refer. Those that claim to do that are most to be suspected, for they offer something which is impossible to give. For the very process of chronicling and cataloguing cannot ever be value-free. That means that we must always be attentive to the processes which produce this particular text in this particular form at a particular time and why it claims the attention of particular readers. The text itself has other stories to tell apart from what we read on the page. Those stories are often difficult to reconstruct but tell the tale, often only very partially, of the psychology of the author, the struggles of her/his world. Any careful reading will want to be alert to such matters as well as to the way in which reading affects individuals and groups and shapes the understanding of 'what the text is actually about'. How can we seek to say more about the ways in which texts have in the past functioned (and continue to function in the present) as part and parcel of the legitimation of the existing order or as challenges to it; and how can we take account of that dialectic between ideas and social formation in seeking to undertand the way in which texts and the interpretation of those texts are social products and manifest conflicting ideologies? We have seen something of the kinds of choices made by liberation exegesis in the interests of its identification with the poor, and it is tempting to suppose that those specific choices have captured what the text *really* means in disclosing what the author intended. That may or may not be the case. What is certain is that the multiplicity of often conflicting interpretations, some of which would most emphatically seek to distance themselves from an overtly 'political' reading, require some caution on the part of those who would seek to ally particular texts to their cause on the basis of the belief that the real meaning has been disclosed.

Similar texts can be used in the service of vastly different causes, as the history of European religion down the centuries has shown. But one text, the book of Revelation, has more often been used in the service of those who have set about subverting the contemporary social order. That is not to deny that the Apocalypse, and the apocalyptic tradition generally, has often been linked to the projects of opponents of social change. Even today it can be found buttressing the projects of those whose quest for utopia is firmly rooted in conventional values and the nostalgic yearning for a golden age of moral perfection based on hierarchy and subservience. In the quest for this, apocalyptic symbolism can serve to undergird a view of the world which supports the conviction of a comfortable elect, that they will ultimately be saved. The outlook of the Apocalypse, with its alternative horizon beckoning towards a different future, enables the maintenance of clearly defined lines between the godly and the godless, capitalism and communism. Also, it can serve to enable the oppressed to maintain a critical distance from reality and to assert in face of the contradictory character of a world of injustice the prospect of the hope of a reign of justice. There is little new in all this. The apocalyptic symbolism has never been the sole preserve of the oppressed and poor. Even in post-exilic Israel in the very years when eschatological hope was being formed there was a common stock of images which two sides in a struggle for power used to achieve pre-eminence for their own positions.[16]

Even allowing for this there can be no denying the way in

which the Apocalypse has proved to be a potent – and, in the eyes of the wielders of political power, a dangerous – instrument of protest and hope. It is a necessary task of those who are involved in seeking to determine the ways in which texts are social products to examine the various ways in which their form and content betray those contradictions and hopes of individuals and groups locked into societies where class and power oppress, marginalize and distort humanity. The point is made quite clearly by Frederic Jameson: 'All works are profoundly ideological . . . all have a vested interest in relation to social formations based on violence and oppression . . . The restoration of meaning of the greatest cultural monuments cannot be separated from a passionate and partisan assessment of everything that is oppressive'.[17]

Texts themselves are going to relate to very particular social situations, as well as to wider social and economic movements whose history is far bigger than the immediate situation in which a text is written. Thus, as well as representing the narrow confines of the struggles and language of a particular group, the text is an individual representative of the struggles between social classes and the contradictions of human existence.[18] Doing justice to the way in which texts form part of the struggles for power and survival depends to a large extent on a knowledge of the particular social situation and general social trends of which they are a part. It is much easier to use this model to illuminate contemporary reading than to illuminate production of texts or meaning in the ancient world. This is because of the greater amount of data available in the contemporary world which enables us to know more of the circumstances in which interpretation takes place. The paucity of information about the peculiar circumstances which might have determined, wholly or in part, the symbolic constellation or narrative of an ancient text makes it a difficult task to ascertain what precisely were the factors which helped form the text as we now have it. We are bound (as biblical scholars have always accepted) to resort to a significant amount of imaginative reconstruction in order to offer answers to the question: In what kind of situation, and as part of what sort of social struggle, did people write this kind of text in this kind of way? That is not to minimize the importance of historical reconstruction, as the main fabric of historical criticism has set itself the task of 'filling the gaps' of the textual remains.[19]

It is necessary, however, to assemble sufficient information to form some picture of the social formation. In order to do this we may frequently find ourselves relying on ideas as indicators of both social location and the relationship of the writer and readers to the wider society and its struggles.[20]

How, then, do texts manifest the ebb and flow of social conflict and the oppression of the weak by the strong? First, in Jameson's view: 'Texts are symbolic acts whereby real social contradictions insurmountable in their own terms find a purely formal resolution in the aesthetic realm.'[21] In other words, texts and rituals can offer solutions which satisfy the imagination of readers or participants when the real world seems to offer no resolution whatsoever. The story which ends happily ever after, or the glorious conclusion to a religious service, contrasts with a world where conflict is the order of the day.

Second, in that conflict, those who exercise power will seek to do so not only in terms of control of wealth-creation but also in terms of the ideas which can justify and support the way in which the world is run to their advantage. The recognition of this process, and the attempt to understand the way in which those who refuse to accept the dominant understanding of the way the world is, forms a central part of the investigation of ideology. A text must be interpreted as part of a struggle between different class interests in which a ruling class ideology seeks to offer itself as 'common sense' or 'normality' and all else as deviant and irrational. So, for example, Jameson can write:

> A ruling class ideology will explore strategies of legitimation, while an oppositional culture or ideology will often in covert and disguised strategies seek to contest and to undermine the dominant value system . . . There is a process of reappropriation and neutralisation by the dominant ideology; also the co-optation and hence neutralisation of the ideas of subordinated groups: so the slave religion of Christianity is transformed into the hegemonic ideological apparatus of the mediaeval system.[22]

When we speak of the Christian tradition, it is easy to identify it with those parts of it which have been accepted by those who have wielded power. Deviant faith and practice have by the consent of the powerful been excluded and branded as unfit for proper ecclesiastical consumption. In some cases we can see why such decisions may have been necessary. But that does not by any means always apply. There is a legitimate task of rediscovering bits of the tradition which have become submerged by dominant ideologies. The canon is in one sense a domestication of awkward ideas; but in another sense, in the very process of domestication it contains within itself the minority opposition ideas. The formation of a dominant ideology involves the incorporation of the opposition ideas – which means that they are not completely lost and are therefore recoverable by means of patient analysis. So the very presence of such ideas continues to provide a basis for the rediscovery of social and ecclesiastical alternatives. The retrieval of a 'subversive memory' is a significant component of the theology of liberation. Thus, for example, we find in discussions of Latin American history a clear desire to tell the story of the ideas and memories which were suppressed by the European conquest. The recovery of Aztec and Mayan culture in Mexico and Central America, and more recently in post-1979 Nicaragua the quest for a popular history are examples of this.[23]

The liberation theology perspective on the story of the Church likewise seeks to activate that present concern with the story of the people's struggle by attempting to recover that story down the centuries. That will mean giving more attention to popular religions as carriers of that subversive memory. No better example can be found than the creative way in which the African religions of the slaves were preserved by means of a creative synthesis with dominant Catholicism.[24] In Brazil, for example, the slaves kept alive their West African culture after their enforced baptisms by identifying the divinities and saints of Christianity with their African gods. Although outwardly the religion may have been Catholic and Christian, what was going on in their heads was a devotion to their cultural origins and a worship of the gods of their ancestors. Truly this was a matter of singing the Lord's song in a strange land. By using the language of the victors to speak their own language of hope and home, they kept alive the alternative horizon of that land across the sea whence their ancestors had been cruelly dragged.

In this respect they parallel the emphasis placed by Walter Benjamin and Theodor Adorno on the power of the past to disturb. 'The past could appear in the form of memory, which kept alive the utopian hopes and critical energies of previous generations. That was a necessary corrective to the 'repetition of the ever-the same' in the guise of the new, the return of the seemingly repressed even amidst apparent enlightenment'.[25] Both Benjamin and Adorno have kept hold of a utopian horizon even in the midst of some of their more pessimistic assessments of the present culture. They resisted the view which asserted that history was cyclical, even if they rejected any simple unilinear, evolutionary or progressivist view of history. The subversive memory could frequently bear witness to those affirmations of utopia 'that seem so out of place against the more frequent note of bleak despair'.[26]

Benjamin emphasized that the cultural monuments celebrated by official history could not be understood outside the context of their origins, a context of oppression and exploitation.[27] Incorporated into the tradition of conventional history, they were no more than booty carried in the triumphal procession of the victors. Just as the cultural object itself would never be free from barbarity, 'so neither is the process of handing down by which it is passed from one to the next'. He spoke of the need to capture a memory 'as it flashed past in a moment of danger'.[28] It is the 'involuntary memory of a redeemed humanity' which contrasted with convention and false tradition. It is necessary to 'brush history against the grain'.[29] The task of each generation is to rescue tradition from the conformity imposed upon it by the powerful: 'In every era the attempt must be made anew to wrest tradition away from a conformism that is about to overpower it.'[30]

In the book of Revelation we have a book which today serves as the potent resource supplying the subversive memory of the poor and oppressed. Its stark contrasts and uncompromising critique can appeal to those who find little hope in compromise with the powers that be and demand something more than a meek acceptance that 'the way the world is' is what God intended.

The New Testament Apocalypse sets out to reveal things as they really are in both the life of the Christian communities and the world at large.[31] In so doing it gives little comfort to the complacent Church or the powerful world. For the powerful and the complacent it has a message of judgement and doom, whereas for the powerless and oppressed it offers hope and vindication.

The characterization of contemporary society in the apocalyptic symbolism of the beast and the harlot is a vigorous unmasking and denunciation of the ideology of the powerful, by which they seek to legitimize their position by persecution and economic exploitation. A critique of the present is effected by the use of a contrast between the glories of the future and the inadequacies of the present. The process of unmasking involves an attempt to delineate the true character of contemporary society and the super human forces at work in the opposition to God's righteousness in the world. Also, the enormous power of those forces which undergird the oppression and unrighteousness of the world order are shown to be unstable and destined to defeat (Rev. 17.16: 'the ten horns . . . will make [the harlot] desolate and naked, and devour her flesh and burn her up with fire'). In contrast, the apparent fragility of the witness of those who follow the way of Jesus is promised ultimate vindication (Rev. 7 and 14).

Revelation seeks to persuade its readers that the present moment is a time of critical importance. The whole of history has to be seen in the light of the Lamb, the symbol of the executed Messiah, whose vindication precipitates the manifestation of judgement begun in Revelation 5. The outline of future history is offered as the basis for a change of heart which will have drastic consequences for the one who reads it. Acceptance or rejection of its message is nothing less than the difference between alignment with the reign of God which is to come or sharing the fate of the beast in the lake of fire. Revelation offers a justification for the cosmic and historical context of divine activity. That view, so deeply imbedded in the Jewish Scriptures, was subordinated in mainstream Christian doctrine to the concern for the individual soul, a process already evident in the New Testament. The book of Revelation has provided encouragement for all those who look for the fulfilment of God's righteousness in human history.

In Revelation 4 the seer is granted a glimpse into the environs of God. Here God the Creator and Liberator is acknowledged, and, as we notice from the following chapter, it is from the God of the universe that the historical process begins which leads to the establishment of a new aeon after the manifestation of divine judgement. In the chapters following Revelation 4–5 we find the picture of a world afflicted but unrepentant (e.g. Rev. 9.20–1; 16.9), indeed, manifesting precisely the kind of misguided devotion to evil which has to be rooted out before God's Kingdom can finally come. In Revelation 4 God is still in heaven, and it is there that the heavenly host sing God's praise and magnify God's name. In a world where righteousness is absent the separation of God in heaven is a necessary way of showing up present injustice and reminding all the world that what passes off as normality is not so.[32]

There is in Revelation 4 a contrast with Revelation 21, where God's dwelling is on earth; it is no longer in heaven. The contrast is between this age and the age to come, with the latter pictured as already existing in heaven but destined to be manifest on earth in the future (Rev. 21.2). God is ultimately in control of human history, but God *appears* to the seer to be removed behind the vault of heaven through which the latter ascends to witness the divine presence and worship.

This contrast between heaven and earth disappears in the new creation. Now the tabernacling of God is with humanity, and they shall be God's people. God's dwelling is not to be found above the cherubim in heaven; for God's throne is set right in the midst of the New Jerusalem (Rev 21.3), where the living waters stream from the throne and God's servants marked with the mark of God will see God face to face (Rev 22.1, 4). It is only in the new age that there will be the conditions for God and humanity to dwell in that harmony which was impossible in all its fullness while there was rejection of the divine righteousness in human affairs. Heaven on earth is what the new age is all about. God is no longer transcendent but immediate – part and parcel of that world of perfection, and evident in it. In the apocalyptic vision, therefore, the contradictions of a fractured existence are resolved in the harmony offered by that vision. Apocalyptic writers were convinced that this divine immanence was not reserved solely for the new age. The glory which the apocalyptic seer enjoyed in his revelation was a matter of living experience here and now for those who confessed Jesus as Messiah and participated in the eschatological Spirit. Already those who possessed the Spirit of God were sons and daughters of God; already those in Christ were a new creation and a temple of the divine Spirit (Rev.1.6; cf. Rom. 8.15; Gal. 4.6).

The Apocalypse can remind readers of early Christian literature that the hope for a reign of God on earth, when injustice and oppression will be swept away and the structures of an evil society broken down, is an important component of the Christian gospel. One can imagine how easy it would have been for the early Christians to have capitulated to their feelings of political power-lessness by concentrating solely on individual holiness. But Paul, for example, speaks of a process of salvation which is firmly rooted in the process of liberation for the whole of creation (see Rom. 8.19ff.). Similarly, the Apocalypse does not easily allow a retreat into the conventicle as the main arena of divine activity, for it persuades the saints to prophesy before the world about the righteousness of God and the dreadful consequences of ignoring its implementation.

The readers of the Apocalypse are not allowed to dream about millennial bliss without being brought face to face with the obstacles which stand in the way of its fulfilment and the costly part to be played by them in that process. Those demands are evident in the letters to the churches which introduce the vision of hope and in the concluding admonitions which stress the authority of the text and the imminence of the fulfilment of its message. The book of Revelation offers a timely reminder in its own form about supposing that its preoccupation with eschatological matters offers an opportunity to avoid the more challenging preoccupations of the present. Thus, the vision of hope inaugurated by the exaltation of the Lamb is set within the framework of the letters to the seven churches. The promise of a part in the New Jerusalem is linked with present behaviour.

Apocalypses are full of different genres; Revelation is no exception. The mixture of epistle and apocalypse, for example, may reflect the ambiguities and contradictions of life. Even the most overtly messianic and historically oriented text of the New Testament cannot but be affected by the contradictions between hope and impoverished reality. The letters which impress on their readers the importance of present action indicate a degree of interest in apparently narrow religious issues[33] (one of the reasons, one suspects, that these letters continue to gain a more ready hearing from contemporary Christian audiences). That concern to recapture one's first love and to endeavour to maintain the purity of one's relationship to the Lord who stands in the midst of his churches (Rev 1.19–20) indicates the emerging preoccupation with personal and ecclesial holiness which is itself part of the reaction to political impotence. The letter form itself, that medium of the Pauline urban Christianity which appears so different from the world of Jesus and the first followers of Jesus, seems also to embody that spirit of urban Christianity, where accommodation with the surrounding culture and acceptance of its priorities led to a growing restriction to the 'religious' realm. In saying this, however, we should not ignore the very political character of some of the issues touched on in Revelation 2–3 as we shall see in a moment.

A text will not usually produce a particular ideology in a 'pure' form, whether it be supportive of the status quo or not. Accordingly, however loud the note of protest in a text, it is going to be shot through with the ambiguities of being part of a world that is itself full of contradiction and pain. Any text's relation to that struggle may well be ambiguous. It will not necessarily stand firmly on one side or another. Sometimes it will manifest the voice of the oppressor and his/her ideology in the process of seeking to articulate an alternative perspective on the world. It is part of the task of interpretation to lay bare the ambiguities and contradictions that are inherent in all texts.

Take the dualism of the apocalypses, for example. First, their contrast between the inadequacies of the present and the glories of the future has the effect of impoverishing the present and life in this world. As a result apocalyptic dualism can easily end up in a kind of self-denying rejection of this world and a disparaging of God's creation. Clearly, the book of Revelation never does this. There is, however, ambiguity in its description of the new age. There are two climaxes in the process of judgement (Rev. 19 and Rev. 20) and two visions of a new age (the millennium, and the new heaven and the new earth). Various attempts have been made to explain this phenomenon. It could be argued that the uncertainty with regard to eschatology provided by the juxtaposition of a this-worldly millennium and an apparently transcendent new creation may reflect an ambiguity with regard to the content of hope. Does the text reflect the despair and the political powerlessness of those who cannot conceive of human history being the arena for the fulfilment of the divine promises? Whatever initially led to the repetition of the themes of judgement and eschatological fulfilment in Revelation 19–21 (and there are good reasons for supposing that one author might have been responsible, as in 4 Ezra 6–7), their presence in this text could be taken to indicate that uncertainty about the locus of eschatological fulfilment which has been part of the Christian tradition throughout the ages: Is the Kingdom of God to come in this world, or is it a radical, other-worldly entity whose coming is entirely in God's hands?

Apocalyptic symbolism strikes us as bizarre today. It would probably have been regarded in the same way by many pagans as well. As such it represents a powerful form whereby the oppressed can keep alive the oppressed culture in the face of a dominant and powerful ideology. Doing this, however, requires an effort on the part of the believer. The role of the follower of the Messiah is not quiet resignation. In the unfolding eschatological drama in the main body of the Apocalypse the involvement of the seer in Revelation 10, when he is instructed to eat the scroll and commanded to prophesy, is a direct call to participate actively as a prophet rather than merely be a passive spectator. Revelation is insistent that the role of the martyr or witness is of central importance.[34] Jesus of Nazareth is the faithful prophetic witness, and his followers have to continue that testimony of Jesus. In Revelation 11 the Church is offered a paradigm of the true prophetic witness as it sets out to fulfil its vocation to prophesy before the world. That prophetic witness takes place in a social scene opposed to God, even though it ends up with martyrdom.

Two of the issues in the letters to the seven churches are 'eating food sacrificed to idols' and 'immorality', almost certainly references to idolatry (Rev. 2.14, 20). The strictures against those who recommend eating food sacrificed to idols indicate the need to create some distance between the conduct of Christians and the typical behaviour of society. The references to idolatry and immorality in these passages are to be understood as standing in the tradition of the Jewish concern for holiness, that distinctive pattern of life over against the nations: 'it shall not be so with you . . .' (Mark 10.43).[35] There is a challenge to the assumption that the disciple is going to be able to take part without too much discomfort in the social intercourse of the contemporary world. There are several counter-cultural strands in Revelation. It resists compromise and accommodation and keeps alive the spirit of Jesus and the apostles by advocating a critical distance from contemporary culture in the character of social relations adopted and the language of religious discourse.

This may be seen in several areas. First, the invective against complacency in the letters to the churches has been interpreted as an indication of growing laxity and lack of rigour. The concern for holiness in Jewish culture was tied up with the maintenance of an alternative culture over against the nations. This can be seen in the repudiation of idolatry, the food laws, circumcision and Sabbath observance. Likewise the call to martyrdom indicates the need for resistance, even if that means non-participation in the Roman economic system.[36]

Second, for Revelation the Spirit and prophecy have a central role, as they were to have in the Montanist movement a century later. By then prophecy was viewed with suspicion, so much so that Revelation's place as part of the canon was challenged. Ambivalence with regard to prophecy has always characterized religion. Revelation stands out against those who would quench the Spirit and despise prophecy (I Thess. 5.19–20). As with the millenarian/apocalyptic tradition, prophecy was too deeply rooted in the Christian memory to be allowed to be anathematized, so that other ways had to be found to domesticate it.

Finally, the apocalyptic imagery and cosmology itself betokens a view of the world where protest and resistance to compromise are the order of the day. The dualistic cosmology encouraged a separatist mentality. The millenarian horizon, with its radical alternative to the present order, showed up the discredited social processes of the present in the starkest possible relief. It was not just a case of relativizing the world order in the light of the glory of the City of God, for it also involved casting the power behind the structures as diabolical and exposing its concerns as oppressive. There is little room for accommodation with the beast and Babylon. Now all this is not to suggest that the apocalyptic outlook could not be 'appropriated and neutralized' by its incorporation into the dominant ideology. Clearly that did happen to some extent, not least by its incorporation into the canon. Religions in particular offer excellent examples of the way in which this process of domestication can take place. Movements of protest born as ways of keeping alive ideas and aspirations contrary to the dominant culture can in the course of time lose their cutting edge and become part of a diffused cultural phenomenon that is incorporated into the dominant economic system. But with apocalyptic such assimilation often remained an incomplete process, for such subversive ideas could never be completely tamed. The language and imagery itself evokes ideas of a different perspective on reality. Apocalyptic demands of its readers that conventional judgements are suspended and an alternative perspective considered. Apocalyptic dualism is, therefore, an indispensable ideological mechanism whereby the distorted form of reality and the contradictions of the world can be seen by those without political power. Those whose existence is on the margins of the contemporary world, can bear witness to the reality of the fragmentation of humanity which they above all experience. Of course, that can easily end up with the 'other world' of any dualistic system becoming a refuge for those who seek to escape the conflicts of the present distorted existence. Religions have all too often performed this role extremely effectively. But the abolition of a dualistic outlook cannot solve the problem of the socio-economic reality which prompts the need to use dualistic language. This is a way of creating distance from the present, offering an alternative horizon to unjust situations and relationships, and enabling the oppressed to voice their discontent at an unjust world.

NOTES

1 H. Harris, *The Tübingen School* (Oxford: Oxford University Press, 1975).
2 L. Boff, *Jesus Christ Liberator: A Critical Christology of Our Time* (London: SPCK, 1979), p. 75.
3 See briefly C. Rowland, *Radical Christianity* (Cambridge: Polity Press/Oxford: Basil Blackwell, 1988), ch. 5, and, on the history of exegesis, see C. Patrides and J. Wittreich, *The Apocalypse in English Renaissance Thought and Literature* (Manchester: Manchester University Press, 1984).
4 P. Richard, lecture in São Paulo, September 1985.
5 See F. Hinkelammert, *The Ideological Weapons of Death* (Maryknoll, NY: Orbis Books, 1986) for suggestive approaches to the critical use of the Christian tradition.
6 K. Mannheim, *Ideology and Utopia: An Introduction to the Sociology of Knowledge* (London: Routledge & Kegan Paul, 1936), pp. 173ff.
7 See below, pp. 148, on Rev. 4 and 21.
8 The Kairos Theologians, *The Kairos Document: Challenge to the Church = A Theological Comment on the Political Crisis in South Africa*, introduced by J. W. de Gruchy (Grand Rapids: Wm B. Eerdmans, 1986).
9 It is instructive to look at the historicizing exegesis of the antichrist idea in the biblical interpretation of the seventeenth century. See, for

example, C. Hill, *Antichrist in Seventeenth-Century England. The Riddell Memorial Lectures, Newcastle 1969* (London: Oxford University Press, 1971).

10 See above, pp. 104ff., and see W. Wink, *Naming the Powers: The Language of Power in the New Testament* (Philadelphia: Fortress Press, 1984) and *Unmasking the Powers* (Philadelphia: Fortress Press, 1986).

11 See C. Rowland, 'Discerning the "Abomination of Desolation"' in A. Race (ed.), *Theology Against the Nuclear Horizon* (London: SCM Press, 1988), pp. 39–51.

12 T. Adorno, *Minima Moralia* (London: Verso, 1974), p. 247.

13 On the need for self-critical caution, see Rowland, 'Discerning the "Abomination of Desolation"', pp. 49–51.

14 See M. Hengel, *Judaism and Hellenism* (London: SCM Press, 1974, vol. 1, pp. 210ff. and C. Rowland, *The Open Heaven: A Study of Apocalyptic in Judaism and Early Christianity* (London: SPCK, 1982), pp. 9ff. and C. Rowland, *Christian Origins: An Account of the Setting and Character of the Most Important Messianic Sect of Judaism* (London: SPCK, 1985), pp. 56ff.

15 See further, C. Rowland, 'Apocalyptic Literature' in D. A. Carson and H. G. M. Williamson (eds), *It is Written: Scripture Citing Scripture* (Cambridge: Cambridge University Press, 1988), pp. 170ff.

16 See, for example, the suggestive comments in P. D. Hanson, *The Dawn of Apocalyptic* (Philadelphia: Fortress Press, 1975).

17 F. Jameson, *The Political Unconscious: Narrative as a Socially Symbolic Act* (London: Methuen, 1981), pp. 98, 299.

18 ibid., pp. 76ff.

19 K. Kautsky, *The Foundations of Christianity* (London: Allen and Unwin, 1925), and G. de Ste. Croix, *The Class Struggle in the Ancient Greek World* (London: Duckworth, 1981), attempt to use a Marxist approach to write the history of early Christianity with due regard to the socio-economic struggles of the time.

20 See D. McLellan, *Marxism and Religion: A Description and Assessment of the Marxist Critique of Christianity* (Basingstoke: Macmillan, 1987).

21 Jameson, *Political Unconscious*, p. 79.

22 ibid., p. 86.

23 On contemporary Latin American history, see E. Dussel, *A History of the Church in Latin America: Colonialism to Liberalism (1492–1979)* (Grand Rapids, MI: Wm B. Eerdmans, 1981).

24 See S. Hall, 'Religious Ideologies and Social Movements in Jamaica' in R. Bocock and K. Thompson, *Religion and Ideology* (Manchester: Manchester University Press, 1985), pp. 273ff.

25 T. Adorno, *Negative Dialectics* (New York: Seabury, 1973), p. 406.

26 See also M. Jay, *Adorno* (London: Fontana, 1984), pp. 104–5.

27 W. Benjamin, *Illuminations*, H. Arendt (ed.) (New York: Schocken, 1978), p. 258.

28 ibid., p. 257.

29 ibid., p. 259.

30 See further, J. Roberts, *Walter Benjamin* (London: Macmillan, 1982), pp. 207–8.

31 What follows is an abbreviation of material used earlier in Rowland, *Radical Christianity*, pp. 66ff., and in C. Rowland, 'Keeping Alive the Dangerous Vision of a World of Peace and Justice' in W. Beuken, S. Freyne and A. Weiler (eds), 'Truth and its Victims', *Concilium* 200 (1988), pp. 75–86.

32 cf. M. Horkheimer, *Critical Theory* (New York, 1972), p. 129, quoted in McLellan, *Marxism and Religion*, p. 124: 'The concept of God was for a long time the place where the idea was kept alive that there are other norms besides those to which nature and society give expression in their operation. Dissatisfaction with earthly destiny is the strongest motive for acceptance of a transcendent being. If justice registers with God, then it is not to be found in the same measure in the world. Religion is the record of the wishes, desires and accusations of countless generations.'

33 Though we may note the points made in A. Y. Collins, 'The Political Perspective of the Revelation to John', *Journal of Biblical Literature* 96 (1977), pp. 241–56.

34 On the idea of witness in Revelation, see the survey in A. A. Trites, *The New Testament Concept of Witness* (Cambridge: Cambridge University Press, 1977).

35 See K. Wengst, *Pax Romana and the Peace of Jesus Christ* (London: SCM Press, 1987).

36 As is suggested by A. Y. Collins in her discussion of Revelation 13.15–17 in 'Political Perspective', pp. 241–56.

5

Liberation Theology in a First World Context

1 ONE WORLD OR THREE?

The report of the Archbishop of Canterbury's Commission on Urban Priority Areas in Britain, *Faith in the City*, made the following familiar comment in the chapter entitled 'Theological Priorities':

> It is often said, and doubtless rightly, that conditions in Western Europe are not such that this kind of political 'liberation' could ever be a comparable theological priority. Liberation Theology is a development that has grown out of political and economic conditions radically different from our own.[1]

The implication of this argument is that liberation theology is inappropriate to Britain, where the 'political and economic conditions' are said to be radically different from those in the Third World.

Another view, expressed by the Bishop of Durham, David Jenkins, is that different conditions in different countries require a variety of liberation theologies. Jenkins sees that 'British essays in liberation theology would not be mere echoes or reflections of liberation theology elsewhere', but also recognizes that there is nothing inappropriate or unnecessary in the idea of a British liberation theology.[2] Indeed the problems of devising one was the subject of his 1985 Hibbert lecture.

Our view is that liberation theology is not simply appropriate to the Third World societies within which it first came to notice in the early 1970s. At the same time, it is clearly important to think through what the theology of liberation would mean, for instance, in a British or North American as opposed to a 'Third World' context

Many of those who have begun to think about the question of a First World theology of liberation have done so by pointing out that First World countries have their own groups of poor, under-privileged and oppressed people. Georges Casalis comments: 'Obviously we are going to have to be active at home ourselves on the battlefronts drawn up against the existence of the Fourth World – that of the marginalised, the hospital and prison worlds, the migrant workers, and ethnic minorities.'[3]

Clearly there is validity in the argument that deprived groups exist in rich nations also, and it may be helpful to introduce the term 'Fourth World' to describe them. But there is a tendency for these considerations of what the theology of liberation means for the rich nations of the world to miss the main point, which derives from their common existence with the poor nations on a single planet ruled by global forces of capital. If we in the wealthier nations of the world start looking for deprived groups in our societies, which in some ways echo the situation of deprived groups in Third World countries, then we are in danger of thinking in national rather than international terms.

The approach to a First World theology of liberation does not need to look for patterns of oppression in rich countries which somehow mirror or echo patterns of oppression in the Third World. The point is that the First World is already intimately involved in the patterns of oppression in the Third World. We do not need to search around for groups in Britain, for instance, who are treated in the way that the South African government treats its black majority. So far as that majority is concerned, the oppressor is not only the South African government but also the governments of Britain, the United States and other wealthy nations who do not manipulate the global economic system in such a way as to make the white minority in South Africa change its policy. No one doubts that there are considerable differences between the political and economic conditions of Britain or the United States and those, for instance, of Brazil. But that is not the point. For Britain and the United States are intimately involved not only in the economic life of their own countries but also in that of Brazil and the rest of the Third World.

A liberation theology is appropriate to Britain, then, not only because there is a British poor as well as a Brazilian poor, but also because of Britain's involvement in the oppression of the Brazilian poor. Liberation for the Third World is not only from its own local patterns of dictatorship but also from the First World which is often responsible for sustaining those dictators in power. The First World cannot escape the theology of liberation, not only because of the injustice which exists within its own borders, but also because of its responsibility for the injustice which exists globally. Whatever the value of labelling different areas of the planet or different groups in it as the 'First', 'Second', 'Third' or even 'Fourth' World, such recognition of various political and economic conditions should not obscure the fact that no country can be insulated from the global patterns of trade that create wealth and poverty throughout the world.

2 CHARITY AND CAPITALISM: PERSPECTIVES ON WORLD POVERTY

A number of recent writers on the theology of liberation have stressed this perspective of interconnectedness between the 'Third' and 'First' Worlds. In *Heralds of a New Reformation*, Richard Shaull has explored the relationship between the poor in South and North America.[4] A useful issue of the international journal *Concilium*, entitled 'Option for the Poor: Challenge to the Rich Countries', contains a number of important articles.[5] Writing on the theme of 'Liberation Theology in the "First World"?', Norbert Greinacher challenges the immorality of a world economic order that allows a constant transfer of wealth from the poor to the rich. He quotes President Julius Nyerere's view that such a transfer is as immoral on an international scale as it is within nations.[6] Tissa Balasuriya has examined the impact of a 'world system' upon the economic life of different countries.[7]

One writer who has a particularly sharp insight into Britain's attitude to world poverty is Charles Elliott. His book *Comfortable Compassion?*[8] represents a devastating critique of the Christian response in Britain to world poverty, a response in which sentiment on the whole fails to give way to effective analysis.

Aided by an international network of communications, the

industrialized nations of the world contain a large number of people who are obviously moved by pictures of poverty and starvation in the Third World. Sometimes it is 'natural disasters' that catch the headlines (although very few are entirely natural; for instance, it is clear that deforestation in the Himalayas contributed to the devastating floods of 1988 in Bangladesh). But there is also some recognition of the chronic poverty, man-made and prolonged, which blights large areas of the world year in and year out. What Elliott calls this 'natural pity' in the industrialized world forms a 'continuing backdrop against which the Western Churches became historically – and become existentially – involved in the process of development'.[9] But how do they make use of this 'natural pity', and how far do they convert it into an active and effective commitment on behalf of those for whom the 'natural pity' is felt?

This is the context in which a British liberation theology can make an important contribution. It can help to supply the systematic analysis and encouragement without which 'natural pity' fails to be converted into any real amelioration of the situation of the poor. What is more, such pity all too easily turns into a 'comfortable compassion', a sympathy for the poor which salves the conscience of the rich without proving of any lasting benefit to the oppressed.

The theology of liberation offers 'systematic analysis' not in the sense of being in some abstract way more organized, but in the sense that it insists upon seeing the situation of the poor in terms of a global system which affects everyone. Thus in the process of converting natural pity into effective commitment, the theology of liberation asks First World Christians some uncomfortable questions about the world economic system that cannot be ignored in any real attempt to end poverty.

In doing so, it is bound to consider the emphasis which the Churches and, in the late 1980s, organizations like 'Band Aid' have placed upon the need to give more to the Third World. Analysis of economic relations between the First and Third World makes it clear that the problem is not so much what the First World fails to give in aid, but what it insists on taking in terms of debt repayments. Greinacher points out that in 1984 Third World countries paid DM 17,000,000,000 in interest repayments (about £5,000,000,000). This was far more than they received in development aid. While the First World highlights its giving, it keeps silent about its taking. The problem for the Churches is whether to settle for a campaign to increase giving by the First World, to highlight the virtue of generosity and raise money to be sent abroad alongside all the other charitable efforts currently in evidence, or to turn the spotlight upon the far larger amounts of money that the First World continues to take from the Third World.

Elliott asks how the Churches will respond to the evidence before them. He considers the example of Kenya, which because of its supposed political stability was a major recipient of aid from church development agencies in the 1960s and 1970s. Studies of Kenya by writers like André Frank and Colin Leys have claimed to show that the role of international capital in Kenya makes development impossible. Elliott cites the particular methods by which underdevelopment is made an inevitable result of the process by which capital is transferred from poor countries to rich ones: ' . . .monopoly profits of transnational corporations, inflated selling prices for capital goods from the rich countries, cheap land grants to foreign investors, agreement between foreign agricultural concerns and local labour élites to keep wages low.'[10]

Frank's conclusion is that underdeveloped countries only have a real chance of developing if they 'opt out of the international economic system altogether' as China and Japan did earlier this century.

Not all economists would agree with Frank, but he does represent a substantial body of opinion on the problems of 'developing' countries. It is a body of opinion already thoroughly explored by the theology of liberation in the Third World. It is well known that the concept of 'liberation' emerged in the 1970s partly as a reaction to the idea of 'development' popularized in the 1960s, when it was felt that as the rich nations became richer the poorer nations would be drawn along in their wake towards greater wealth. The rejection of that idea in the face of the greater disparities in wealth between rich and poor nations, and the widening of a gap that according to 'development' theories ought to be closing or at least remaining stable, led to the formation of new and more radical ideas about the workings of the global economy. 'Development' models gave way to 'dependency' models. The new argument was that international capital required a rich centre and a poor periphery. Those at the centre of economic power – the institutions of international capital, the multinational banks, the multinational corporations – would all draw wealth away from the periphery, including the wealth created by church development agencies. Against the 'development' view that all, both rich and poor nations, would increase their wealth together, the 'dependency' model suggested that the process by which the rich became richer was inseparable from that by which the poor became poorer.[11]

Against the idea of 'development', that of 'liberation' entailed a fundamental break with the prevailing patterns of international trade, which could not, it was argued, improve the situation for the world's poorer nations. Countries that had won political independence from the West in the eighteenth and nineteenth centuries, although often only by replacing external élites with internal ones, now sought an economic independence too. Having expelled foreign rulers, administrators, and armies, they now sought to expel foreign banks, businesses and corporations. However impractical it might have been to opt out of the economic system, when the beneficiaries of that system could place enormous pressure on its victims to accept it, this was the context within which liberation theology emerged in Central and Latin America in the 1970s. It is the *Sitz im Leben* of a decade which saw considerable political upheaval, and whose story is focused upon the experience of countries like Chile, Cuba and Nicaragua.

Charles Elliott, however, makes it clear that the problems raised by the discussion over 'development' and 'dependence' are as pertinent to the experience of First World Christians as to that of Third World Christians. They cannot escape the debate simply by living in relative affluence. For if it is true that the international economic system must fail to solve the problems of world poverty, then that undermines First World giving as much as it undermines the efforts of Third World Christians to abolish poverty in their own countries. It puts a question mark against the efforts to inspire individual and national generosity towards the Third World by giving even relatively large sums of money in charitable aid, and it undermines the work of church development agencies in the Third World. If it is impossible to give capitalism a 'human face', then this is a problem as much for

Britain and the United States as for a struggling Third World country, even if the implications for the former are different.

The theology of liberation has insisted that the Christian gospel contains at once an individual and a social dimension, and that the two are inseparable. 'Liberation' conveys the fact that salvation is at once of persons and their communities. It is impossible for the Kingdom of God to come on earth within the hearts of individuals, without its being expressed in the social relations that govern their lives as individuals. Jesus pronounces judgement not simply upon individuals who fail to meet the will of God (e.g. the rich young man), but also upon nations and cities that fail to do so (e.g. Matt. 11.20ff.). Liberation theology makes clear that the Christian language of 'sin' and 'salvation' applies not only to individuals but also to communities and to the social relations that connect them, which may become 'sinful structures'.

Although associated with a liberationist approach, the idea of 'sinful structures' also informs 'orthodox' church documents. It can be seen in the encyclical *Populorum Progressio* (1967) whose twentieth anniversary was commemorated in a new encyclical, *Solicitudo Rei Socialis*, in which John Paul II himself talks of 'structures of sin'.[12]

The witness of Jesus cannot be isolated from the earlier witness of the prophets addressed to the whole community, to its failure to support the weak and deprived (the 'widows and orphans' of so much Old Testament commentary) or to turn from the worship of wealth and greed.

In its approach to the interpretation of Scripture, the theology of liberation is alive to the emphasis which the New Testament places upon external powers that constrain and frustrate the efforts of individuals to respond to the gospel. Of course, no scholar has been able to overlook the references to powerful external forces in the New Testament – the demons with whom Jesus is in conflict in the Gospels, the 'principalities and powers' referred to by Paul, the tapestry of cosmic forces woven around the image of the redeeming blood of the Lamb in the Apocalypse. But there has been considerable disagreement over the way in which these external forces are to be understood. In an earlier chapter we contrasted Bultmann's understanding of a 'pre-scientific' mentality, which simply thought of them in terms of supernatural beings, with Dorothee Sölle's political interpretation. Sölle identifies them more as powerful social rather than supernatural forces, and sees in the challenge to them a message of rebellion against the unjust exercise of power. Liberation theology interprets these texts today in a *Sitz im Leben* which is acutely conscious of the way in which individuals who attempt to live out the gospel find powerful external forces ranged against them, often in a way that threatens them with persecution and death.

While the experience of such forces is not the same in the First World, Christians in the affluent West may find that their determination to live the gospel is also constrained. If their own efforts to help the poor are as enfeebled by the international economic system as the efforts of the poor to help themselves, then they too have to challenge the 'principalities and powers' of their day. In the First World, understanding Christian commitment exclusively in terms of individual giving makes sense only so long as the exercise of charitable power within the present international economic system is effective. But what if it is not? What if it can do nothing to alleviate the plight of the poor? Then the challenge of the gospel to Christians in rich nations forces them too to take account of the powerful structures that determine the lives of individuals.

The issue of poverty is not a national one, but an international one.[13] Whatever the variations in economic and social conditions between different countries, the international character of the problem cannot be neglected. The same system that makes the poor of the Third World powerless to be helped makes many of the rich in the First World powerless to help. The same determination to perceive the structural forces which frustrate Third World countries as they seek to receive help needs to be matched in First World countries by those who seriously want to give help. Indeed the perception of social and political forces ranged against the practice of the Christian gospel is arguably most necessary now in the First World, for it is the countries in this part of the globe which ultimately have the most power to affect the international economic order. It is for them to determine whether the apparently ceaseless toll of victims from starvation can be brought to an end by aid programmes operated from within the old system, or whether the only practical means of change is through a radical challenge to the international economic system.

The observation that sometimes effective action can come only through a radical break with the past, rather than by attempting to graft something new on to the old order, allows us to apply an existing tradition to the new situation of global poverty:

> No one sews a patch of unshrunk cloth on to an old coat; for then the patch tears away from the coat, and leaves a bigger hole. Neither do you put new wine into old wine skins; if you do, the skins burst, and then the wine runs out and the skins are spoilt. No, you put new wine into fresh skins; then both are preserved. (Matt. 9.16–17, NEB)

3 CHARITY AND CAPITALISM: A NATIONAL PERSPECTIVE

In the previous section we questioned the effectiveness of international aid which attempts to use the existing economic system as a channel for relief to the poor. In this section we attempt to outline ways in which a similarly ineffective form of aid is directed at the poor in Britain, and we add some comments about the similar but not identical experience of the United States.

One of the consequences of living on an offshore island, all too ready to believe that our own British experience of life in the late twentieth century must be far removed from anyone else's, is that we tend to isolate the political and social changes of the 1980s in Britain from those which are taking place or have already taken place elsewhere. In a sophisticated analysis, Nicholas Boyle makes the following point in his article 'Understanding Thatcherism':

> Thatcherism is simply the local British form taken by the global process of the flexibilisation of human material; the Thatcher government is simply the local political solvent applied to British society not just by multi-national companies but by the entire multi-national currency and capital markets whose degree of integration was briefly and embarrassingly glimpsed on Black Monday in 1987.[14]

Mrs Thatcher represents, Boyle argues, the 'Europeanisation' of Britain, the clearing away of those intermediate institutions between central government and individual citizens that frustrate the process whereby British society is integrated into the global market. The 'nationalism' of the British government in the 1980s represents, in Boyle's view, a mere front. Far more important than outbursts against a single European state, or statements of commitment to British nationhood and sovereignty, are the ways in which this administration has firmly integrated Britain into the world economic order.

The institutions that have been weakened during the 1980s – trade unions, local authorities, even universities and the professions, are those which might hold back that integration. A trade union which frustrates a multinational company like Ford, and forces it to go elsewhere by refusing single-union agreements, is not acclaimed for its stand on workers' rights in Britain. It is attacked for a lack of realism in turning down the conditions set by a foreign company for British workers to adhere to. International capitalism, like international communism, knows no national boundaries and baulks at national loyalties.

But what is the effect of this process of integration? It is not only to remove as many barriers as possible to the unbridled operation of international capitalism in this country, but also to identify that operation with the 'natural order', with 'realism', and thereby avoid any penetrating moral questions that might be addressed to it.

In 1989 it is no longer possible for those local authorities which have not simply been abolished by central government to refuse a contract to a company that invests in South Africa or has a notable shortage of women in top management. Indeed local government, which has in some cases been one of the most effective brakes upon capitalism, represents the social organization most severely mauled by central government in Britain over the last ten years.

But certain institutions cannot be abolished or have their powers determined by government legislation. Among them are the Churches. The Churches cannot be forced to support capitalism; they must be persuaded by argument. A Prime Minister who wishes to bring them into line must go to them in all humility and speak to them of her faith, as the Prime Minister, Mrs Thatcher, did to the General Assembly of the Church of Scotland on 21 May 1988.

The speech to the General Assembly was highly significant. It sought to commend a form of Christianity that was compatible with the removal of all barriers to capitalism in this country, ensuring the submergence of Britain in what any liberation theologian – from any country – would view as an international system of injustice. That form of Christianity was one in which an approach to national poverty mirrored the approach to international poverty, namely one of individual giving to relieve the suffering generated by a collective system. Charity, after all, begins at home.

The speech rejected any notion that spiritual revolution could be separated from social reform. But the question was: How do you achieve social reform? Its answer to that was clear. Most Christians would consider it 'their personal Christian duty' to help their fellow men and women. As an example of 'personal duty' the speech cited helping children, and then it continued: 'These duties come not from any secular legislation passed by Parliament, but from being a Christian.'

The key argument here was the wedge between secular legislation and Christian belief. Apparently Christians were to understand the obligations of their faith in terms of helping others at a personal level, but never in terms of seeking social change that might require 'secular' legislation in order to make it effective. This principle appeared to be confirmed in the part of the speech that was most remarked upon by commentators at the time: 'It is not the creation of wealth that is wrong, but the love of money for its own sake . . . the spiritual dimension comes in deciding what one does with the wealth.'[15]

The unanswered question behind this comment is: Whose wealth? The presumption is that it is the individual's wealth that is being referred to. But why not the wealth of nations, or the wealth of the world? From the perspective of those who reject capitalism, it is a truism that the creation of wealth is not wrong, and equally a truism that the spiritual dimension comes in deciding what one does with the wealth. But the creation and distribution of the wealth are thought of not in terms of individuals but of nations, and even in terms of the whole planet. For that reason, it would be perfectly reasonable to see the 'spiritual dimension', which the Prime Minister herself sees expressed in deciding what one does with the wealth, encapsulated in what she calls 'secular legislation'. How else can one decide what to do with the wealth of a rich nation like Britain?

The Prime Minister, however, could conceive of the 'spiritual dimension' only in terms of individual wealth. The idea of a spiritual dimension to what one did with the national wealth, the billions of pounds in the national exchequer, seemed to be beyond comprehension. Yet in an astute response to her speech the Chairman and Secretary of the Church of England's Board for Social Responsibility perceived that this was an idea that couldn't be ignored:

> On the question of how wealth is used, we cannot restrict the matters of justice or generosity to personal, individual action. Is it not unrealistic to think that the needs of the poor can be met in our sort of world by individual charity alone? Indeed, to leave the poor dependent on the charity of others threatens their dignity.[16]

From what we have tried to argue in the previous section, it certainly is unrealistic to think in terms of the needs of the international poor being met by individual charity alone. Increasingly, however, we see the ideology of individual charity, already established in the popular mind as a way of helping the poor abroad, being employed as an approach to poverty in Britain. As the economy of Britain is increasingly subordinated to the global market, so the situation of the rich and poor in Britain increasingly mirrors that of rich and poor internationally. In 1988 the dichotomy became more clearly recognized than ever in this country, through a budget marked by tax cuts for the rich and benefit cuts for the poor. As in the world generally, so in Britain in particular, an economic system is in place that produces considerable inequalities of wealth and makes life difficult, if not unbearable, for large numbers of people.

But just as the poor of the Third World cannot be effectively helped by acts of individual charity, or even by grand enterprises in giving like Band Aid, so long as they remain victims of a system which ensures that more will always be taken from them by the rich than handed to them, so the poor of Britain cannot be effectively helped either. Individual charity cannot plug all the gaps in social provision initiated by the present government. You cannot run a health service on donations from the rich. In the end, a concern for 'realism' and 'rationalism', those buzz words of the present order, has to argue for the morality of public provision as the only rational way of organizing the nation's health or education. The 'spiritual dimension' to what one does with one's wealth has to apply to the wealth of countries and not simply to the wealth of its individual citizens.

The example of the United States provides interesting parallels with, and important differences from, that of Britain.[17] On the one hand, there is much in the history of the United States to support the idea of government intervention to promote investment in the national economy. Without it, the demand of the American Constitution that the government 'provides for the general welfare' can hardly be met. The experience of the Great Depression between 1929 and 1933, when production halved and unemployment rose to 25% (at a time when there was no universal system of benefit payments and the jobless were forced to rely largely upon private charity), made it clear that a government which acted merely as a spectator rather than as a participant in the national economy was neglecting its duty. The direct relief programmes, work projects and construction to build up the nation's infrastructure under President Roosevelt's 'New Deal' anticipated in practice much of what Keynes was to describe in theory in *The General Theory of Employment, Interest and Money* in 1936.[18] The ideal of a 'New Deal' has remained an appealing slogan in American politics, and it would be wrong to think of the United States in terms of a simplistic model of commitment to government non-intervention in the economy. Indeed it was the Republican President Richard Nixon who made the renowned comment two decades ago: 'We are all Keynesians now.'

At the same time, the situation in America has changed in the last ten years under Ronald Reagan. The idea of the government using its spending power to stimulate the economy has been replaced by the idea that the government interferes too much, and that it should be taken 'off the backs' of the American people and the business community, particularly through a lowering of tax rates. The 'supply-side economics' of the 1980s has argued that investment is stimulated not by the government doing more but by its doing less. Tax cuts may reduce government spending and public programmes, the argument goes, but it also releases the business community to demonstrate new initiatives and invest more through the reduced burden of taxation.

What evidence there is suggests that this strategy has failed to produce the investment and economic expansion that were heralded as its benefits. Moreover, a distinctive characteristic of the 1980s in the United States, matched to a much lesser degree in Britain, has been an increasing commitment to military expenditure, which in 1987 reached a massive 36% of the federal budget. Spending on arms is inflationary (because it means pumping money into the economy through wages but puts no new products into it) and it diverts capital from the domestic economy. As a result of the combination of greater military expenditure and lower tax revenues the United States government in the 1980s has had to cut domestic welfare programmes (as well as run up a huge budget deficit) in a way that exceeds even the cuts made by Thatcher in Britain. The government has been both financially unable, and ideologically unwilling, to stimulate the economy in a Keynesian manner.

The result has been greater inequality between rich and poor. In 1950 the poorest 20% of the population in the United States had 4.5% of the wealth; by 1970, partly because of programmes in the 1960s like the 'War against Poverty', that figure had risen to 5.4%. By the mid-1980s it had fallen to the 1950 level. On the other hand, whereas in 1963 the richest 0.5% of the American population owned 25% of the national assets, by 1983 that figure had risen to 35%. The effect of partial government withdrawal from regulating the economy (for it is a myth that the government ever withdraws entirely) was simply to make the poor poorer and the rich richer. Comparable figures show that the same is true in Britain under Thatcher.

In Western Europe and Japan the devastation wrought by the Second World War made the state's role in the regeneration of the nation's economy obvious. It may be that in the United States and in Britain (which suffered neither occupation nor defeat) this lesson was not so clearly learnt as elsewhere. Even though every economy, including capitalist economies, is to some extent planned (in the United States tobacco and grain, for instance, have federal price subsidies, and peanuts have acreage allotments – what is that if not national economic planning?), Britain under Thatcher and the United States under Reagan appear to have succeeded in suggesting that a government's role in the domestic economy is a passive rather than an active one, spectator or possibly umpire but never participant and initiator.

However, such an approach is out of step with important traditions in both countries, whether it be the anticipated Keynesianism of the 'New Deal' in America or the principles of the Welfare State in Britain. Against these traditions, recent leaders in both countries have sought to introduce the idea that governments should reduce the level of their social provision, leaving the needs of the poor to be met increasingly from private charitable sources. Such a 'withdrawal' of the government, which is never a complete one, has removed an important brake upon social and economic inequality, and has generated increased poverty in both countries. The lessons for both will probably be learnt painfully in the 1990s.

There is an interesting difference between the United States and Britain which, if anything, highlights the need for a Christian morality to incorporate economic and social structures within its area of concern even more sharply. That difference is the pressure that has been notable in America since the mid-1970s for a return to protectionism in one form or another. The United States has been to some extent shaken by the very progress of the West European and Japanese economies which, immediately after the Second World War, it helped to encourage through initiatives such as the Marshall Plan. It has seen its economic dominance of world trade diminish, and faces the prospect of increasing inroads into its domestic markets by foreign competitors. As a result it has been prepared to consider and, in some cases, to implement protectionist measures which the more *laissez-faire* approach of the British government has been unwilling to contemplate.

It is when the protectionist policies of a capitalist government are examined that the hypocrisies of the international economic system become apparent. For now the problem of the global economy appears less that of its being unregulated than that of its being regulated by the rich in their own interests. It is not even as though the rich nations had the justification of believing that the economic system cannot and should not be regulated. They do regulate it, but in their own interests rather than in the interests of the poor. The less developed nations are largely exporters of primary products such as coffee beans and sugar, and importers of manufactured goods. Should they seek to set up manufacturing industry at home, they face protectionist measures from the First World.

Tariffs for foreign imports in the United States are lowest for raw materials and highest for finished products. Brazil, for instance, exports coffee beans to America, but all sorts of pressures are applied to prevent it moving in on the processed coffee market. It would be in the interests of the less developed nations to free their plantations to supply the home market, where people are often desperately short of food, and to produce manufactured goods for export. But the rich nations, fearing the implications for their own industries, do everything they can to prevent it. The International Monetary Fund, which is effectively in the hands of the wealthy nations since the voting power of member nations is determined by the amount of money each participant puts into the fund, becomes the instrument of economic regulation in the interests of the rich, encouraging poor nations to reduce their debts by wage controls and lower government spending (a procedure that hits the poorest in those poor nations most). The very commitment to government-led investment and social programmes which has been an important tradition in the American economy is firmly denied to the poorer nations as they attempt to escape a crippling burden of debt.

If it has been difficult for a 'Keynesian' approach to be maintained in national economies like those of Britain or America, it has been virtually impossible to apply the idea to the global economy. Principles of stimulating investment and supporting increased welfare provision in the less developed nations run precisely counter to those which are insisted upon as a condition of essential financial assistance when the IMF deals with the poorer nations. The example of America, far more strongly than that of Britain, shows that capitalism is not an economic system which fails to understand a role for government in controlling the economy, but that it understands that role in a certain way, one which produces increasing inequality and poverty both nationally and internationally.

From this perspective a different approach would appear less as one of government involvement where previously there was none, but of a different form of government involvement, both in the national and the international economy – one that sought to promote international justice rather than to serve the interests only of those who were wealthy, whether the wealthy élite within nations or the wealthy élite of nations.

In the previous section we argued that a real concern for the poor of the world had to face the challenge of an international economic system that frustrated attempts to help them. The contrast between a biblical notion of hostile 'principalities and powers' and the individually based charitable intentions of Christian giving could hardly be clearer than in the daily evidence of our incapacity to solve the problem of world poverty. A world so technologically developed remains unable to prevent billions of its citizens from dying an agonizing and unnecessary death. We can only face up to this scandal as Christians if we accept that we are challenged by more than our own failure to be generous. We are challenged by an economic system that makes so many of our efforts to relieve world poverty useless.

In this section we have raised the possibility that the situation may move in a similar direction in First World countries. The poor of Britain and America will become a problem minority which government will claim to be beyond its powers of assistance. Appeals will be made to individuals, particularly those individuals made richer in the last few years, to reach into their pockets on behalf of the poor. But the systems of social provision which previously operated to provide a public service for all citizens – the health service, education, housing, benefits – will wither away. No moral value will be attached to them. The institutions supporting them, such as local government, will have been weakened and their powers reduced. The national poor, like the international poor, will be a helpless and powerless band of people dependent upon sympathetic television pictures for occasional hand-outs.

The Church of England's Board for Social Responsibility has questioned whether either the dignity or the needs of the poor can be met through individual charity alone. Those needs, both nationally and internationally, can be met only if there is a just and effective system of public provision. Such a system must be recognized as a proper object of Christian moral concern.

Unless Christians in the First World accept that the economic and political structures of their communities cannot be somehow left out of consideration as they attempt to put faith into practice, their efforts can hardly expect to be effective. Individual consciences of the rich may be salved, but the problems of the poor will not be solved. Without a systematic appraisal of the conditions that promote poverty both at home and abroad, the 'Christian giving' of individuals will always be less than the 'Christian taking' of those same individuals as beneficiaries of the economic system. For this reason social analysis, which some feel has been forced upon Third World Christians because of the uniquely harsh social conditions of their own countries, is if anything more necessary here in the West. But can such analysis make any headway in a country like Britain, encouraged by its leaders to extol the virtues of private charity, and suffering the erosion of those public services of which forty years ago it had learnt to be proud?

There is an area of Christian concern where such analysis has been adopted by some of the Churches. This is in meeting the challenge of apartheid. On this issue, a number of Christians have found it necessary to use language that recognizes the reality of 'sinful structures'. They have not been prepared to isolate Christian morality from a challenge to the social system which they see as responsible for most of the suffering endured by individuals. By examining the treatment of apartheid by Christians in South Africa, we may gain some insights into the nature of an approach to the gospel that is unable to view Christian morality in the way that the British or American governments hope the Churches will understand it.

4 APARTHEID AND 'PROPHETIC THEOLOGY': A STUDY OF *THE KAIROS DOCUMENT*

In 1985 a group of South African theologians produced *The Kairos Document*, sub-titled 'Challenge to the Church'. Describing itself as 'A Theological Comment on the Political Crisis in South Africa', the Document was not the work of a church-appointed commission, unlike earlier documents such as the Belhar Confession of Faith issued by the Dutch Reformed Mission Church. It was generated from the grassroots of the Church, rather than fed down from above. It emerged out of the townships in and around Johannesburg, from discussion groups in Soweto and elsewhere that initially had no intention of writing and publishing a formal document.

Even when, in the course of three months from June to September 1985, the publication came into being, it was emphasized that it was only a provisional document, a response to circumstances that would necessarily change and thereby generate new documents. It was born with a principled obsolescence, arguing that by its very nature 'no theological statement of this kind could ever be final'.[19]

Despite this insistence, the Document has been highly influential. On publication, it was immediately supported and signed by 150 South African theologians and church leaders, black and white, from several different denominations. It has generated discussion and response from both within and outside South Africa.[20] It has implications not only for Christians in South Africa but also for Christians in other countries who contend with their own forms of oppression.

The Document examines three theologies, which it names State Theology, Church Theology and Prophetic Theology. State Theology is defined simply as 'the theological justification of the status quo . . . It blesses injustice, canonises the will of the powerful and reduces the poor to passivity, obedience and apathy'.[21] It quotes Romans 13. 1–7 in order to claim that any established political order exists by divine will and should be obeyed. Indeed the idea that the apartheid state exists by God's command is very important to its rulers, and the name of God is invoked in the new apartheid constitution. 'State Theology' is regarded by *The Kairos Document* as both heretical and blasphemous.

The second form of theology considered by the Document is 'Church Theology'. Unlike the first form, this form does not claim that apartheid is God's will, but its criticism of it is said to be 'limited, guarded and cautious'. Indeed, *The Kairos Document* considers that the criticism offered by Church Theology is counter-productive: ' . . .instead of engaging in an in-depth analysis of the signs of our times, it relies upon a few stock ideas derived from Christian tradition and then uncritically and repeatedly applies them to our situation'.[22]

An example of one of these stock ideas is that of 'reconciliation'. Church Theology talks attractively of the need for all South Africans to come together, for white and black to meet and resolve their differences. It treats the problem as if it were analogous to two angry and recalcitrant neighbours who refused to sort out their differences over a garden fence. But is that the right analogy for the conflict between white and black in South

Africa? *The Kairos Document* argues that it is not, because of the structural dimension to the conflict – that is to say it is a conflict between rich and poor, armed and unarmed, oppressor and oppressed. In such circumstances, no reconciliation is possible without justice. The tradition of Jesus saying 'Do you suppose I came to establish peace on earth? No indeed, I have come to bring division' (Luke 12.51, NEB) can be readily applied to the situation in South Africa, where a desperate and justified longing for reconciliation can all too easily lead to a desire to avoid the condition of reconciliation, the abolition of an evil social system.

The Kairos Document feels that it can no more condemn the armed struggle against apartheid and call for peace at any price, than it can call for reconciliation at any price. Furthermore, it feels that if Church Theology seriously wished to see an end to all violence, it would condemn the conscription of white males into the army as much as it condemns the formation of armed black gangs in the townships. Too often violence against the state is attacked as terrorism, while violence by the state is defended as legitimate policing.

'Church Theology' does at times recognize that reconciliation and peace cannot simply be plucked from the skies, but have to grow in the soil of a just society. But it is noticeable that when 'Church Theology' does talk of justice, it thinks of it as something that can be introduced 'from above', through a change of heart on the part of those in power rather than through radical change from below. *The Kairos Document*, however, does not hope for much from the attempt to convert those in authority:

> The problem that we are dealing with here in South Africa is not merely a problem of personal guilt, it is a problem of structural injustice. People are suffering, people are being maimed and killed and tortured every day. We cannot just sit back and wait for the oppressor to see the light so that the oppressed can put out their hands and beg for the crumbs of some small reforms.[23]

'Church Theology', the Document concludes, lacks social analysis. It applies pre-formed theological categories like 'reconciliation' to any and every situation, with little attempt to analyse what is actually happening in society. After all, if you can throw a theological principle at any problem, you hardly need to make the effort to understand what the problem is.

The lack of social analysis and political awareness in 'Church Theology' is attributed by *The Kairos Document* to 'the type of faith and spirituality that has dominated Church life for centuries'.[24] Social and political affairs have often been regarded by the Church as worldly concerns, separate from the spiritual concerns of the Church, which have been conceived in a private, individualistic and other-worldly manner. As a consequence, the Church now finds it difficult to integrate its spiritual with its social concerns. It does not understand how to connect its theological principles, like reconciliation, not simply with a private dispute between individuals but with a social and political conflict into which all the individual citizens of South Africa are inevitably drawn. It is very difficult for 'Church Theology' to apply to the contemporary situation of an apartheid state biblical traditions (such as Rom. 8.18–24) that integrate a person's private with his or her public life.

The Kairos Document calls for a third form of theology, which it terms 'Prophetic Theology'. 'The first task' of such a theology, the Document states, must be 'an attempt at social analysis or what Jesus would call "reading the signs of the times" (Mt 16:3)'.[25] Such an analysis reveals the situation in South Africa to be less a racial war than a system of oppression, one from which a minority benefits in terms of wealth and a high standard of living, while the majority is paid very little and suffers from injustices like the migratory labour laws.

The Kairos Document believes that the situation facing South Africa today, with a social system that can either be maintained or overcome but cannot be reformed, is one in which Christians can renew the biblical tradition of resistance to oppression. The Bible is full of vivid and concrete descriptions of oppression. As the Document puts it: 'The Bible describes oppression as the experience of being crushed, degraded, humiliated, exploited, impoverished, defrauded, deceived and enslaved. And the oppressors are described as cruel, ruthless, arrogant, greedy, violent and tyrannical and as the enemy.'[26]

Israel itself was born out of the experience of oppression. The biblical traditions which speak of it are the fruit of such an experience. The description of it makes no suggestion of reconciliation between oppressor and oppressed. When God chooses Moses as the liberator of Israel, he does not reconcile the Hebrew slaves with their Egyptian rulers. 'Oppression is sin and it cannot be compromised with, it must be done away with.'[27] God sides with the oppressed rather than playing the role of umpire in their dispute with the oppressor.

In the New Testament too, Jesus sides with the oppressed from the moment when he stands in the synagogue in Nazareth and renews the tradition of Isaiah's prophecy in the situation of first-century Galilee:

> The spirit of the Lord has been given to me,
> for he has anointed me.
> He has sent me to bring the good news to the poor,
> to proclaim liberty to captives
> and to the blind new sight,
> to set the downtrodden free,
> to proclaim the Lord's year of favour. (Luke 4.18–19, JB)

The Kairos Document understands 'Prophetic Theology' as a message based on – to recall von Rad's understanding once again (see pp. 61ff.) – the renewal of biblical tradition in the light of new situations that demand a contemporary expression of Christian hope. The expectation expressed in the prayer for God's Kingdom to come, for the will of God to be done on earth as in heaven, is now focused on the struggle to overcome apartheid.

In the final section of the Document, entitled 'Challenge to Action', certain practical steps are commended to Christians who 'side with the oppressed'. These include: support for popular campaigns like consumer boycotts and stayaways; church programmes and campaigns which support the popular struggle – as opposed to campaigns that might present the Church as a 'third force' between oppressor and oppressed; and involvement in civil disobedience against the 'moral illegitimacy of the apartheid regime'.[28] In contrast to the 'State Theology', the 'Prophetic Theology' of *The Kairos Document* insists that 'A Church that takes its responsibilities seriously in the circumstances will sometimes have to confront and to disobey the State in order to obey God.'[29]

5 'PROPHETIC THEOLOGY' AND BRITISH CAPITALISM

Britain is not South Africa. Capitalism is not apartheid, whatever connections may be drawn between the two. But as we found earlier in this chapter, recognition of the particular needs and situations of different countries has to be balanced by perception of their common participation in an international order. One interesting feature of *The Kairos Document* is the way in which its arguments have been taken up and used in other political contexts since its publication. The question as to how far this 'manifesto' of resistance to South African oppression strikes chords elsewhere in the world cannot be ignored.

We find, for instance, the three theologies described in the Kairos Document taken up in Duncan Forrester's recent study *Theology and Politics*.[30] Indeed his concluding chapter on 'The Responsibilities of Political Theology' appears to owe more to *The Kairos Document* than to almost anything else. It is interesting that the discussion of 'political theology', which Forrester conceives to be broader in its meaning than that of the various liberation theologies which he has considered earlier in his book, should be so closely informed by the principles of a document produced out of the challenge of apartheid. It would suggest that there is something in *The Kairos Document* which 'addresses the moment' not only in South Africa but elsewhere too. This is the possibility that we shall investigate further in the present chapter.

Is there evidence, for instance, of what *The Kairos Document* calls 'Church Theology' in a British context? Is there a tendency to replace social analysis with general ideas from Christian tradition which are flung uncritically at any social and political situation confronting the British Church? Does the character of the Church in Britain, for instance the particular nature of Anglicanism as the 'Established' form of Christianity, in some ways lend itself to the approach of a 'Church Theology'? Not that 'Church Theology' need arise only in the context of an 'Established' Church. American readers might ask how far the arguments in this section apply to their own situation, where the looser concept of 'civil religion' introduces an establishment-oriented theology across several denominations.

It is certainly fair to say that the wealth of publications by

Anglican, Roman Catholic, Methodist, United Reformed, Baptist, Quaker – and other! – bodies over the last ten years cannot be fairly summarized in any single section. Britain contains a plurality of groupings within a plurality of denominations within a plurality of religions. To some extent it could be argued that one noticeable weakness in Britain is the failure of a large number of religious groups to unite around a common programme. *The Kairos Document*, for instance, was signed by at least a dozen different Christian denominations, and thereby achieved an ecumenical status which few documents have managed to do in this country.

One of the contributions of a British liberation theology could be to interest ecumenical bodies in social questions around which different denominations might achieve an 'orthopraxis', and divert their concerns a little from the search for an 'orthodoxy' reflected in common consent to doctrinal propositions.[31] The application of the liberation theologian's notion of 'truth as praxis' has its place here, and although it raises issues which go beyond our present discussion, it clearly addresses an important question to the British Churches, and to the bodies endeavouring to unite them: Does it make sense to concentrate efforts to achieve church unity on what might be called matters of right belief, and not put a greater emphasis on achieving a common practice? Is there not reason to believe from biblical tradition that it is a common practice that provides the true foundation of Christian unity? Could not the hope of one Church be realized around a common commitment to change society, as in South Africa, rather than around a common consent to propositions about the nature of Christian belief?

Important questions of truth and meaning are raised here, which should not be neglected. But it is difficult to avoid the view that the absence of a British *Kairos Document*, reflecting an interdenominational approach to and analysis of the social and political task of Christians in Britain today, itself contributes to the disunity that the ecumenical movement, with limited success, is striving to overcome.

No discussion of a British liberation theology can avoid the question of 'establishment'. The existence of an 'Established Church', even though it is one of many denominations, places a question mark against the possibility of an Anglican 'Prophetic

Theology' as the Kairos Document describes it. Can a Church linked by establishment to the status quo really renew the biblical tradition of prophetic challenge to an unjust society in the situation of contemporary capitalism?

Certainly the main Christian denomination in Britain is capable of criticizing government policies. One can see this in *Faith in the City*, the 1985 Report of the Archbishop of Canterbury's Commission on Urban Priority Areas, to which we have already referred in this chapter and which has been the subject of considerable interest, both within and outside the Churches since its publication.

Faith in the City, unlike *The Kairos Document*, reflects a perspective 'from the top down' rather than 'from the bottom up'. It is the product of concern for the poor, rather than expressing the concerns of the poor.[32] The Report recognizes this; indeed it is quite candid about the structural shortcomings of the Anglican Church:

> . . . it is clear that the Church of England has traditionally been mainly middle class in character: it never attained the kind of pervasive influence, transcending the boundaries of class, that was achieved by Catholicism in Ireland or nonconformity in Wales. Equally, as it moved into the twentieth century, it carried with it a clerical paternalistic legacy; of a male-dominated Church in which the clergy held the power.[33]

Moreover, even as a document self-consciously written by a Church conscious that it is more representative of the privileged than the under-privileged, *Faith in the City* does not shun practical proposals for what amount to changes in government policy. It demands a rise (in real terms) of the Rate Support Grant (an idea now somewhat overtaken by the Poll Tax) to local authorities, an increase in child benefit, financial help for the long-term unemployed, an expanded public housing programme, and argues against the unfairness of mortgage tax relief.[34]

Can there be any criticism of a Church, even an 'Established Church', so prepared to admit its class limitations, and at the same time so prepared to challenge government policies in clear and practical ways? Does it matter that *Faith in the City* was not born out of inner-city struggles in the way that *The Kairos Document* was born out of the Soweto uprising?

Unfortunately, there are severe weaknesses in the Report, and it is in considering these that our consideration of the context in which the Report was produced becomes relevant. For one thing, its criticism of the nation and its leaders is much more evident than its self-criticism of the Church. The section on 'The Challenge to the Church' addresses few fundamental questions. No talk, understandably enough, of disestablishment. Only a passing reference to the role of the Church as a major landlord and landowner in British society, including the inner cities. These issues require sustained social analysis, but the Report appears far happier when discussing questions such as the need to consult community groups before selling redundant churches, or ways of making vicarages 'accessible' to local people. The problem of the way in which the Church of England has historically been woven, or has woven itself, deeply into the web of British capitalism remains untouched.

Of course the benefits or otherwise of establishment are a controversial issue for Anglicans. Some, for instance Peter Hinchliff in *The Study of Anglicanism*, feel that it does not automatically mean support of the political status quo by the Church, and even that it will give a proper sense that religion belongs in the public domain.[35] Others, like John Habgood, feel that although there may be a situation in the future when disestablishment becomes necessary – and it may be at the instigation of the state rather than of the Church – no such situation exists at present.[36]

Neither position can remain unchallenged from the perspective of the 'Prophetic Theology' outlined in *The Kairos Document*. Habgood suggests that the experience of closeness to those in power, and some 'first-hand knowledge of the complexity of the actual choices facing them', has what he calls 'a devastating effect on prophetic certainties'.[37] In other words, if we knew how difficult and tough things were at the top, we wouldn't criticize. It is hard to think of a more patronizing argument. Such a view reflects the outlook of a Church that has more practical contact with those in power than with the suffering of those without it.

If we accept that the status quo is in need of more than a channel by which to explain the difficulties it faces in governing, then we come to Hinchliff's argument that establishment permits, and even facilitates, criticism of the government. But the problem is not simply one of bringing religion into the public domain, as

Hinchliff highlights it, but of what position religion takes when firmly put into that domain. Our argument on the basis of *Faith in the City* is that the Church of England finds it very difficult to challenge the iniquities of an economic and political system for which it is in many respects itself the beneficiary. A 'Prophetic Theology' is not easily engendered when it entails biting the hand that feeds you.

Being the 'Established Church' arguably creates in British Anglicanism characteristics of what *The Kairos Document* calls a 'Church Theology'. This is shown most clearly if we recall a central point in *The Kairos Document*'s critique of 'Church Theology', that which concerned the crucial concept of reconciliation.

At one level the established character of the Church of England may not appear very significant. A few seats in the House of Lords do not provide much political clout; perhaps a modified Prime Ministerial role in appointments to bishoprics does not provide a great deal of political accountability, although it certainly represents a measure of interference by the state in the life of the Church. At another level, however, its involvement with the state undoubtedly does bring a particular character to the Anglican Church. It becomes an 'institution' of society, which conceived of itself as having a special responsibility to speak for the nation as a whole. It is expected to reflect a cultural and religious solidarity of the English (as opposed to British) people, whose spirit it incarnates. As the 'Established Church' it is able to unite and reflect the spirit of a people, a rationalization of a single religion for a single nation which can be traced back through the Tractarians to the Elizabethan Settlement of the sixteenth century.

Habgood recognizes this consequence of establishment in a most disarming way: 'One almost inevitable consequence of disestablishment would be the alienation of large numbers of people whose residual allegiance to the Church of England is bound up with the perception that in some obscure way it represents "England".'[38] He makes it clear that he regards the prospect of their loss to the Church as a tragic one. Less clear to him is the possibility that this rationale for Anglicanism as a 'folk religion' might dull the edge of any prophetic challenge to the very nation whose 'English' nature it represents.

As W.S.F. Pickering points out in *The Study of Anglicanism*,[39] the 'genius' of Anglicanism, its 'blending of Christian traditions – its comprehensiveness', is offset by a less welcome downside, which he calls the 'flabbiness' that leads to an exodus of dissatisfied groups who feel that it lacks coherent theological identity. Such a criticism is undoubtedly irritating to those who have argued that Anglicanism does have such an identity.[40] However, few of those who attempt to discuss the identity of Anglicanism manage to move beyond questions of doctrine to a candid examination of social and political influences upon its cohesion as a religion. It is as if the search for theological identity reflects a desire to obscure the true ground of unity between groups with very little in common doctrinally.

In an interesting comment Habgood remarks:

> He [Clifford Longley] has argued that divisions between Catholics and Protestants, conservatives and radicals, within the Church of England are so deep that it is in effect held together only by the fact of being established. A common concern about fulfilling a national role serves to paper over the cracks.[41]

The Archbishop comments that 'This is an exaggeration, as anyone who knows the Church of England from within must surely realize.' But is it so clear that this is the case? Is it so clear that the toleration of a wide spectrum of theological opinion within the Church of England is any more than a reflection of the fact that the ground of its unity lies in its social and political role rather than in a supposed doctrinal coherence?

It is arguable that its established status makes the Church of England particularly susceptible to the attitude towards reconciliation outlined in *The Kairos Document*'s description of 'Church Theology'. It is worth recalling again what the description given by *The Kairos Document* is. It speaks of 'a few stock ideas derived from Christian tradition and then uncritically and repeatedly applied . . . to our situation'.[42] In other words, reconciliation becomes an ideology. It becomes a principle not derived from, but thrown at, the present situation of the Church. Can the Church of England renew the traditions of biblical Christianity in the context of contemporary English society, when for many of its adherents its purpose is to 'speak for' England rather than to address the message of the gospel *to* it. Can it renew the challenge of the prophets in such a context?

Reconciliation is an obvious aim of any Christian. But at the same time it is clear that the means to reconciliation will encounter hostility from those who do not wish to give up privilege. The Bible introduces us to the way in which obedience to God invites persecution from humanity. Whether it is Moses before Pharaoh or Jesus before some of the Pharisees, it is clear that the Judeo-Christian tradition continually illustrates the words of its most well-known prophet: 'I come not to bring peace but a sword' (Matt.10.34).

This is not to say that the Christian does not seek to reconcile, but that the way to reconciliation is a hard one, inevitably leading to opposition. Reconciliation becomes an ideology, however, when that difficult means to its achievement is denied, and the hostility which true commitment to reconciliation must entail is avoided. Instead, the leadership of the Church utters bland generalities about healing the divisions of society, without consideration of the method by which that healing can be made possible. The Church cannot reconcile the privileged with the under-privileged without seeking the abolition of privilege.

Christianity seeks reconciliation through an acceptance rather than a denial of conflict. Jesus in the Sermon on the Mount speaks of loving enemies, but not of there being no enemies to love. Christianity, by siding with the poor and oppressed, will make enemies of those among the rich and powerful who are not prepared to renounce their privilege. Can an 'Established Church', a Church committed to the view that it can somehow reflect a whole nation, accept the divisions within that nation that its very commitment to reconciliation will necessarily open up?

The position of a 'Prophetic Theology' as outlined in *The Kairos Document*, is clearly one of challenge to the existing social and political order. The prophetic tradition is renewed in the present day by those who call the whole community to repentance and to a new form of existence as a society. It is difficult to see how the Church of England could begin to renew this tradition in the contemporary world. The idea that it reflects the whole nation, that in some sense it speaks for England, means that when it talks of reconciliation the Church of England has to do so in such a way that both the privileged and the under-privileged in society can assent to what is said. It is thereby bound to talk in terms of platitudes, generalizations about the need for tolerant or compassionate attitudes, rather than in terms of the social analysis spoken of by *The Kairos Document* – analysis which will clearly have the effect of dividing society. The responsibility of the 'Established Church' to speak for the whole nation becomes a rationalization for speaking in such a way as to please everyone in it, and this can only be done in the blandest of terms.

Whereas *The Kairos Document* is deeply conscious of a system of oppression, and of the deeply divisive effect which that system has upon society as a whole, *Faith in the City* is not. It challenges certain government policies, about which it is certainly very specific. But it does not attempt the sort of social analysis that might provide a critique of these policies. It does not see particular instances of injustice as a product of capitalism in the way that the South African *Kairos Document* sees them as a product of apartheid.

It may, of course, be argued that the situation in England does not admit of such a social analysis. Capitalism, it may be said, is not the 'villain' that apartheid obviously is. Yet if our comments on the problems of an international economic order earlier in this chapter have any validity, then there is an economic system which has global structural shortcomings, a system to which Britain has over the last decade become more firmly wedded than ever. In such circumstances, the Christian task of reconciliation can be achieved only by changing that social and economic order which introduces poverty and division into the country.

This chapter began by raising the possibility that there existed a global problem which required what the Sri Lankan theologian Tissa Balasuriya has called a 'planetary theology'. Of course any language which talks, with Balasuriya, of a 'world system', is prey to generalization and to overlooking the particularities of Asia, Africa, Latin America or Britain. At the same time, there is a danger that respect for differences will become a reason to avoid the social analysis that is necessary to a proper understanding of the global context within which the affairs of each particular country are conducted.

Apartheid is a phenomenon linked to one part of the world only. Yet *The Kairos Document*, generated by the particular situation of that country, has been appropriated and used as a crìtique of the Church in other countries with very different problems. At the very least, Christians are discovering that in circumstances where they find themselves confronting systematic injustice, the challenge to the Church is the same – that of renewing the prophetic tradition of the gospel in a situation where it must confront its enemies with love, but not present love in such a way as to deny that such enemies exist.

6 CONCLUSION

In this chapter we have tried to explain why we cannot accept the view of *Faith in the City* that conditions in Western Europe make it unnecessary to develop a theology of liberation here. Not only is there poverty in First World countries too – the so-called 'Fourth World' referred to by Casalis and others[43] – but the wealth of the rich nations is inseparably bound up with the poverty of the poor nations. One cannot be considered apart from the other. In the global market, the First World is as responsible for overcoming the poverty of the Third World as is the Third World itself – however necessary it may be to avoid a patronizing attitude towards 'helping' the poor. The very emergence of the theology of liberation in the late 1960s, around a discussion of 'dependence' and 'development' theories of the relationship between rich and poor nations, reflected an awareness of what Balasuriya recognizes as the 'global system' of international trade and finance, a system calling for a 'planetary theology'.[44]

Moreover, just as the study of conditions in Latin America in 1968 revealed the intimate connection between social and economic prospects for the poor there and the impact of global forces, so the study of conditions in Britain in 1988 reveals a similar connection. The British poor, like the poor of the world as a whole, are increasingly being seen as objects of private charity rather than public provision. As Britain itself becomes assimilated to international capitalism, and as the national institutions resisting such assimilation are weakened and made ineffective, so the idea of curing poverty through a system of social provision becomes as inappropriate at home as it is abroad. Once the assimilation is complete, individual charities will be organizing aid programmes for the British poor in the way that they organize such programmes for the poor of the Third World. Indeed, some like Oxfam are already thinking in these terms.

How prepared is Christianity in this country to read 'the signs of the times'? It is true that there is a resistance to thinking in terms of oppressive 'systems', and to the sort of social analysis that is prepared to discuss the causes of poverty rather than satisfy itself with relieving the symptoms. At the same time, however, language which talks of 'sinful structures' should not be represented in an exaggerated way as foreign to the whole thinking of the established Churches. As we have seen, it is part of the Catholic social tradition represented by *Populorum Progressio* and the recent encyclical of John Paul II, *Solicitudo Rei Socialis*. And as we have also seen, it is accepted by the highly influential *Kairos Document* as appropriate to the condition of Christians in South Africa. It is difficult not to see at least some of the experience of Christians there having an important message for Christians in Western Europe.

The call of *The Kairos Document* for a 'Prophetic Theology' is an intrinsic part of that message. In the last section of this chapter, it was argued that the established character of the main Christian denomination in Britain made such a commitment to prophecy particularly difficult. The harshness of the Christian gospel is easily made subservient to an ideology of reconciliation, which manipulates the principle of Christian love into a means of resisting any real challenge to the established order. Denying one's enemies is easier than loving them.

In the memory of the Christian communities who formed the texts of the New Testament was the recognition of a man whose public career survived barely three years before he suffered a violent death at the hands of the state. They remembered him as one into whose mouth it was not felt inappropriate to put words like 'As for the man who is a cause of stumbling to one of these little ones who have faith, it would be better for him to be thrown into the sea with a millstone round his neck' (Mark 9.42, NEB). It is noteworthy that the peasants of Solentiname read the references to the children as references to the poor,[45] since both find themselves in a situation of helpless dependence, and yet both aspire to winning independence in the future.

The memory of one who came not to bring peace but a sword (Matt. 10.34), who talked of offending limbs being cut off if they frustrated obedience to God's will (Matt. 5.30), doubtless represents the 'creative fidelity' spoken of by Boff,[46] and not necessarily the actual words of Jesus. At the same time, such words in Scripture, even when taken as part of a whole which includes the reminder that 'my yoke is good to bear, my load is light' (Matt. 11.30, NEB), make clear the harsh and uncompromising character of the call to discipleship. Even a light yoke is a burden that has to be borne. In the comfortable *Sitz im Leben* from which the contemporary Church in Britain so often presents the gospel, or from which the United States televangelists present a sentimental message of personal comfort, so much of the teaching about Christ appears hardly to begin to interpret the anger and suffering of Christ for our situation today. What would it mean for us as Christians in the First World to share the insults, mockery, persecution, and uneasy insecurity to which he so clearly challenged the disciples in his own time? It is arguable that we can have no understanding of this unless we are prepared to interpret the nature of the 'principalities and powers' which are a stumbling-block to the gospel in our own time.

NOTES

1 The Archbishop of Canterbury's Commission on Urban Priority Areas, *Faith in the City: A Call for Action by Church and Nation* (London: Church House Publishing, 1985), 3.34, p. 64.
2 D. Jenkins, 'The God of Freedom and the Freedom of God', *Hibbert Lecture*, 1985.
3 G. Casalis, *Methodology for a Western European Theology of Liberation*, in V. Fabella and S. Torres (eds), *Doing Theology in a Divided World* (Maryknoll, NY: Orbis Books, 1985), p. 114.
4 R. Shaull, *Heralds of a New Reformation: The Poor of South and North America* (Maryknoll, NY: Orbis Books, 1984).
5 L. Boff and V. Elizondo (eds), 'Option for the Poor: Challenge to the Rich Countries', *Concilium* 187 (1986).
6 N. Greinacher, 'Liberation Theology in the "First World"?', in Boff and Elizondo (eds), 'Option for the Poor', *Concilium* 187 (1986), pp. 81–90.
7 T. Balasuriya, *Planetary Theology* (London: SCM Press, 1984).
8 C. Elliott, *Comfortable Compassion?: Poverty, Power and the Church* (London: Hodder & Stoughton, 1987).
9 ibid., p. 100.
10 ibid., p. 103.
11 The 'dependency school' has both Marxist and non-Marxist

adherents (Elliott, *Comfortable Compassion?*, pp. 102–3). See the discussion in Part 1 of Boff and Elizondo (eds), 'Option for the Poor', *Concilium* 187 (1986).

12 *Solicitudo Rei Socialis* (London: Catholic Truth Society, 1988). See p. 77 for the reference to 'structures of sin'. The encyclical also contains discussion of problems caused to poor countries by the system of international trade and finance. While it clearly rejects Marxism, and is suspicious of the theology of liberation, the encyclical does contain many ideas and themes familiar to the liberation theologian.

13 See 'The Christian Churches and the World System' in Balasuriya, *Planetary Theology*, ch 7.

14 N. Boyle, 'Understanding Thatcherism', *New Blackfriars* 69/818 (July-August 1988), pp. 307–25.

15 The speech was printed in the *Guardian* on Monday 23 May 1988.

16 The text of their letter of response was printed in *The Times* on Tuesday 24 May 1988.

17 Material in this section is dependent on W. L. Owensby, *Economics for Prophets* (Grand Rapids, MI: Wm B. Eerdmans, 1988).

18 J. M. Keynes, *The General Theory of Employment, Interest and Money* (Basingstoke: Macmillan, 1936).

19 The Kairos Theologians, *The Kairos Document: Challenge to the Church = A Theological Comment on the Political Crisis in South Africa*, introduced by J. W. de Gruchy (Grand Rapids: Wm B. Eerdmans, 1986), p.9.

20 It is, for instance, an important model for Duncan Forrester's discussion in his book *Theology and Politics* (Oxford: Basil Blackwell, 1988), which is a general study of political theory, not one limited to a particular part of the globe.

21 *Kairos Document*, p.17.

22 ibid., p.25.

23 ibid., p.29.

24 ibid., p.35.

25 ibid., p.37.

26 ibid., p.39.

27 ibid., p.40.

28 ibid., pp. 47–51.

29 ibid., p. 50.

30 See note 20.

31 Interestingly, this is very much the thrust of Don Cupitt's latest work, *The New Christian Ethics* (London: SCM Press, 1988). It would be a useful enterprise to discuss what links there are between Cupitt's 'liberal agnosticism' and the theology of liberation. Both put the emphasis on praxis, one from the stand-point of a metaphysical agnosticism about the possibility of understanding God, the other from the stand-point of a perception of God's will as commanding faith in action rather than speculation. But both arguably arrive at the same point.

32 This point highlights the need for a British *Kairos Document* generated by the poor themselves, a document (in Ian Fraser's words) that would be 'doing theology as the people's work'. Useful in this context also is Carlos Mesters' contribution 'The Use of the Bible in Christian Communities of the Common People' in N. K. Gottwald (ed.), *The Bible and Liberation: Political and Social Hermeneutics* (Maryknoll, NY: Orbis Books, 1984).

33 Archbishop's Commission, *Faith in the City*, 2.18, p. 31.

34 ibid., 3.13 (pp. 52–3), 3.16–17 (pp. 54–6), 8.55 (p. 181), 9.90–1 (pp. 220–1), 10.98 (p.257).

35 P. Hinchliff, 'Church-State Relations', in S. Sykes and J. Booty (eds), *The Study of Anglicanism* (London: SPCK, 1988), pp. 351–63.

36 J. Habgood, *Church and Nation in a Secular Age* (London: Darton, Longman & Todd, 1983).

37 ibid., p. 105.

38 ibid., p. 109.

39 W. S. F. Pickering, 'Sociology of Anglicanism', in Sykes and Booty (eds), *Study of Anglicanism*, pp. 364–75.

40 See S. Sykes, *The Integrity of Anglicanism* (Oxford: Mowbrays, 1978). Even here, however, the discussion of comprehensiveness hardly touches on the social and political constraints which we have mentioned.

41 Habgood, *Church and Nation*, p. 110.

42 *Kairos Document*, p. 25.

43 See note 3.

44 See note 7.

45 E. Cardenal, *The Gospel in Solentiname*, 4 vols (Maryknoll, NY: Orbis Books, 1977–84), vol. 3, ch. 24, 'The Rich Epicure and Poor Lazarus', pp. 251–7.

46 See C. Boff, *Theology and Praxis: Epistemological Foundations* (Maryknoll, NY: Orbis Books, 1987).

Conclusion: Two Disturbing Texts

In the course of this book we have argued that patterns of disturbance exist both in society and in the sacred text of Scripture. Ideas of 'conflict', 'disorder', 'division', 'separation' and even 'dualism' have appeared frequently. By way of contrast, opposite notions of 'peace', 'harmony' and 'unity' have been less noticeable. Moreover, at times, as in the idea of an 'ideology of reconciliation', these latter notions have been made to suggest not so much an ideal for which Christians are rightly striving as a temptation to short-circuit the painful demands of the gospel. Too often, we have indicated, the peace which Christians seek is a false peace.

One example of this 'false peace' lies in our attitude to the Bible. It cannot be assumed that this library of sacred literature, the product of at least a millennium of Jewish and Christian experience, is a perfect unity at peace with itself. It is all too easy to approach it, not least because of the way it is now published as a single book, as one work by one author with one message.

Such an approach is common to fundamentalist attitudes to Scripture. Even 'radical' fundamentalists present themselves as highlighting parts of the Bible that other fundamentalists tend to devalue or omit, such as passages in which Jesus appears to commend pacifism or in which the apostles pool their wealth and appear to renounce private ownership. The 'radicals' only claim to be presenting the other side of a single coin, a neglected counterpoint in the scriptural harmony.

The theology of liberation, on the other hand, perceives a divided text. It argues that the biblical tradition is not homogeneous. For example, Fernando Belo's treatment of Mark's Gospel[1] sets out to contrast two traditions within a single text. One, the 'messianic narrative', presents Jesus going up to Jerusalem not to die but to preach in the Temple, proclaiming that in the light of his rejection the vineyard would be given to others – in other words that his message was about to be taken to the pagans. The other tradition, one of 'theological reflection', presents an ideological justification for Jesus' death on the cross. Rather than an unforeseen hitch in the progress of his teaching, Jesus' death is instead presented as the foreseen and predetermined climax to his ministry, and the occasion of reconciliation between God and humankind. For Belo, both these contrasting traditions are woven into the fabric of the same text.

Similarly, George Pixley's treatment of the Old Testament[2] contrasts textual traditions rooted in the oligarchic projects of the monarchy and the Temple with traditions rooted in Israel's tribal past. Again, we have discussed the possibility that the existence of two climaxes to the judgement of the world and two visions of the new age, in the book of Revelation, may reflect a conflict in the understanding of God's Kingdom on earth. In each case, rather than presume that the texts contain a single internally coherent account, we have explored the possibility of conflicting accounts, either between texts or within a single text.

The historical-critical method has been alive to the possibility of such internal disagreement. But in explaining such conflict it has tended to concentrate on the influence of later 'redactions', claiming to discern the influence of writers who have added to the work of an 'original author'. The approach of the theology of liberation, on the other hand, is not to speculate on individual authorship, but rather to perceive in textual conflict the reflection of social discord. Belo's 'materialist' reading of Mark, for instance, identifies conflict between followers of Jesus attempting to maintain their ideals in the face of Roman power and those in the emerging Christian communities who favoured a measure of compromise with socio-economic realities. The formation of the canon is seen less as the drawing together of a unified Christian kerygma than as a process by which awkward ideas are domesticated. In the process of domestication the awkward ideas are often included, but in such a way as to bring together a number of different traditions under the umbrella of sacred Scripture.

The traditions of the powerless are forced to cohabit for

survival with the dominant traditions of the powerful within a single text. They are compared in this book to the traditions of Aztec and Mayan culture, or to the African traditions of slaves taken to America, which were maintained as a 'subversive memory' within the dominant Catholicism of the European settlers.

Of course, the idea that the Bible presents no single coherent message is not new. For a century the attempt to separate the historical Jesus from the Christ of ecclesiastical confession has involved claims about various conflicting ideas contained within the biblical text. The 'Quest of the Historical Jesus' has spawned a number of theories contrasting the 'early Catholicism' of the Petrine and Deutero-Pauline texts with the authentic letters of Paul, or the teaching of Paul with that of Jesus recorded in the synoptic Gospels. A great deal of traditional Old and New Testament scholarship could be described as highlighting ideological conflict within Scripture.

However, this scholarship has tended to concentrate on religious conflict as the ground of disagreement within the text, rather than the wider social and political conflicts that have been highlighted by the theologians of liberation. Concentrating on these wider conflicts produces a very different interpretation of the differences made apparent by a study of the text.

A good illustration of the impact of this wider contextual criticism is once again provided by the book of Revelation. We would not agree with those who treat it as an appendix to the New Testament rather than as a mainstream contribution to the Christian kerygma. We cannot accept that its mythological language can simply be dismissed as an example of 'primitive' traditions of thought, while its concern with practicalities of Christian life is rejected as slight or non-existent.

The theology of liberation presents a very different understanding of this traditionally marginalized work. It offers a perspective that highlights both the political character of myth and the positive character of dualistic language as a way of distancing the Christian's hopes for this world from the present form of society. In the context of a political situation within which the established order was presented as the only conceivable order for society, an empire based on Rome, whose boundaries and influence extended virtually throughout the known world, those who challenged that order were inevitably driven to the use of dualistic language. Their rejection of the present form of the world appeared to be a rejection of the world as such. The language they used to distance themselves from an unjust order appeared to be distancing them from reality. When the *Pax Romana* was the only peace available, the Christian hope for a peace beyond human understanding could easily be misinterpreted as a peace that could be realized only in another world.

Dualistic language creates the distance which allows for an 'unmasking' of present reality, a rejection of the demonic character of the present order ruled by 'the beast' Nero and centred on 'the great harlot' Rome. It opens up space for the future hope of the Christian, focused on the Kingdom of the Lamb who was slain, the reign of God whose will is at last done on earth as it is in heaven.

The theologian and the biblical critic need to examine carefully what is meant by those who contrast the 'universalism' of Jesus (who was, however, at times reluctant to help Gentiles – e.g. Matt. 15.21ff.) with the 'separatism' of his opponents. The Pharisees, their very name implying separation, come to be presented as a grouping of legalistic rigorists in contrast to the Jesus movement with its search for universal reconciliation based on love. The attachment of some Christians to food laws and circumcision is seen as a failure to appreciate the universal character of the Christian message, and an attachment instead to Jewish exclusivism. Such a presentation fails to recognize the positive challenge to the established order represented by much early Christian concern to preserve a separate identity in the world, something that Jesus himself recognized in his attitudes.

It is a presentation that carries over into Christianity's conception of its task today, when theological language is used in an abstract manner to encourage a bland unity rather than to unearth sources of conflict. It does not analyse the forces opposed to the Kingdom of God. It espouses an ideology of reconciliation that seeks to unite everyone around theological ideas whose engagement with present reality it fails to explore. We have discussed the critique in *The Kairos Document* of the lack of social analysis presented by what it calls 'Church Theology' in South Africa. We may suggest that the criticisms offered by *The Kairos Document* have implications elsewhere, and may indeed be addressed to the

Churches in our own country. In Britain itself the notion of an 'established Church', whose remit is to unite and speak for a whole nation, makes it particularly unlikely that that Church will attempt the sustained analysis which highlights deep, structurally rooted sources of conflict in a community whose united voice it is supposed to present.

The theology of liberation in the Third World is grateful for the wells of European scholarship at which many of its leading exponents have drunk in the course of their lives. It is also grateful for the sustained analysis provided by Christian tradition, and considers its own approach to the text to be consistent with aspects of that tradition. Thus Carlos Mesters insists that liberation approaches to exegesis have much in common with the methods adopted by patristic commentators on the text.[3] Indeed we have argued that the Jewish methods of exegesis practised by the biblical writers themselves provide a tradition within which the theology of liberation can justifiably claim to belong (see p. 61ff.).

Once disconnected from a historical-critical approach which thinks only in terms of recapturing the author's original intention, the liberation theologian is able to introduce the socio-political context of his or her own day into the process of exegesis. Most liberation theologians write from a perspective of Third World experience. However, there is no reason why the experience of First World academics cannot also be relevant to the work of exegesis. Indeed, First and Third Worlds belong together as different poles in the interplay of global forces with which both have to come to terms.

Our own experience discerns in the contemporary world a socio-political situation within which the Christian challenge to the present order and its hope for a future reign of God on earth are given new content. Forces of capital oppress our own world and divide it with conflicts as universally as the forces of imperial Rome did in the first century. The sinful structures of the present order, identified (if not analysed) even by the official documents of the Churches, create the injustice that makes peace on earth unrealizable. The Lamb continues to be slain in the sufferings of the poor. The beast continues to occupy the throne of the Lamb, and to substitute for the form of God's world the form of this world. The powers whose pervasive oppressiveness gives them a character to be described as 'demonic' continue to make examples of individual goodness and giving limited in scope and even counter-productive in effect. Their name is now not Legion but other, deadlier forms of warfare.

The vision of wholesale destruction and the vision of the Kingdom compete as alternative futures. A world that has learnt to master the forces of technology and capital has learnt that they are not demonic, that they are not powers beyond our control but within our control. But when these forces are experienced by so many of the powerless as controlling them, their demonic character remains. For the millions in this world who are starving to death, the millions in Britain who are becoming poorer while a minority becomes richer, the millions who perceive the threat of destruction, by war or by pollution, which the earth faces, Christian language of harmony, peace and unity has its place only in the context of a rejection of the present state of our planet. They are people who have no hope for the future unless it be in the context of a judgement addressed to the present.

Jesus of Nazareth, one interpretation of a parable offered in this book suggests, asked for a coin because he came from a part of the world, Galilee, which lay outside Roman jurisdiction. He had no money himself, and his followers were sent out with none. His life was not dominated by money, although money brought about his death. When he said, in one of the most famous lines of Scripture, 'Render to Caesar the things that are Caesar's, and to God the things that are God's' (Mark 12.17), he was not marking out the boundaries of two complementary worlds. He was explaining that those who, unlike himself, participated in the Roman economic system had no choice but to pay taxes to Caesar, whose head was inscribed on every coin, an image to affront every devout Jew. On the other hand, those who recognized the supremacy of God would keep their distance from Rome and its idolatrous practices. Serving God entails the rejection of Mammon, not a complementary service to things spiritual alongside the service of things material.

The theology of liberation argues that Christians today serve God by rejecting an economic system that dominates the global economy and encroaches on the lives of all who live on this planet. If many who write in the West prefer not to attempt any systematic analysis of their own *Sitz im Leben*, that may in part be because they are on the whole the beneficiaries of that system. They reject language which describes the present order as demonic because its demonic aspect never touches them. They reserve such language for the hellish aspects of their own European past, rather than those of the global present. 'Theology after Auschwitz' affects them in a way that 'Theology in the face of Ethiopia' does not.

The integration of Britain under Thatcherism into the network of global capitalism represents a twentieth-century assimilation to forces of injustice. In the first century the area of the world within which Jesus carried out his ministry was similarly undergoing a process of assimilation which culminated in the destruction of the Temple after the Jewish War of AD 66–70. In one sense that assimilation made easier the spread of the Christian gospel throughout the Roman empire. In another sense it perhaps made easier the eventual assimilation of Christianity to the values of that empire, and the establishment of a medieval theocracy which was in many ways marked by continuity with the traditions of ancient Rome. Therefore, the history of Christianity itself justifies concern for a constant unmasking of reality, a constant application of the traditions found in the Bible to new empires and new forms of human pretension.

It is possible to feel that a means can be found of realizing the ethics of the Christian gospel within the parameters laid down by an unjust social order. Such a feeling was already present among Christians soon after Jesus' death, and finds its voice in some of the traditions found in the New Testament. The traditions applied by the theology of liberation, on the other hand, may seem less to do with the Christian hope for reconciliation than with the necessary conflicts which Christians must engage in to achieve it. But if it is true that Christianity has constantly sought to by-pass that difficult means to a true peace, then such an emphasis may not be altogether unjustified.

Christians engaged in 'reading the signs of the times' can hardly be sanguine about the prospects for global peace and survival. Their reading of the Bible is correspondingly aware that the hope for God's Kingdom was often based on a negative rejection of the present order. But rejection of that order is always a ground for hope in a future that men and women are able to realize if they are prepared to will the means to its realization. The negative is always the condition of a greater positive, the cross a condition of the resurrection. No greater empowerment can be offered than that which reveals a way of life so far barely glimpsed through the constant disappointments of those who have proclaimed the gospel of Christ in history.

We are not condemned by nature to live under the shadow of the beast, and to worry daily about demonic forces outside our control – the arms race, pollution, starvation, runaway levels of inflation and unemployment. We condemn ourselves to live under their shadow. That realization is a condemnation and a judgement, but also an opportunity. What we have ourselves made we can ourselves unmake, if we have the courage to make an analysis that will inevitably force us to endure conflict with those holding power in our society. Even in the present age, we possess the opportunity to encounter the age to come. Our claim is that the theology of liberation expresses that opportunity in terms which come from the depths of Christian history, and from traditions woven deeply into the fabric of its sacred literature.

NOTES

1   F. Belo, *A Materialist Reading of the Gospel of Mark* (Maryknoll, NY: Orbis Books, 1981).
2   G. Pixley, *God's Kingdom: A Guide for Biblical Study* (London: SCM Press, 1981).
3   C. Mesters, 'The Bible in Christian Communities' in eds. S. Torres and J. Eagleson *The Challenge of Basic Communities* (Maryknoll, NY: Orbis Books, 1982).

Indexes

Index of Biblical References

Index of Names and Subjects